LADDERS TO LITERACY

LADDERS TO LITERACY

A Kindergarten Activity Book

by

Rollanda E. O'Connor, Ph.D.
University of Pittsburgh
Pittsburgh, Pennsylvania

Angela Notari-Syverson, Ph.D.
Washington Research Institute
Seattle, Washington

Patricia F. Vadasy, M.P.H.
Washington Research Institute
Seattle, Washington

·P A U L · H·
BROOKES
PUBLISHING C⁰

Baltimore · London · Toronto · Sydney

Paul H. Brookes Publishing Co.
Post Office Box 10624
Baltimore, Maryland 21285-0624
www.brookespublishing.com

Typeset by A.W. Bennett, Inc., Hartland, Vermont.
Manufactured in the United States of America by
Versa Press, East Peoria, Illinois.

The project on which this book is based was funded by Grant #H024B20031 from the U.S. Department of Education, Office of Special Education and Rehabilitative Services, Early Education Program for Children with Disabilities. The content, however, does not necessarily reflect the position of the U.S. Department of Education, and no official endorsement should be inferred.

The illustrations throughout this book are provided, with permission, from the following individuals: Lauralee Brainard, Darby Cieply, Brianna Coen, Mary Delaney Gallien, Heidi Gainer, Linda Gil, Matthew Jarvis, Bryan Johnson, Ben Laughlin, Rod O'Connor, and Jonathon Zaborowski.

The clipart on pages 127 and 130 is courtesy of Corel Corporation.

The bingo card on page 142 was compiled using images from ClickArt by T/Maker Company, Mountain View, California.

Second printing, December 1999.
Third printing, August 2001.

Library of Congress Cataloging-in-Publication Data

O'Connor, Rollanda E.
  Ladders to literacy : a kindergarten activity book / by Rollanda E. O'Connor, Angela Notari-Syverson, Patricia F. Vadasy.
    p.   cm.
  Includes bibliographical references and index.
  1. Handicapped children—Education (Preschool)—United States.   2. Reading (Kindergarten)—United States.   3. Kindergarten—Activity programs—United States.   4. Literacy—United States.   I. Notari-Syverson, Angela.   II. Vadasy, Patricia F.   III. Title.
LC4028.5.O36   1998
371.9'0444—dc21   97-37861
                                                                                          CIP

British Library Cataloguing in Publication data are available from the British Library.

Contents

About the Authors

Rollanda E. O'Connor, Ph.D., Assistant Professor, Department of Instruction and Learning, University of Pittsburgh, 4H01 Forbes Quadrangle, 230 South Bouquet Street, Pittsburgh, Pennsylvania 15260   Dr. O'Connor is a reading specialist and an assistant professor at the University of Pittsburgh and has a doctoral degree in special education from the University of Washington in Seattle. Dr. O'Connor taught reading in special and general education classrooms for 16 years, directed an in-service consortium for general and special educators on strategies for educating children with disabilities in general education classes, and conducted research to develop literacy skills for young children with disabilities. Dr. O'Connor's research has focused on two themes: the feasibility and effectiveness of incorporating phonological awareness instruction into programs for children at risk for reading difficulties in general education classes and factors that influence accessibility of reading instruction. She has taught teachers to use activities designed to improve the reading development of their children during large- and small-group instruction. The factors identified in these studies have been incorporated in the activities in *Ladders to Literacy.*

Angela Notari-Syverson, Ph.D., Research Associate, Washington Research Institute, 150 Nickerson Street, Suite 305, Seattle, Washington 98109
Dr. Notari-Syverson is a research associate at the Washington Research Institute in Seattle. Dr. Notari-Syverson holds degrees in child psychology and language disorders from the University of Geneva, Switzerland, and a doctoral degree in early childhood special education from the University of Oregon in Eugene. In Geneva, Dr. Notari-Syverson worked in a clinical setting with children with a variety of oral and written communication disorders. In the United States since 1985, she has directed or co-directed federal research, model demonstration, and outreach projects at the Washington Research Institute and at the University of Washington in Seattle focused on early language and literacy intervention. She has published chapters and journal articles on early intervention assessment and curriculum as well as on language, literacy, and cognitive development of young children with disabilities.

Patricia F. Vadasy, M.P.H., Research Associate, Washington Research Institute, 150 Nickerson Street, Suite 305, Seattle, Washington 98109   Patricia Vadasy is a research associate at the Washington Research Institute in Seattle. She has published extensively in the areas of early childhood special education and family support programs during her work at the University of Washington's Experimental Education Unit. Since 1989, she has directed federal research and demonstration projects at the Washington Research Institute in programs for students from differing ethnic backgrounds and early reading instruction.

Foreword

Learning to become literate begins long before children receive formal reading lessons. This fact, which seems obvious, was not always so readily recognized. Since the mid-1970s, however, researchers have succeeded in tracing the foundations of literacy learning to early childhood. Vague conceptions of "reading readiness" based on unexamined assumptions about maturity, mental age, and IQ score that dominated the educational landscape have yielded to an improved understanding of the cognitive and language pillars on which literacy learning is built.

Literacy is founded on three developmental pillars. The first of these is receptive and expressive language. Fortunately, this aspect of language develops quite naturally. It does not require detailed planning, formal training, or carefully orchestrated lessons. All that is needed is an environment that includes other, more capable language users who are willing to interact with young and eager language learners.

Establishing the other two pillars, however, places far greater demands on the environment. In the absence of special conditions, neither of these pillars develops at all, or, if conditions are not optimum, then they develop insufficiently. History makes this point forcefully. Humans lived successfully for millions of years and even developed sophisticated forms of communication before anyone thought about representing spoken language with an alphabetic system. Literacy is contrived, not natural. Therefore, if children do not participate in specific, contrived language and literacy activities before they encounter formal reading and writing instruction, then they face a daunting learning challenge that some are unable to meet.

The second pillar consists of an awareness and understanding of the structure and functions of print. Children who have acquired this understanding realize that print is written language and that individual spoken words can also appear on pages of books, sides of buildings, cereal boxes, coins, television screens, t-shirts, and so forth. Print is everywhere. We use it for all sorts of purposes. We make lists as a memory device to remind ourselves about things to do and purchase. We look at print in newspapers, television guides, directions, schedules, and time tables to get information and make decisions. We use print to send and receive messages in those cases in which voice communication won't suffice. And perhaps most important, we use print for enjoyment. Developing an awareness and appreciation of print—knowing how to look at books, noticing that some words look like other words, seeing that words are composed of letters, recognizing there are spaces between words, and discerning that language in books is similar to but not the same as the language we use in talking—are critical insights that facilitate later literacy learning. Developing concepts about print depends on the nature and quality of experiences children have with print. It cannot be taken for granted.

The importance of oral language and print awareness to the development of literacy has such strong face validity it is nearly self-evident. Delayed development in either of these areas should be a cause for concern to parents and teachers. Not so for the third pillar of literacy; its importance was missed until only recently. I refer here to the development of phonological awareness or the conscious ability to hear and manipulate the individual sounds that make up words. Phonological awareness is composed of several dimensions that can be represented in the following tasks: identifying and producing rhymes (e.g., "ran" and "man"), recognizing that two words begin with the same sound ("sat" and "sick") or end with the same sound ("lock" and "chunk"), combining separate sounds into a word (/m/ /a/ /n/ to "man"), and segmenting words into smaller parts (e.g., "man" to "m-a-n" or "m-an").

Individual differences in phonological awareness are more predictive of children's success in beginning reading than any other language or cognitive skill. Children develop phonological awareness when their attention is drawn to the *sound* of language, away from its usual focus on meaning. Rhyming games and books facilitate the development of phonological awareness, but many children do not develop the level of phonological sensitivity needed for learning to read. These children require more explicit instruction if they are to acquire this important ability.

Heretofore, a comprehensive, developmentally appropriate curriculum was not available to aid teachers in addressing the emergent literacy needs of young children. Kindergarten and preschool teachers chose between two unattractive alternatives. They could begin formal reading instruction ahead of schedule, pushing the primary school curriculum down to inappropriate levels; or they could, working by themselves, use their intuitions to cobble together a set of emergent literacy activities in hopes of producing a reasonably comprehensive and effective set of lessons.

I am happy to report that a much better alternative is now available. *Ladders to Literacy* provides teachers the comprehensive and developmentally appropriate emergent literacy curriculum they seek. This curriculum addresses the three principal areas of development that serve as the foundation for learning to read and write. Moreover, each lesson and activity in *Ladders to Literacy* provides practical teaching adaptations for a range of learners so that all students (struggling, average, and advanced) can participate together. In addition, it is classroom friendly and delivers on its claims.

Ladders to Literacy was forged from the accumulated research knowledge on early literacy learning. Field-tested across a broad spectrum of kindergarten classrooms, the curriculum underwent a rigorous 3-year implementation trial. Successive generations of the program were informed by the results of children's literacy acquisition and teachers' feedback and suggestions. Annual comparisons of classrooms with and without *Ladders to Literacy* showed strong effects for the program, and follow-up studies into first grade indicated lasting benefits from the curriculum.

For many children, the literacy gap between home and school is enormous. Not all families manage to provide sufficient language and print experiences to prepare their young for literacy instruction. Yet formal literacy instruction begins in first grade, ready or not. That leaves preschool and kindergarten teachers with the job of filling the literacy gap. *Ladders to Literacy* gives teachers the tool for helping children mount those first critical rungs on their journey to literacy.

Joseph R. Jenkins, Ph.D.
Professor of Special Education
University of Washington
Seattle

Acknowledgments

Our thanks to kindergarten teachers Judy Hasselmann, Antoinette Jacobs, Gail Forsythe, Susan Sager, Gail Wedner, and Nancy Desch for their assistance in field-testing these activities and for their many helpful suggestions. Thanks also to the following kindergarten teachers in Pittsburgh: Stephanie Hornick, Helen Holt, Susan Sevel, and Holly Blackburn; and to Jim Weaver, Gloria Johnson, Janet Richards, and the teachers and administration of the Lake Huron Intermediate School District in Bad Axe, Michigan, for participating in experimental tests of the effects of these activities on the literacy development of young children. We are especially grateful to Mary Delaney Gallien for her invaluable contributions in the typing, design, and preparation of the many experimental versions of the manuscript. Finally, the development of this curriculum would not have been possible without the support of the federal government.

LADDERS TO LITERACY

SECTION I

Theoretical Framework
for Early Literacy

Chapter 1

Introduction
The Development of Early Literacy

The most critical academic task that children accomplish in the primary years is the development of literacy. However, many children enter kindergarten and first grade without critical literacy skills. *Ladders to Literacy* is designed to develop early literacy skills through engaging activities that can be incorporated into programs for children at risk for reading failure—including children with disabilities and their typically developing peers. These activities target the factors that research suggests are *most* strongly related to later reading development—print awareness, oral language, and phonological awareness. The activities promote the competence that helps children become receptive to beginning reading instruction in the early grades. The activities in *Ladders to Literacy* were field tested in kindergarten settings with small and large groups of children reflecting a range of interests and abilities. Each activity provides suggestions for encouraging participation from students along a continuum of developmental levels.

THEORETICAL BASES FOR THE DEVELOPMENT OF *LADDERS TO LITERACY*

The activities in *Ladders to Literacy* reflect two theoretical perspectives: Vygotsky's (1978) social-interactionist perspective that emphasizes the role of scaffolded interactions with adults in the child's learning process and converging evidence on the role of cognitive processes (metalinguistic and phonological awareness, oral language, and knowledge about print) in reading acquisition (see Beck & Juel, 1992; Blachman, 1994; Share & Stanovich, 1995, for reviews). Since the mid-1980s, educators and researchers have revised their views regarding how and when children begin to learn about literacy. Known as the *emergent literacy perspective,* this view considers literacy a complex sociological, psychological, and linguistic activity. Learning about literacy begins in the very early years and is a continuous process that is directly linked to early oral language and social interactions. It is an integral and functional component of everyday living (Teale, 1984). Several lines of evidence suggest that a child's experience with literate activities prior to first grade makes a significant difference in the child's later literacy skills (Dickinson & Smith, 1996; Maclean, Bryant, & Bradley, 1987; Scanlon & Vellutino, 1997; Scarborough, Dobrich, & Hager, 1991; Snow & Weisman, 1996; Wells, 1985; Whitehurst, 1996; Whitehurst et al., 1988). A study of factors contributing to successful reading found that the best first-grade readers came from kindergarten classes in which more time was spent on phonological awareness, spelling, and writing activities (Scanlon & Vellutino, 1997). Early exposure to literacy events (e.g., listening to stories, talking about books) and metaphonological aspects of language (e.g., recognizing similarities among sounds in spoken words) is important for successful performance in school-based literacy activities. The acquisition of literacy results from the interaction among these experiences (Sulzby & Teale, 1991), which can be broadly categorized into three major areas: print awareness, phonological awareness, and oral language. Instructional programs based on stimulating these areas have been successful in promoting the literacy development of children in kindergarten (Blachman, Ball, Black, & Tangel, 1994; O'Connor, Notari-Syverson, & Vadasy, 1998).

SUPPORTING LITERACY DEVELOPMENT IN YOUNG CHILDREN

Ladders to Literacy provides teachers and parents with the knowledge and skills to understand the development of literacy in young children, to provide a literacy-rich physical environment in the school and home, and to promote early literacy through child-responsive teaching strategies. For each activity, information is provided on child development and applications of literacy research to ensure a thorough understanding of the processes involved in the development of literacy in young children. This book provides recommendations for materials, activities, and organization of daily routines that support children's literacy experiences in school and at home, such as participating in storybook readings and informal and structured writing activities, playing sound manipulation games, and visiting the class and school libraries. The activities provide teachers and parents with information on the use of child-responsive teaching strategies based on the concepts of scaffolding and social-interactionist research (e.g., Diaz, Neal, & Vachio, 1991; Pellegrini, Perlmutter, Galda, & Brody, 1990; Snow, 1983; Wertsch, 1985). Examples of child-responsive teaching strategies include varying levels of task demands and support in response to the child's level of competence, facilitating language through information talk, expanding on the child's utterance, asking open-ended questions, following the child's lead, and taking turns.

Activity Features

The following features of *Ladders to Literacy* enable teachers and parents to use the activities in a variety of settings and with children at different stages of literacy development:

- **Ecologically sensitive**—*Ladders to Literacy* emphasizes the importance of providing children with a broad, literacy-rich environment (physical and social) both at school and at home. Teaching is activity based (Bricker & Cripe, 1992), and literacy is encouraged within meaningful everyday experiences.
- **Developmentally appropriate**—Activities encourage children to experience and experiment with literacy along a continuum of levels, materials, and sophistication. Adults can select activities to work with a child at a particular developmental level and to fit the child's level of play and language skills.
- **Responsive to individual differences**—Activities are designed specifically to respond to the particular needs of young children across a range of abilities. The concept of scaffolding provides a useful framework for addressing the variety of task difficulties experienced by children at risk for reading difficulties and children with special needs learning with their peers. Literacy experiences that have been associated with school success are introduced not as isolated segments but through a rich series of activities in which each child can participate and learn at his or her individual level of functioning. To facilitate learning, activities propose developmentally appropriate teaching strategies, with adults assisting and arranging tasks and situations as a function of the goals of the interaction and the individual child's understanding of the tasks (Wertsch, 1985). The development of teaching strategies and adaptations for specific needs of children with learning difficulties is guided by the notion of scaffolding (Pressley, Hogan, Wharton-McDonald, & Mistretta, 1996; Wood, Bruner, & Ross, 1976), a dynamic process of adult–child interactions during which the adult provides high levels of support and low demands to assist the less-competent child's performance (see Figure 1 in Chapter 2). Such an approach allows for individualization in a child-responsive manner, making it ideal for an inclusive program with children of many ability levels grouped in the same classroom.
- **Multiculturally sensitive**—Literacy is deeply embedded in the culture of the family and the community (Heath, 1982; Sulzby & Teale, 1991). *Ladders to Literacy* offers activities and materials that are meaningful across a variety of cultures and ethnic groups and has been field tested in culturally diverse classrooms.

Instructional Features

The following features derive from our work in real-world kindergartens in which concerns of instructional efficiency and effectiveness are paramount:

- **Useful in group instruction; adaptable to heterogeneous groups**—The activities are designed to ensure that children of different ability levels can be served in inclusive groupings. Each activity includes suggestions for engaging a range of developmental levels so that teachers can respond to individual differences.
- **Supports and can be integrated with other curricula**—This curriculum will enhance rather than replace existing curricula. This makes the activities flexible and easy to integrate with classroom curricula and routines.
- **Developmentally appropriate**—Activities are functional and meaningful for the child and facilitate behaviors in multiple areas. Each educational activity identifies a developmental sequence of engagement and expectations to accommodate children of different developmental levels.
- **Provides guidelines for child-responsive teaching strategies**—For each activity, guidelines for teaching strategies are described to facilitate children's participation and to allow for adjustments of demands and support according to the child's level of task competence.
- **Provides suggestions for including parents**—A series of activities in Appendix A are available specifically for use by parents. These suggestions are integrated with classroom activities in the Home Link section at the end of each activity.
- **Facilitates individualized education program (IEP)/individualized family service plan (IFSP) goals and objectives**—The educational activities contain examples of behaviors that can be facilitated during the activity to assist teachers and parents in identifying goals and objectives for IEPs and IFSPs.
- **Grounded in research theory**—Effective implementation of any instructional routine depends on a solid understanding by the users of the philosophy and principles on which it is founded (Adams, 1990). Each teaching activity is accompanied by relevant theoretical and empirical information to enable users to understand its purpose.

EFFICACY OF *LADDERS TO LITERACY*

We have tested the effects of conducting activities in this volume under research and practical conditions since 1992. Specifically, we have considered the possibility of improving the reading outcomes of children who are hard to teach by increasing their experiences with metaphonological and other literacy-related tasks in kindergarten. We explored the feasibility of teaching young children with mild disabilities to rhyme, blend, and segment the sounds in words (phonological awareness tasks) prior to formal reading instruction (O'Connor, Jenkins, Slocum, & Leicester, 1993); in Head Start classrooms, we tested whether ordering instructional tasks differently (i.e., teaching blending prior to segmenting or vice versa) resulted in more efficient learning for the children (Slocum, O'Connor, & Jenkins, 1993); and we considered the relative advantages to be gained by teaching minimal sets of tasks (i.e., blending and segmenting) or by teaching a more global array of phonological manipulations to small groups of kindergartners in general education classes (O'Connor, Jenkins, & Slocum, 1995). Since 1993, we have taught teachers of kindergarten classes that included children with mild disabilities and other risk factors to use activities designed to improve the literacy development of their children during large- and small-group instruction (O'Connor, Notari-Syverson, & Vadasy, 1996)—the activities compiled in *Ladders to Literacy*. A total of 31 teachers and more than 700 children participated in field testing and experimental trials to explore the feasibility of activity implementation and the effects of these activities on the oral language, phonological awareness, and print awareness of the children. Classrooms were primarily general education kindergartens that included children with mild disabilities, although four self-contained special education classes and two classes for children repeating kindergarten also participated.

The Activities

During the 6-month intervention in kindergarten, teachers learned to implement the activities in *Ladders to Literacy*. We monitored the activities and their frequency of use in each of the participating classes. Activities in the first 2 months stimulated oral language and word and syllable awareness (e.g., teachers conducted finger-point reading, labeled classroom materials, played syllable clapping games, made a chart of the day's activities, and wrote words and a morning message dictated by children). Activities in the third and fourth months stimulated rhyming, first sound isolation, and onset-rime level blending and segmenting. Children played Guess the Word (Blending) ["I'm thinking of an animal: sn-ake"], matched rhyming pictures in card decks, and touched the adjoining rectangles of Elkonin boxes (Elkonin, 1973) as they said words in onset-rime format. They drew pictures; labeled them with letters or "pretend writing"; and shared the pictures with classmates, teachers, and parents. In the last 2 months, we added letter sounds to the phonological activities ["Find the letter that starts Max"], showed children how to use a letter sound to match pictures that start with the same sound, and made the auditory blending and segmenting games more sophisticated by separating each spoken phoneme. Teachers in these classes used between one and three activities daily over the course of the kindergarten year, with a minimum of 100 activities during the 90 days of monitoring, and selected a balance among the three types of activities. Teachers reported that they and their students enjoyed the activities. Teachers found the activities developmentally appropriate, culturally sensitive, and easy to integrate within their daily routines.

The Results

The short-term results of this work (reported in O'Connor et al., 1996) demonstrated that general education kindergarten teachers and special educators can increase the literacy skills of their children across a range of abilities through whole-class and center-based activities. Children in the *Ladders to Literacy* classes made significant gains in reading and writing over children who were in classes that used standard kindergarten prereading programs. Other studies have reported similar findings (Blachman et al., 1994; Byrne & Fielding-Barnsley, 1993); however, our study differed along two dimensions. First, teachers (not research personnel) conducted the activities with their children; and second, classes included children with mild disabilities. A follow-up study of children in the *Ladders to Literacy* and control classes 1 year later found sustained significant differences between groups (O'Connor et al., 1998). For children who began kindergarten with low literacy skill levels, these activities continued to stimulate significant benefits more than 1 year later on standardized measures of reading and writing and on oral reading fluency and spelling. We found these long-term effects regardless of the setting (general or special education) in which children received the *Ladders to Literacy* activities.

We expanded the field test during the 1996–1997 school year to 23 new classrooms. The end of kindergarten effects from this larger study mirror the results of our earlier field test. We present these activities to you with confidence in their efficacy.

Chapter 2

The Role of Scaffolding

Scaffolding is a metaphor first introduced by Wood et al. (1976) to describe a process observed in parent–child interactions. In scaffolding, the adult guides and supports the child's learning by building on what the child is able to do. The notion of scaffolding was later applied to classroom practice (Tharp & Gallimore, 1988) and language intervention (Norris & Hoffman, 1990). Because it is highly responsive to the individual characteristics of children and emphasizes the importance of the social environment, scaffolding has valuable applications for teachers and other professionals working in inclusive settings in which adults interact with children who are functioning at diverse developmental levels. Scaffolding approaches have been used successfully to assess and teach language and literacy skills to young children with language delays (Olswang, Bain, & Johnson, 1992), children at risk (Juel, 1996), and children from diverse cultural backgrounds (Gutierrez-Clellen & Quinn, 1993).

The notion of scaffolding derives from Vygotsky's (1978) concept of the zone of proximal development (ZPD). Vygotsky observed that children could improve their performance on tasks when provided with adult assistance. He used the term *ZPD* to refer to the difference between what a child can achieve independently and what the child can achieve with assistance. Teachers provide the necessary amount of support to help the child master emerging skills as defined by the child's ZPD. Only if tasks are at an appropriately challenging level within the child's ZPD will scaffolding be successful in moving the child to a more advanced level (Olswang et al., 1992; Pressley et al., 1996). The ZPD is different for each child, varies as a function of context and task, and changes constantly as the child learns new skills (Bodrova & Leong, 1996; Pressley et al., 1996). Some children may require high support and make small gains, whereas others learn quickly with minimal assistance. The same child may respond differently to different types of assistance and in various areas of development. Teachers need to be sensitive to both the level of task difficulty and the competence of the child. The amount of scaffolding or support the adult provides should be inversely related to the child's level of task competence. The more difficulty the child has in achieving a goal, the more directive the intervention of the adult (Fry, 1992). Effective scaffolding is flexible, is responsive to the child, draws on a variety of strategies, and may vary considerably across cultures (Berk & Winsler, 1995). The scaffolding process involves active coparticipation of the adult and the child. The amount and type of support is adjusted to the child's behavior and is gradually reduced as the child assumes more responsibility for learning (Bruner, 1983; Rogoff, 1986; Tharp & Gallimore, 1988).

Applications of scaffolding range from low-structured approaches with minimal adult assistance (e.g., asking questions to help children discover their own solutions) to highly structured approaches with more direct and explicit modeling and instruction (e.g., elicitation questions, giving directions) (Norris & Hoffman, 1990; Peña, 1996). Figure 1 shows the categories of scaffolding arranged from the least-intensive levels (upper left corner) to the most-intensive support (lower right corner). Means of assistance can be verbal, visual, or physical, including words, symbols, drawings, maps, arrangement of materials, and shaping (Bodrova & Leong, 1996; Tharp & Gallimore, 1988). Adults should vary the degree of support, providing minimal guidance at first and increasing assistance as needed by the child.

SCAFFOLDING CATEGORIES

Following is a *description* for each of the different scaffolding strategies organized from lower to higher levels of support and grouped into six main categories. (Each scaffolding strategy has a corresponding icon that will be used throughout the book for easy reference to the strategy.)

Open-ended questioning   The adult asks questions that encourage children to elaborate on their own ideas and communicate them to others. Open-ended questions are questions with unknown answers that have no one correct response. These include questions that relate to the immediate context ["What do you see?"], questions that relate to past events ["What happened?"], questions that require explanations ["Why?"], questions that help the child go beyond the here and now by relating events to his or her own experiences ["Did this ever happen to you at home?"], and questions that require hypotheses about novel situations and cause-and-effect inferences ["What should we do next?" "What if?"].

Providing feedback   The adult provides information on the child's performance to increase the child's sense of competence (e.g., encouragements,

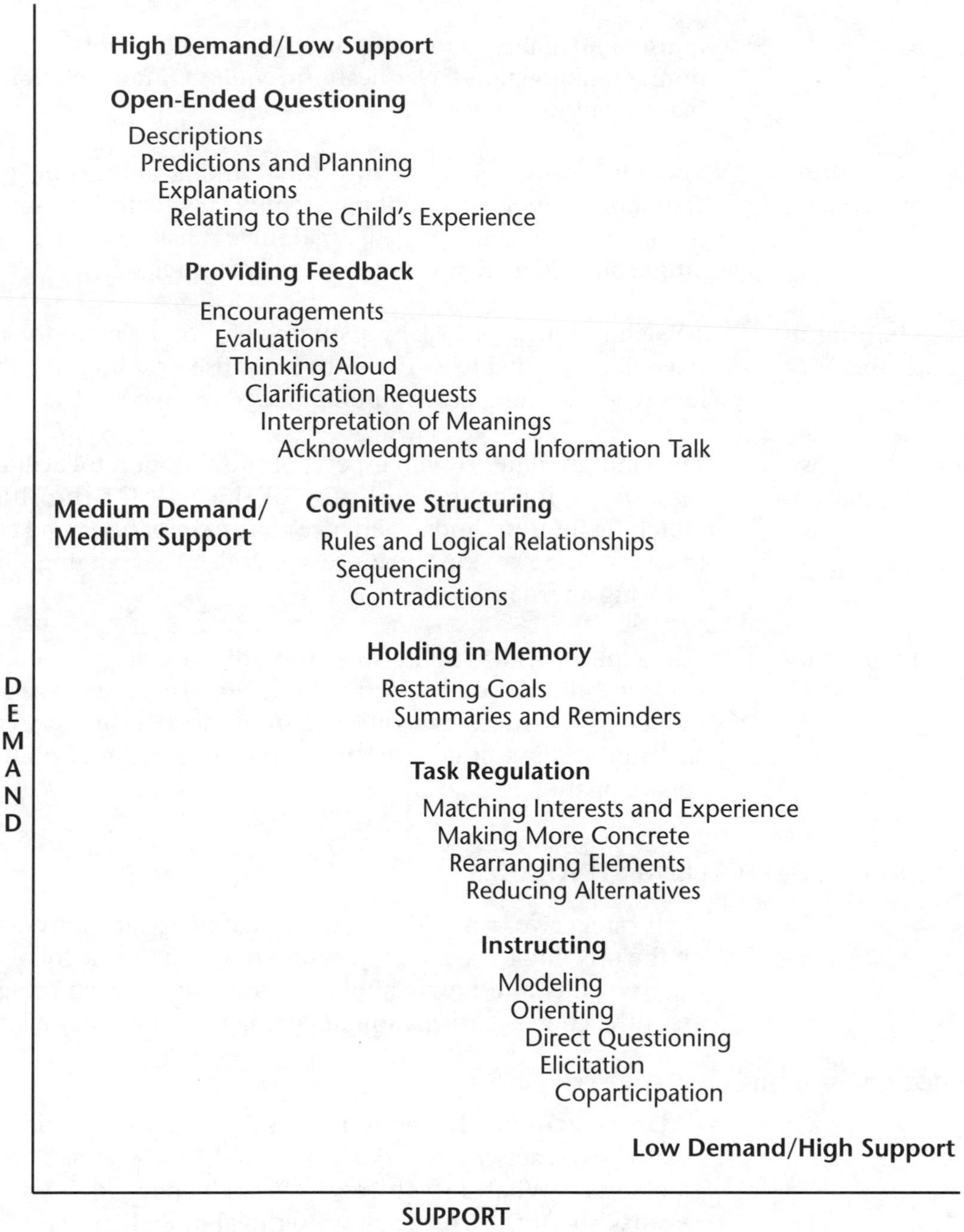

High Demand/Low Support

Open-Ended Questioning

Descriptions
Predictions and Planning
Explanations
Relating to the Child's Experience

Providing Feedback

Encouragements
Evaluations
Thinking Aloud
Clarification Requests
Interpretation of Meanings
Acknowledgments and Information Talk

Medium Demand/
Medium Support   **Cognitive Structuring**

Rules and Logical Relationships
Sequencing
Contradictions

Holding in Memory

Restating Goals
Summaries and Reminders

Task Regulation

Matching Interests and Experience
Making More Concrete
Rearranging Elements
Reducing Alternatives

Instructing

Modeling
Orienting
Direct Questioning
Elicitation
Coparticipation

Low Demand/High Support

D
E
M
A
N
D

SUPPORT

Figure 1.   A continuum of scaffolding strategies.

praise) and ability to monitor and regulate behaviors (e.g., evaluations, thinking aloud, clarification requests, interpretations, information talk).

 **Cognitive structuring**   The adult provides a structure for thinking and acting (Tharp & Gallimore, 1988) and facilitates children's logical reasoning and problem-solving abilities (e.g., making explicit rules and logical relationships, sequencing, pointing out contradictions).

 **Holding in memory**   The adult shares the task by assuming part of the memory demands to enable the child to focus on the response or solution to the problem (e.g., restating goals, summaries, reminders).

 **Task regulation**   The adult modifies certain aspects of the situation to facilitate child mastery by increasing the value of the task for the child (e.g., matching interests and experience) or by simplifying and clarifying the task (e.g., making it more concrete, rearranging elements, reducing alternatives).

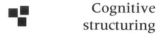 **Instructing**   The adult provides highly structured direct assistance that has an explicit influence on the child's behavior. These strategies include modeling, orienting the child's attention to relevant aspects of the situation, asking direct questions, and prompting elicitations and coparticipation.

DESCRIPTION OF SCAFFOLDING STRATEGIES

Each category of scaffolding has a range of applications depending on the task and the child's understanding of it. In the following section, we illustrate how scaffolding strategies in each category can assist the child's participation in language and literacy activities.

Open-Ended Questioning

- **Descriptions**—The adult helps the child initiate and maintain a topic or activity by asking the child to talk about events and objects ["What do you see?" "What happened?" "What's this story about?" "What shall we write about?"].
- **Predictions and Planning**—The adult helps the child go beyond the immediate context, generalize to novel situations, predict and plan future events, propose alternatives, hypothesize about possibilities, and anticipate eventual difficulties ["What are the things we need to do?" "What else could we use to reach up to the cupboard door?" "What else could you use to count the number of points you earned?" "What do you think might happen if . . . ?" "What could go wrong?" "How could you do this at home?" "Let's think about words to describe your pet"].

- **Explanations**—The adult helps the child provide explanations and explain causes ["Why do you think that happened?" "How is this different from what we saw yesterday?" "What did the wheel do when you poured the water?" "What did you do to make a sound with the drum?"].
- **Relating to the Child's Experience**—The adult helps the child relate a new or strange situation to something the child may have experienced directly ["Has this ever happened to you before?" "Have you ever seen something like this?"].

Providing Feedback

- **Encouragements**—The adult offers simple verbal and nonverbal encouragements and praise on an ongoing basis to increase the child's confidence and sense of self-competence ["That's a good idea!" "That's interesting!"].
- **Evaluations**—The adult encourages the child to check the results of his or her own actions and to judge the appropriateness of his or her own actions ["Did it work?" "Did it move when you blew on it?" "Does that look right?" "Which sound did you hear first?" "You said /t/ and chose a p. Is that right?"].
- **Thinking Aloud**—The adult helps the child describe aloud what he or she is doing or thinking to encourage awareness of the processes involved in solving problems ["Tell me what you are doing," "Talk about spelling that word"].
- **Clarification Requests**—The adult encourages the child to provide reasons for his or her ideas and actions in order to help solve a problem or asks for more specific information to make an action or message clearer ["Why did you put the piece that way?" " Why are you writing to Safa?"].
- **Interpretation of Meanings**—The adult offers interpretations and explains underlying meanings to help the child complete a task, reach a solution, or understand reasons for success or failure of an action ["I don't think Katie understood what you said," "The lady was upset because you talked too loudly in the library," "Tyler and Timmy both start with T. Do you hear other sounds that could help you decide which name this is?"].
- **Acknowledgments and Information Talk**—The adult acknowledges the child's actions and statements by making appropriate comments or verbally describing the child's actions ["Now you're pouring water into the big jar," "You have a c and an a so far"].

Cognitive Structuring

- **Rules and Logical Relationships**—The adult makes explicit underlying rules and helps the child notice relationships (cause and effect, similarities and differences) between events and characteristics of objects ["Did you notice that when the blue one gets smaller, the red one gets bigger?" "These two are the same size," "A husky and a poodle both are dogs," "Cat, rat, fat. They rhyme; they all have -at"].

- **Sequencing**—The adult helps the child find a starting point or continue an action or narrative in a correct sequence ["Which puzzle piece should you choose first?" "What comes after the green one?" "Touch the first box. Which sound came first in milk?"].
- **Contradictions**—The adult helps the child recognize inconsistencies and contradictions between actions, events, and facts ["You said mouse. Does mouse start with /t/?"].

Holding in Memory

- **Restating Goals**—The adult reminds the child of the activity's purpose and of the behaviors expected ["Remember, we are writing this card to tell Tim about our visit to the zoo," "We're listening for the last sound"].
- **Summaries and Reminders**—The adult summarizes events and actions and offers important information to help the child complete a task ["Remember, the one we saw was soft and fuzzy," "We've decided that we are going to the museum of natural history tomorrow and we are going to take the bus. What else?" "You're writing *stop*. You have /s/ /t/ . . . "].

Task Regulation

- **Matching Interests and Experience**—The adult modifies aspects of the task to match closer the interests of the child (e.g., substitute blocks with toy dinosaurs), relate the task to the child's experience ["That's cold like ice cream"], or make the task more familiar by using familiar materials or teaching tasks in a familiar setting or routine (e.g., rhyming words within familiar storybook reading routines) ["Tara brought cookies for snack; before we eat the cookies, let's describe them"].
- **Making More Concrete**—The adult modifies a situation by decreasing the level of symbolic representation and memory demands, for example, by providing visual and other nonlinguistic cues (e.g., making gestures, substituting written words with pictures and real objects) ["I'm thinking of a jungle animal. Guess my word: /t/ /i/ /ger/"].
- **Rearranging Elements**—The adult changes the arrangement of materials to help the child complete the task or solve the problem (e.g., together place puzzle pieces that go together; turn objects in the right directions) ["See, I put a dot in the square for the first sound"].
- **Reducing Alternatives**—The adult simplifies the task by reducing the number of choices ["Should we pick the yellow or

the blue?" "Is this for real or pretend?" "Is this an animal or a bird?" "Here's m and s. Which letter begins mmmmilk?"].

Instructing

- **Modeling**—The adult models problem-solving strategies and oral and written communication by demonstrating or pairing the child with a more experienced peer so that the child learns through observation and collaboration. The adult may, for example, write words for the child to copy, name letters, label objects, reword an incorrect sentence, or recast or expand on the child's utterances by adding new information ["Watch me find the first letter. Here's f. /Fff/. Now you find f"].

- **Orienting**—The adult proposes appropriate tools or strategies to facilitate the child's performance, verbally describes how to perform a task, or draws the child's attention to relevant aspects of the situation ["How about using a typewriter?" "Do you think we could paste them together?" "I would push the green one," "You could ask Dave to help you," "Look at the top of the page," "Shake and cake rhyme. Say shake/cake"]. (Child repeats.) ["They rhyme because shake/cake both have -ake at the end. Let's look for more words that rhyme with shake and cake. More -ake words"].

- **Direct Questioning**—The adult directs the child to a specific action or response by asking questions ["What's the name of this animal?" "Which letter?" "Which sound?"].

- **Elicitation**—The adult directly requests a specific action or verbalization ["Juice. Say juice," "M says /mmmm/. Say /mmmm/"].

- **Co-participation**—The adult encourages the child to accompany the adult in performing an action (e.g., reciting a nursery rhyme together) ["House. /H/ /ou/ . . ."] or filling in the blanks in an utterance ["The eagle flew to the top of the . . .?"].

EXAMPLES OF SCAFFOLDING INTERACTIONS

Adults will use a variety of strategies to teach a skill. Two major guidelines are useful in choosing strategies: 1) observe the child's responses and determine which type of support will best suit the child's needs in that specific situation, and 2) begin with the least intensive assistance and progressively provide more support as needed.

Scaffolding a Word Reading Task

The following example illustrates an adult (A) helping a child (C) read a word in the presence of a peer (P):

A: What are we eating today? (**Open-ended questioning**/*predictions and planning*)

C: (Points to a word)

A: That's a complicated word. Let's look at the letters I wrote down here. First, here's a s, then there's a p—sp. (**Cognitive Structuring**/*sequencing*)

C: Sp.

A: Here's a g, which makes which sound? (**Task Regulation**/*matching interests and experience*)

C: /G/. That starts my name!

A: Right. (**Providing Feedback**/*encouragements*)

A: For Graham. (**Instructing**/*modeling*)

A: Right at the end—What are these letters? (**Cognitive Structuring**/*sequencing*)

P: I and t. (**Instructing**/*modeling*)

C: Oh, you know what? That last one is an i.

A: Great. (**Providing Feedback**/*encouragement*)

A: We put all these sounds together to read the word. (**Cognitive Structuring**/*rules and logical relationships*)

C: (waits)

A: Spa . . . (**Instructing**/*modeling*)

C: Spaghetti. They're really short letters.

A: You think it's a short word? (**Providing Feedback**/*interpretation of meaning*)

A: Let's count the letters. 1-2-3-4-5-6-7-8-9. Is that short? (**Cognitive Structuring**/*contradictions*)

C: Nine letters is a long word.

Working on Multiple Goals

The scaffolding suggestions following each activity are designed to help teachers support their students sufficiently to achieve the primary learning goal targeted by the activity (e.g., to segment words into individual sounds). With the broad range of abilities in today's kindergartens, there may also be times when it is appropriate to aim for achieving different goals with individual children; nevertheless, teachers rarely have the time to conduct multiple activities simultaneously. We have structured *Ladders to Literacy* to allow teachers to address multiple goals within a single activity.

Imagine, for example, choosing Shared Storybook Reading as a center activity in November. The group of seven children arrives at the center, and for five of the children, the goals and procedures outlined in the activity description are appropriately engaging and challenging. One of the children, however, has begun to independently read high-frequency words and to search for letter–sound clues in those words. For that child, providing several opportunities to read individual words on the page and to explain to the other children how he or she reads the word (the goal of The Transition to Reading Words—an activity too difficult at this stage in the year for the other children) is appropriate and easy to provide within the

Table 1.   Early literacy and language behaviors and concepts across curriculum areas

Print awareness	Phonological awareness	Oral language
Print • Book conventions • Awareness of graphic symbols • Letter identification • Writing Letter–sound correspondence • Single sounds/letters • Words	Perception and memory for sounds • Environmental sounds • Words • Phrases • Phonemes Word awareness • Words Phonological skills • Rhyming • Alliteration • Blending • Segmentation	Vocabulary • Words and sentences Narrative skills • Narrations of real events • Books • Narrations of fictional story Literate discourse • Conversations • Categorical organization • Decontextualization • Interpretive/analytic discourse

Shared Storybook Reading activity the others are enjoying. Now, assume that the seventh child in the group is just learning color names—a vocabulary goal that is much too easy for the other group members. The Shared Storybook Reading activity, because of the colorful pictures in the big book, also gives the adult frequent opportunities to direct color identification questions and support to this child within the natural context of reading aloud with everyone ["Find green on this page," "Here's purple. Can you find something that's purple?" "Which color is that monster?"]. Thus, while the goal of the activity for the group is to learn concepts about print, the adult can also incorporate another child's goal of reading words and another child's oral language goal. Teachers will often find meeting goals for individual children within a single activity useful in addressing the needs of a broad range of learners. To make it easier to select activities that facilitate this kind of individualization, we have placed the concepts each activity addresses near the beginning of each activity. Table 1 shows the entire range of concepts developed across all sections of activities. By selecting activities across the three sections, teachers can facilitate a foundation for successful reading.

Chapter 3

Implementing *Ladders to Literacy*

The collection of activities in the *Ladders to Literacy* curriculum is intended to provide vehicles for developing concepts about literacy and preparing for reading and writing instruction in ways that are developmentally appropriate and sensitive to the diversity in kindergarten classrooms. By promoting abilities known to influence later reading development (e.g., phonological awareness, letter knowledge), we can increase the likelihood of a successful transition to first grade and beyond. Within each of the sections to follow, activities have been sequenced loosely by difficulty. It is not necessary to complete all of the activities in one area before proceeding to another; rather, activities can be selected to enhance ongoing classroom routines and special events. Because the three areas are interrelated, teachers will want to include activities across areas in their weekly planning.

ABOUT THE ACTIVITIES

Although the activities lend themselves to teaching a range of early literacy and language skills, each activity has been assigned to one primary area: print awareness, phonological awareness, or oral language. We recommend teachers focus on teaching skills in the designated primary area. Given the range of ages and abilities in inclusive and special education settings, teachers often need to address multiple educational goals within a single activity. Within the primary area (e.g., print awareness), we provide recommendations for how children with different needs can be taught concepts and behaviors that are developmentally appropriate to their individual levels. For each level of support, we suggest teaching strategies to facilitate the individual goals.

Components

Each activity includes a purpose statement with a list of behaviors the activity facilitates, a description of the activity procedures and materials, suggestions for specific child objectives or levels of participation and adult assistance for achieving these objectives, adaptations for specific disabling conditions, and ideas for home activities and parent involvement.

Main Purpose

The main purpose describes the major goals of the activity and how these goals promote the use of literacy and language in daily life settings. It also includes a list of concepts and behaviors across the three major areas of the curriculum (print awareness, phonological awareness, and oral language) stimulated by the activity.

Materials and Description of the Activity

Suggestions are provided for organizing materials, setting up the activity, and encouraging children to participate.

Adult–Child Interactions

The Adult–Child Interactions section describes how, through participation in the same activity, children functioning at diverse levels may learn new concepts and behaviors that are developmentally appropriate to their individual needs and characteristics. We outline three levels of support for achieving the learning objectives (these are the task demands) with corresponding teaching strategies: high demand/low support, medium demand/medium support, and low demand/high support. The skills selected were the behaviors that are the most likely to occur naturally as children participate in a particular activity. As a result, levels of demand may vary from one activity to another. For each level of task demand, we suggest specific facilitation strategies to support the child's learning. Facilitation strategies are organized from low to high support. In general, the more competent child will require minimal guidance from the adult, whereas other children will need more intensive assistance and higher levels of support. Therefore, low-support strategies are the most appropriate for children ready to master a task at a high level of demand. Children learning tasks with lower demands are more likely to benefit from high-support strategies. For each child participating in the activity, the teacher may determine the most appropriate level of demand based on the child's performance and/or the teacher's recent observations of the child. After determining appropriate levels of task demands for each child, teachers should select two or three teaching strategies to assist the child in accomplishing the task. The teacher should begin by using the least-intensive support strategy (usually the first listed). If this does not help the child learn the skill, then the amount of support should gradually be increased. It is important to remember that children will respond differently to different types of support, with some children benefiting from more direct assistance and others from less direct assistance. Children who are ready to take on high-demand tasks may, at times, need high-support teaching strategies (e.g., explicit instructing). In some situations, low-support strategies (e.g., open-ended questioning) might be sufficient for children learning low-demand tasks. During the teaching interactions, adults should evaluate and revise decisions about appropriate levels of support based on the individual child's responses to prior types of assistance.

Adaptations

Recommendations are provided for adapting materials and activity procedures to facilitate the participation of children with visual, motor, or hearing impairments.

Home Link

For each kindergarten activity, we suggest a corresponding activity from the Early Literacy Activities for Children and Their Parents (Appendix A). These activities help parents reinforce learning concepts and behaviors similar to those taught in the classroom.

HOW TO START

All of the activities have been field tested by teachers working in a variety of inclusive and self-contained kindergarten classrooms with children who are at risk, children with disabilities, and children who are typically developing. The classrooms included children from ethnically and culturally diverse backgrounds (African American, Native American, Asian American, Hispanic, and Arabic). The activities span a range of projects and tasks from those directly involving language and literacy skills (e.g., looking at books, writing letters, learning the alphabetic principle) to those in which language and literacy skills are incorporated as fundamental components (e.g., conducting science projects, identifying story grammar). Implementation of activities will depend on the individual teacher's educational philosophy, classroom routines, and material resources. Many activities require minimal preparation and can be conducted daily (e.g., Shared Storybook Reading, Morning/Afternoon Message and News, My First Journal, Clap the Syllables, Nursery Rhymes). Some require more extensive preparation and may be best implemented weekly or monthly (e.g., Science Projects, Musical Instruments, Foreign Languages: Let's Say it Another Way!, Brainstorming). Some activities describe rarely conducted projects (e.g., Following Recipes, Long Jump, Interviews) or are ongoing and long term (e.g., Let's Find Out!).

It is recommended that teachers begin with activities that can be easily integrated within current classroom routines on a frequent basis and with minimal preparation. If looking at picture books and drawing are already a part of the daily class routine, then it will be easy to implement Shared Storybook Reading or My First Journal. If circle time usually involves singing and musical activities, then Listening to Songs and Nursery Rhymes and can be easily used. Beginning with familiar activities allows teachers to focus on facilitating and teaching behaviors rather than implementing procedures. As teachers become more familiar with the instructional strategies, new activities may be added, preferably balancing the activities across the three literacy areas. Activities can be planned to correspond to certain themes and events during the school year (e.g., using My Dream near Martin Luther King, Jr., Day, using Foreign Languages: Let's Say it Another Way! on Cinco de Mayo, using Classroom Post Office on Valentine's Day). Other activities may emerge from unplanned events. An unusually severe snowstorm can lead to a science project on snow. A child's personal experience may lead to a brainstorming session or a special Show and Tell. We suggest the following implementation sequence:

1. **Begin with Print Awareness:** Shared Storybook Reading; Morning/Afternoon Message and News; My First Journal; **Phonological Awareness:** Listening to Songs; Clap the Syllables; Nursery Rhymes; Sound Isolation; **Oral Language:** Show and Tell; Food Talk; Portraits; What Did You Hear?

2. **By mid-year, introduce Print Awareness:** Snack/Lunch Treat Menu; I Found . . .; Classroom Post Office; Fill in the Blanks; Making Books; Photography; Science Projects; **Phonological Awareness:** Rhyming Games; Letter Sound of the Week; First Sound Song; Guess the Word (Blending); **Oral Language:** Treasure Boxes; Book Review/Story Grammar; Book Buddy; My Dream.

3. **During the second half of the year, try Print Awareness:** Following Recipes; Sorting Objects; Long Jump; Landscapes and Maps; The Transition to Reading Words; **Phonological Awareness:** I'm Thinking of a . . . (Blending by Category); Word to Word Matching Game: First Sound; Segmenting with Onset-Rime Boxes; Segmenting into Three Phonemes; Onset-Rime with First Letter. **Oral Language:** Feeling Objects; From This to That; Interviews; Movie Reviews; Foreign Languages: Let's Say it Another Way!; Special Words; Brainstorming.

Table 1 shows the month-by-month implementation schedule for six teachers who participated in research on the effects of *Ladders to Literacy* and who achieved significant gains in literacy for their students. Once activities were introduced, teachers used many of them in an ongoing fashion over several months. Some of the activities (e.g., Following Recipes, Long Jump, Landscapes and Maps, Let's Find Out!) were not included in the first field tests.

Table 1.   Implementation schedule for the activities in *Ladders to Literacy*

Month	Print Awareness	Phonological Awareness	Oral Language
September	Shared Storybook Reading[a]	Musical Instruments Listening to Songs	Food Talk[a] What Did You Hear?
October	Snack/Lunch Treat Menu[a] Morning/Afternoon Message and News[a]	Sound Isolation Rhythmic Activities Clap the Syllables	Enacting Story-books Feeling Objects
November	I Found . . .[a] Fill in the Blanks[a]	Nursery Rhymes Letter Sound of the Week[a] Guess the Word (Blending)[a]	Show and Tell Treasure Boxes
December	Sorting Objects	Rhyming Pictures First Sound Song[b] Pretend Play with Miniature Toys[b]	Portraits From This to That
January	Making Books[a] My First Journal[a]	Rhyming Triplets[a] I'm Thinking of a . . . (Blending by Category)[a] Word to Word Matching Game: First Sound[a]	Interviews Special Words[a]
February	Photography Classroom Post Office[a]	Sing a First Sound[b] Segmenting with Onset-Rime Boxes[a]	Book Review/ Story Grammar[a] My Dream
March	Science Projects	First Sound Bingo[b] Segmenting into Three Phonemes[a]	Book Buddy[a] Brainstorming
April	The Transition to Reading Words[a]	Onset-Rime with First Letter[a]	Movie Reviews
May–June	Integrating Spelling and Reading[a]	Continue blending and segmenting games	Foreign Languages: Let's Say it Another Way!

[a]Once introduced, these activities were used frequently throughout kindergarten.

[b]Once First Sound tasks were learned, teachers used the same games to teach the last sound in words, and then the medial sounds.

SECTION II

Print Awareness

During the preschool years, children become aware of print and books, and this knowledge becomes a foundation for much of later school instruction (McCormick & Mason, 1986; Snow & Ninio, 1986). Children develop a model (schema) of what it means to be literate in our[1] culture and come to understand that 1) reading and discussing text are ways to acquire knowledge, 2) reading and writing allow communication with others, and 3) the sounds of alphabet letters can be combined to represent words in everyday speech. At an early age (1–3 years), children learn vocabulary from interaction with adults and from books (Ninio & Bruner, 1978). When they are a bit older (2–4 years), children acquire more complex linguistic knowledge such as syntax and idiomatic expressions (Snow & Goldfield, 1983). As they become more familiar with storybooks, children learn aspects of narrative structure (Heath, Branscombe, & Thomas, 1986; Sulzby, 1985), acquire more complex real-world knowledge (Crain-Thoreson & Dale, 1992), and learn to appreciate the enormous potential of literacy as a learning tool. Story reading with parents is the most common informal literacy event for young children and has been linked concurrently and predictively to later literacy and language measures (Bus, Van Ijzendoorn, & Pellegrini, 1995). Frequency of story reading in the home and the amount of parent–child engagement during story reading are correlated with later literacy achievement (Chomsky, 1972; Crain-Thoreson & Dale, 1992; Wells, 1985). Teaching parents to read more interactively with their children enhances language development in both typically developing children (Whitehurst et al., 1988) and in young children with disabilities (Dale, Crain-Thoreson, Notari-Syverson, & Cole, 1996; Swinson & Ellis, 1988). Katims (1991) found that young children with mild to moderate delays made significant gains on formal and ecological measures of literacy after a year-long exposure to structured literacy activities involving daily storybook reading by adults, a classroom writing center, and visits to the classroom library. As children enter kindergarten, parents and teachers begin to draw children's attention to print conventions and letter names and sounds, often in the context of writing activities or manipulating magnetic letters (Clay, 1993; Morrow, 1989; Snow, 1983). These activities help children become aware of formal print conventions (e.g., letter shapes, directionality). Children's knowledge of such print conventions is an important predictor of later literacy achievement (McCormick & Mason, 1986; Wells, 1985). In kindergarten, children's abilities to name alphabet letters, particularly to name them fluently, increases the likelihood that reading will develop adequately in first grade (Share & Stanovich, 1995; Wagner, Torgesen, Laughon, Simmons, & Rashotte, 1993; Wolf, 1991).

---

[1]"Our" culture in this book refers to the United States. These experiences, however, are common to children in many other literate societies.

This section provides suggestions for teachers and parents on how to highlight the child's interest in letters and words while reading stories and how to interactively help the child acquire knowledge. Strategies describe how to target questions to the child's developmental level, monitor comprehension, and remain flexible and responsive to the child's interpretations. These strategies enable teachers to use just one activity to address the diverse needs of a group of children in an inclusive setting. Activities assist adults in encouraging children to actively participate in constructing meaning by asking appropriate questions, making comments, modeling active comprehension processes, and talking about how ideas in books relate to the children's real-world experiences. The activities immerse children in authentic literate practice with teachers, other adults, and peers acting as readers and scribes. In this way, children learn to use print and books to communicate as they learn to formally read and write. When children make pictures and talk about them, teachers can forge the print–meaning connection by writing what the child says on the picture. This act of translating children's meaning into print is a powerful practice in beginning literacy; it is one of teaching children that meaning can be preserved by writing and re-created by reading.

Children are encouraged to send messages to each other. These messages may be pictures, invented spellings, or real words, as they are all ways to transcribe the child's thoughts into print. When adults model these communicative functions of literacy by reading these messages and encouraging children to read them, children begin to understand the relationships among language, print, and communication (McLane & McNamee, 1990). Writing, even more than reading, helps us to think, organize our thoughts, and remember events and ideas (Wells, 1985, 1990). This is the most sophisticated expression of literacy in our culture, and it forms the basis for the more disciplined ways of thinking that are introduced in the upper elementary grades. Writing is essential for scientific thinking because it helps us to classify, measure, and remember observations. The idea that writing helps us to think, in simplified form, however, can be introduced successfully to children in kindergarten (McCormick, Kerr, Mason, & Gruendel, 1992; Wells, 1990). Teachers can model these processes by using lists to keep track of whose turn it is, record the weather, or perform a classroom task. Children can learn to find their own name and check it off when their turn arrives. The teacher or child can make tick marks next to the child's name to keep track of how many times a child has played with certain toys or conducted activities. These tallies integrate ideas about quantity and keeping records, again teaching children very basic notions of scientific ways of thinking.

Children's acquisition of print conventions follows a developmental progression. Children who do not yet understand that we have a sound-based writing system have difficulty learning sound–symbol correspondences (Byrne, 1992; Dyson, 1984; Stahl & Murray, 1994). A fundamental goal of *Ladders to Literacy* is to prepare the child to relate phonological awareness to letter sounds, forming a conceptual understanding of how print represents language. By participating in the activities contained in the print awareness area, the child learns 1) conventions of representing language in print, 2) the sound-based nature of our writing system, and 3) how to use letter sounds to read and write words. These goals are accomplished in the context of authentic literacy activities tailored to the child's developmental level.

- **Conventions of representing language in print**—Children need to understand the specific conventions of our writing system. For example, English is read from left to right and from top to bottom. Words are units that we separate with spaces, even though there are no such breaks in oral language. Children are encouraged to pretend to write. Even if the writing is scribbling or the spelling is unconventional, teachers and parents can encourage children for their efforts.
- **Sound-based nature of our writing system**—This aspect of *Ladders to Literacy* goes hand in hand with the phonological awareness activities. As children are immersed in literate activities that help them to hear and manipulate words and sounds, they prepare to make the connection between print and spoken language. Children discover how a word written in a book is a representation of a spoken word. They become interested in learning that letters stand for individual sounds in the language.
- **How to use letter sounds to read and write words**—As children demonstrate interest, adults can help them read and spell words and write messages or label pictures. When children attempt to translate their ideas into print, teachers can introduce all of the formal aspects of our writing system within functional, meaningful contexts.

EARLY LITERACY SKILLS

Many activities in this section address multiple aspects of print awareness or combine print with phonological awareness or language development. Nevertheless, we designed each activity to highlight a particular literacy concept. Following each print awareness concept, we have listed the activity (or activities) in this section that will assist in teaching that concept to children.

Print

- **Book Conventions**—Child will turn pages. Child will orient book correctly and indicate where the book begins and ends. Child will know that print, not pictures, tells the story. Child will know that text begins at top left corner of page and is read from left to right.

Activity: Shared Storybook Reading

- **Awareness of Graphic Symbols**—Child will read environmental print (e.g., logos, road signs, cereal boxes). Child will recognize familiar words and names in print; child will read simple words.

  Activities: Following Recipes; Landscapes and Maps

- **Letter Identification**—Child will name single letters and their common sounds.

  Activities: Snack/Lunch Treat Menu; I Found . . .

- **Writing**—Child will copy shapes, letters, and words. Child will write name independently. Child will write letters and words. Child will use invented spelling (e.g., related letters) to write messages.

  Activities: Morning/Afternoon Message and News; Classroom Post Office; Making Books; Photography

Letter–Sound Correspondence

- **Single Sounds and Letters**—Child will say most common sound for all letters. Child will select a letter to represent a sound.

  Activities: Sorting Objects; Long Jump; My First Journal

- **Words**—Child will use letter sounds to read and write words.

  Activities: Fill in the Blanks; Science Projects; The Transition to Reading Words; Integrating Spelling and Reading

SHARED STORYBOOK READING

Main Purpose   To develop concepts about print

Through story reading with adults, children learn about objects, people, and events in the real world. Cognitive development is facilitated by looking at books that focus on concepts such as colors, numbers, opposites, time, and space. Personal interactions with adults and peers around story reading, as well as reading books about people and feelings, contribute to children's social and emotional development. Through books, children also learn new vocabulary, syntax, narrative structure, and conventions about written language.

Materials   Big books (e.g., *I Can Read Colors* [Edge, 1988], *The Opposite Song* [Edge, 1988]); little books; cards with pictures or words that match those of text

Description of the Activity   Use big books to read to a large group of children during circle time or to a small group as a center activity. Talk about the relevant concepts in the book (e.g., colors, opposites). Call attention to the title, author, and illustrator. Read the story aloud, tracking the print by pointing a finger at each word read. After reading aloud, ask children to recall important points and to find the corresponding part in the text. Draw children's attention to relevant features (e.g., names of colors, words that rhyme, opposites, letters that begin alliterative phrases). Use visual aids (e.g., separate sheets with isolated print or pictures) to help children focus on specific words. Have children mime or sign when appropriate (e.g., rhymes, opposites, other frequently recurring words or pairs). Involve children by having them take turns in reading to each other or teaching their peers and asking them to label pictures or read words. Encourage children to comment on the pictures and the story and to fill in repetitive words and phrases. Ask them to predict what might happen next, to provide explanations, and to relate events to their own experiences. Invite children to mime and to dramatize the stories. After several shared reading experiences with the same text, give children their own little book—a smaller copy of the big book. While you read the big book, encourage children to turn the pages of their little books, read along with you, and point to the print in their little books that corresponds to selected words in the big book. Send a copy of the little book home for children to share with families. Encourage children to look at books during the daily private book reading time in the classroom library area.

This activity develops the following behaviors and concepts that are related to early literacy:

Print Awareness	Print—book conventions, awareness of graphic symbols, letter identification; letter–sound correspondence—single sounds and letters, words
Phonological Awareness	Perception and memory—words, phrases; phonological skills—rhyming, alliteration
Oral Language	Vocabulary—words and sentences; narrative skills—narrations of fictional story

ADULT–CHILD INTERACTIVE BEHAVIORS

High Demand/Low Support

Children listen to the story and look at their little books. They will:

> read simple words and name letters that are contained in the text

Support Strategies

?	Open-ended questioning	Ask for information not portrayed in the illustrations, and encourage children to help you find words on the page that provide that information.
	Cognitive structuring	Show children a short word composed of letter sounds they already know, and encourage children to sound out the letters. > Let's look at the letters in this word. Which letters do you see? If you say the sounds for those letters, then you can read the word. Point out distinctive features, similarities, and differences between the targeted letter or word and other letters or words. > You said this is a b. Does it look the same as this other b here? Look carefully. On which side of the circle is the stick?
	Holding in memory	Have children look for letters to match a target; keep touching the target to provide the visual model while they are searching for matches. > Let's look for more fs on this page.
	Task regulation	Visually isolate a letter or word from the rest of the text by highlighting or underlining. Increase interest in the task by having children select a word or letter to highlight and read. Increase meaningfulness of the task by selecting a word or letter that relates to a main character or event of the story. Ask children to name letters in their names or other letters they have already learned.

Instructing

Model sounding out a few short decodable words, and have children sound them out with you.

> Let's look at this word. The letters say /d/ /a/ /d/. Dad. Do that with me.

Model by reading the word or letter, and then repeat the request.

> This is an m. Show me another m.

Medium Demand/Medium Support

Children listen to the story and look at their little books. They will:

> read simple words and name letters that are contained in the text

Support Strategies

Open-ended questioning

Ask for information not portrayed in the illustrations to help children realize that the information is conveyed throughout the text.

> What is the fox thinking? We can't see that in the picture. What tells us what he is thinking?

Holding in memory

Encourage children to find words on the page that start with a target sound they have already learned.

> Let's find all the p words on this page. I'll make the sound of /p/ while you're looking.

Slowly point to each word, saying /p/ /p/ /p/ to remind children of the letter sound they are trying to match.

Cognitive structuring

Provide verbal information that helps identify the word.

Task regulation

Simplify the task by selecting the first or last word on the page for the children to identify. Highlight or underline specific words for children to read.

Instructing

Ask children to identify words that are in the classroom environment, for example, on posters and labels. Read the word, and have children imitate. Model sounding out frequently occurring decodable words, and lead children through decoding them with you.

Low Demand/High Support

Children listen to the story and look at their little books. They will:

> read simple words and name letters that are contained in the text

Support Strategies

?	**Open-ended questioning**	Encourage children to describe what they see. What do you see in this picture? Show them words that accompany their descriptions.
	Cognitive structuring	Provide verbal information that helps identify the word, for example, bee. The busy, buzzy . . .
	Holding in memory	Remind children to turn the pages of their little books while you turn the pages of the big book. Let's look for more fs on this page. With one hand, touch under the letter that you wish to emphasize. Then keep pointing to that letter (e.g., the f in frog) to provide the visual model while children are looking for matches.
	Providing feedback	Reinforce reasonable responses to the storybook and your questions. Yes, this is a frog. Point to the word on the page, such as frog. Frog starts with /f/. Here's the f that starts f-f-f-frog.
	Task regulation	Increase interest by having children choose pictures to name and link with printed words. Decrease the size of your group (e.g., read to three to six children as a center activity as well as to the whole

group) to encourage participation. Increase meaningfulness of the task by selecting a picture representing a main character or event of the story or that relates to children's own experiences.

Instructing

Ask children directly to name pictures.

What's this?

Show the children the accompanying word(s) to read along with you and then to read by themselves. Model turning pages slowly, and tell children directly to turn the page of their little books. Ask children to show where the book begins and where it ends.

Comments/Adaptations

Comments

Alternative reading materials include newspapers and magazines with photographs and children's diaries, notebooks, and messages.

Link with Phonological Awareness

Use words from the story to encourage auditory blending (Guess the Word [Blending]), segmenting (Segmenting with Onset-Rime Boxes), or first sound/letter matching (Word to Word Matching Game: First Sound).

Adaptations

For children with visual impairments, prepare relief picture sequences or little books that correspond to the story being read. Select important words that appear in the story (e.g., names of main characters), translate them into braille, and give them to children to hold and feel during the story reading. Use props. For children with hearing impairments, use sign language to communicate the main events and characters of the story. Make sure pictures are visible to children.

More Ideas

Send home little books; send home videotaped storybook readings for parents to view.

Home Link

Parent Activity: Going Places—The Library; Print in the Home; Storybook Reading Routines

SNACK/LUNCH TREAT MENU

Main Purpose

To use print as a communication tool

Children learn that print is a tool to communicate with others. This activity prepares children to understand that print contains information about objects and is used pragmatically to allow readers to make choices, such as when reading a menu in a restaurant.

Materials

Cards with words and pictures or a large sheet on flipchart; snack foods

Description of the Activity

Set out cards with labels and pictures or photographs of the day's snack, lunch foods, or special treats on the table before you present the actual foods. Ask the children to identify words and pictures in order to anticipate the snack and make choices as appropriate. During snack, ask the children to associate specific items with their corresponding labels or pictures. Encourage discussions about where foods come from or how they are made ["How do you think we make muffins?" "Where do bananas grow?"]. Encourage children to describe foods, to recognize the larger categories in which they belong, and to express their likes and dislikes. Parents may occasionally bring in special treats or foods for birthdays or holidays. Provide parents with a model menu (e.g., using words and pictures), and ask the parents to make a menu for the foods they bring to class. Keep these menus in a notebook for children to use during play times.

This activity develops the following behaviors and concepts that are related to early literacy:

Print Awareness

Print—awareness of graphic symbols, letter identification

Phonological Awareness

Perception and memory—words, phonemes; phonological skills—alliteration, segmentation

Oral Language

Vocabulary—words and sentences; literate discourse—conversations, categorical organization, decontextualization

ADULT–CHILD INTERACTIVE BEHAVIORS

High Demand/Low Support

Children read the menu to find out what will be served for snack or lunch. They will:

    read simple words and name single letters and sounds

Support Strategies

?	**Open-ended questioning**

Show the written menu to the children before the food is presented. Ask children to predict which foods will be served by reading words on the written menu. Emphasize how the written menu allows them to predict which foods will be served.

> What are we having today?

Ask children to choose a food or drink to talk about by reading words on the menu.

> Which food shall we talk about today?

▪▫	**Cognitive structuring**

Show how the letters in the printed word correspond to the sounds in the spoken word. Touch under each letter as you sound out the word.

> Apple. Here's how I know this word is apple. It starts with a, and that says /aaa/. Here's p, and it says /p/. /Aaap/. Now see the l? That says /lll/. Now we have /aaapll/—apple.

Point out distinctive features, similarities, and differences between the targeted letter or word and other letters or words.

> Look. Here's spaghetti and here's sauce. How do these words start? Can you tell which word is spaghetti?

Provide verbal information about food.

> It's a fruit that monkeys like to eat.

◉	**Task regulation**

Have children touch under individual letters as they sound out the word. Increase familiarity of task by asking children to name individual letters in their names and other words with which they are familiar.

> Yes, you read banana. Tell me the name of a letter in the word banana.

Highlight or underline specific letters.

i	**Instructing**

Provide names of new letters, and have children look for a same letter in another word.

> This is a b. Can you find another b?

Encourage children to help you write the menu labels for foods.

> I need to write banana on today's menu. How shall I start that word?

Medium Demand/Medium Support

Children refer to the menu during snack. They will:

> recognize familiar words and name letters and sounds

Support Strategies

Cognitive structuring

Show children how to use first-sound cues.

> See the b? That tells me the word starts with the sound of b: /b/.

Provide verbal information that helps identify the food.

> It's yellow.

Task regulation

Ask children to identify words for foods that they like or dislike based on pictures. Have children highlight or underline specific words to read. Provide children with choices.

> Does this word spell melon or spaghetti?

Instructing

Read the word, and have children imitate. Show how the letters in the word correspond to the sounds in the spoken word that is pictured.

> Here's how I know this word is apple. (Point to the a.) It starts with a, and that says /aaa/. Here's p, and it says /p/. /AAAp/. Now see the l? That says /lll/. Now we have /aaaplll/—apple. Do that with me.

Touch under the letters as children sound the word out with you.

Low Demand/High Support

Children will:

> identify objects and foods represented in pictures and use first-sound cues to identify pictured words

Support Strategies

Open-ended questioning

Show children the menu with pictures, and ask them to guess the foods that will be served.

> What will we be eating today?

Providing feedback

After children correctly predict the foods using pictures, show children the words on the menu that correspond to the pictures.

Task regulation

Increase interest by having children choose pictures to name. Have children label pictures in the presence of the actual food or drink.

Instructing

Orient children's attention to a picture.

> Look at what we are having today for snack.

Ask children directly to name pictures.

> What's this?

Label the picture, and have the children imitate. Demonstrate how the first letter captures the first sound in the pictured food.

> You said we'd have muffins for snack, and here's the word muffin. What's the first sound you hear in m-m-m-muffin? Here's the letter that says /mmmm/. It's m.

Comments/Adaptations

Comments

Ideas for recipes include playdough (flour, water, nontoxic food colorants), Jell-O, cornbread, banana bread, guacamole, tacos, and cookies. Recipes can be entered into the computer and printed out to give each child his or her own copy. Sequences of actions can be organized as flowcharts.

Adaptations

For children with visual impairments, apply glue around the contours of drawings or paste figures cut out in thick cardboard so that they can feel the shape of the objects. Print names of the objects in braille. Use props.

More Ideas

If the school provides a lunch menu, then ask parent volunteers to illustrate commonly served foods. These labeled illustrations can also be used by the children to develop concepts of food categories.

Home Link

Send home copies of menus for children to describe to their parents.

FOLLOWING RECIPES

Main Purpose To use print as a tool of thought

Children learn that print can be used to label and identify objects, to record and remember sequences of steps, and to guide individual and collective action. This activity focuses on the function of the written recipe and the object labels. The teacher should repeatedly refer to these two forms of print to show the children how print may serve as an organizational framework for individual and collective activities.

Materials Ingredients; containers; utensils; the recipe, written in large print on a big sheet of paper (*Note:* Write each step of the recipe in a different color, accompanied by a picture representing objects and actions involved in each step.)

Description of the Activity Arrange the ingredients for making favorite foods (e.g., cornbread, guacamole, gelatin) or other products (e.g., playdough) on a table. Explain the activity, referring to the recipe written on a large sheet displayed close to the table vertically. Ask the children to identify each ingredient, and write the names of the ingredients on labels attached to the corresponding objects. Have the children prepare the foods, and assist them, as necessary, in following the recipe. Once the activity is completed, encourage the children to reconstruct the sequence of actions involved in preparing the recipe. This activity can be easily linked to others, such as science projects and learning about other cultures. Making guacamole, for example, provides an opportunity to discuss Mexican culture and to learn Spanish words. The pit from the avocado can be used to start a plant and to watch it grow. Facilitate language by having children discuss aspects of the activity, label objects, and talk about the foods. Encourage children to think of words that rhyme with the ingredients (e.g., flour, power) and the colors (e.g., red, Fred).

This activity develops the following behaviors and concepts that are related to early literacy:

Print Awareness Print—awareness of graphic symbols, letter identification

Phonological Awareness Perception and memory—words, phrases; phonological skills—rhyming, blending, segmentation

Oral Language Vocabulary—words and sentences; literate discourse—categorical organization; decontextualization

ADULT–CHILD INTERACTIVE BEHAVIORS

High Demand/Low Support

Children follow and refer to the written recipe with little guidance from the adult. They will:

> read simple words and follow print conventions of reading from top to bottom, left to right

Support Strategies

?   **Open-ended questioning**

Ask children to describe the activity using the written recipe as reference.

> How are we going to make the dough?
> Which ingredients will we need?

Ask children to make predictions based on the information in the written recipe.

> What do you think will happen when you mix the flour and the water?

Have children make cause-and-effect inferences.

> Why is the dough green now?

Task regulation

Have children focus on specific parts of the written information by sequencing actions while pointing to each individual step on the recipe.

> What should we do first?

Holding in memory

Remind children to refer to the written recipe and pictures to guide their actions.

> What does the recipe tell us to do next?

Medium Demand/Medium Support

Children refer to the written recipe and participate in the entire process with some guidance from adults and peers. They will:

> recognize familiar words and use first-sound cues and labels to identify ingredients

Support Strategies

Cognitive structuring

Explain how print provides the information.

> I can find out what to add next by looking at this word.

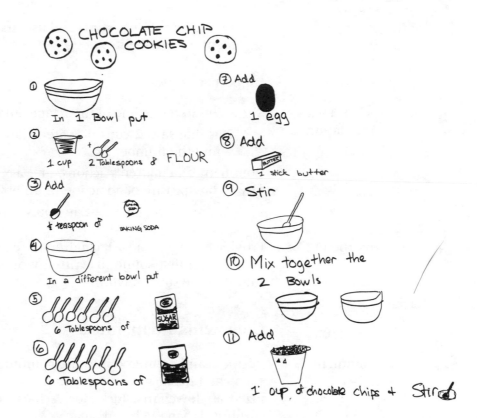

Task regulation

Make the task more concrete by having children describe what they are doing and associate actions and objects with words on the written recipe.

> Here's some water. Can you find the word water on the recipe?

Highlight or underline specific words for children to read. Isolate the portion of the recipe that contains the correct word by covering part of the recipe with a blank sheet of paper. Provide choices.

> Is this word water or salt?

Instructing

Provide a model (e.g., a written label on a card), and ask the children to match it with the corresponding word in the recipe. Model matching the first sound in written and spoken words. Show children how to use their knowledge of first sounds in words to find printed words.

> We're looking for the word f-f-f-flour. How does f-f-f-flour start? Can you find a word in this recipe that starts with f?

Low Demand/High Support

Children refer to the written recipe and participate in the entire process with some guidance from adults and peers. They will:

recognize familiar words and use first-sound cues and labels to identify ingredients

Support Strategies

Task regulation

Show children one line of the recipe, and ask them to find a word.

> This line says 2 cups of water. Can you find water? Can you find the number 2?

Comment on children's actions, and ask them to identify the corresponding picture of an action or an object on the recipe.

> You're pouring water. Can you show me a picture of that?

Instructing

Provide a model, and ask children to repeat. Encourage children to identify the first sound in written words and match it to the first sound in the spoken word.

Comments/Adaptations

Comments

Recipes can be entered into the computer and printed out to give each child his or her own copy. Sequences of actions can be organized as flowcharts. Ideas for recipes include playdough, Jell-O, cornbread, banana bread, guacamole, soup, and cookies.

Link with Oral Language

Later in the day or week, ask children to recall and retell this experience. Write the steps that they remember, and encourage children to consider the sequence of steps and other words that describe what they did.

Adaptations

For children with visual impairments, prepare cut-outs of the ingredients that children can explore tactually, and print the names of ingredients in braille. Use Velcro fasteners or tape to facilitate the participation of children with motor impairments who can easily tape the cut-outs onto the recipe sheet.

More Ideas

Compile a cookbook of favorite foods that children have made in class and distribute to parents.

Home Link

Ask parents to send ideas for simple recipes, especially for dishes that are culturally diverse.

Reference Materials

Katzen, M., & Henderson, A. (1994). *Pretend soup and other real recipes: A cookbook for preschoolers and up*. Berkeley, CA: Tricycle Press.

MORNING/AFTERNOON MESSAGE AND NEWS

Main Purpose

To use print as a communication tool

Children learn that print is a tool to communicate with others. Thoughts and messages can be translated into print and preserved for others to read and reread. Children are made aware of the process of translating meaningful oral language into print.

Materials

Paper; blackboard; markers; chalk

Description of the Activity

Each day during the large-group circle, with the participation of the children, write a message that describes an important event that will take place in the classroom that day. At the end of the day, ask the children to share a significant event that occurred in the classroom that you record and read the following day. You can also ask the children to comment on important events in the community or on their weekend experiences. Write the message on a large sheet of paper or on the chalkboard. Add pictures and objects. Draw children's attention to the process of translating oral language into print, and discuss the advantages of recording written messages and news. Repeat readings of the message and have children retell the message to one another ["Jamie, tell Cindy what we are going to do today"]. Help children read along by pointing with your finger at each word read. Encourage children to read the message along with the adult and discuss the message or the news. Encourage children to make evaluations and express opinions ["What did you think of the muffins that we baked today?"], to investigate cause and effect ["Did you enjoy the trip to the train station?"], to solve problems ["Why didn't it work?" "What could we have done differently?"], and to make predictions ["What are you planning to do this weekend?"].

This activity develops the following behaviors and concepts that are related to early literacy:

Print Awareness

Print—book conventions, awareness of graphic symbols, letter identification; letter–sound correspondence—single sounds and letters, words

Phonological Awareness

Perception and memory—words, phrases; phonological skills—alliteration, blending, segmentation

Oral Language

Vocabulary—words and sentences; narrative skills—narrations of real events; literate discourse—categorical organization, decontextualization

ADULT–CHILD INTERACTIVE BEHAVIORS

High Demand/Low Support

Children offer ideas and dictate coherent narratives. They participate in writing the message by helping to spell selected words. They will:

> name individual letters, identify corresponding sounds, select letters to represent sounds, and use letter sounds to write words

Support Strategies

Open-ended questioning

Ask children to volunteer to spell a word that they dictated.

> Yesterday we had snow. How do we write snow?

Providing feedback

Encourage children to self-evaluate and correct responses by asking them for clarifications.

> Mmmmmilk. Do we need a t in milk?

Cognitive structuring

Have children identify one letter or sound at a time.

> How do we write cat? What's the first letter?

Help children make distinctions and comparisons of relevant features of letters and sounds.

> How do we write a b? On which side of the circle is the stick?

Task regulation

Stretch ["Ssssunday"] or iterate ["T-t-t-today"] sounds to help children identify them. Provide choices.

> Does cat start with c or s?

Instructing

Ask children to help spell words by identifying single letters and sounds.

> What's the first letter in snow?

Fingerpoint, and read one sentence at a time. Then ask children to read that sentence with you as you point to the words.

Medium Demand/Medium Support

Children offer ideas and dictate coherent narratives. They participate in writing the message by helping to spell selected words. They will:

> name individual letters, identify corresponding sounds, select letters to represent sounds, and use letter sounds to write words

Support Strategies

?	Open-ended questioning	Ask children if they would like to add anything to the message.

> Nathan said that it's cloudy today. What else?

Write the additional comments, and ask children to read a word.

Cognitive structuring — Demonstrate the one-to-one correspondence between a child's utterances and the printed words by pointing to each word while reading it aloud.

> Beth said, "I went sledding in the park." And here are the words, *I went sledding in the park.*

Provide strategies for how to identify a printed word.

> Each word is separated from other words by empty spaces.

Help children make relevant distinctions.

> Timmy and Tyler both start with t. How shall we tell which is which?

Task regulation — Circle or highlight with a color marker a word proposed by the child, and ask the child to read it. Circle or highlight names of children in the class or add them at the end of the message as authors, and ask children to identify them. Provide visual cues by drawing a picture or showing an object that corresponds to the chosen word.

Instructing — Point out important words before reading with the children.

> This sentence was about Bro's trip to the hospital. Let's read the word Bro together.

Model reading the word.

Low Demand/High Support

Children attend to the writing of the message. They will:

> participate in dictating and reading the message

Support Strategies

Open-ended questioning — Ask children to recall what the message was about.

> We began, "Today is (blank)." Do you remember what we said today is?

Instructing — Draw children's attention to the link between the oral dictation of the message and the print by pointing to the text while reading the message. Ask them to show that print conveys the message.

> Where does it tell us what we are going to do today?

Circle names of children in the class, and model associating printed and spoken names with classmates represented in the message. Model sounding out a decodable word that appears several times in the message, and encourage children to sound it out with you.

Comments/Adaptations

Comments

The message can also be written on the computer, and individual copies can be printed out for each child.

Adaptations

Messages can be translated into braille for children with visual impairments or into a sequence of signs for children with hearing impairments who are not yet able to read.

Home Link

Parent Activities: Scribbling; Writing Messages

I FOUND . . .

Main Purpose To use print as a tool of thought

Children use what they know about letters and words to make sense of written messages. They practice identifying features of print.

Materials Previous day's "message of the day"; color markers

Description of the Activity Display the large message that the class wrote together from the day before. Ask for volunteers to find something familiar in the writing, such as a child's name, a letter, a word, or a punctuation mark. Children will select a variety of features, depending on their sophistication with print and memory of the previous day's message.

This activity develops the following behaviors and concepts that are related to early literacy:

Print Awareness Print—awareness of graphic symbols, letter identification; letter–sound correspondence—single sounds and letters, words

Phonological Awareness Perception and memory—words, phrases; phonological skills—blending, segmentation .

Oral Language Vocabulary—words and sentences; narrative skills—narrations of real events

ADULT–CHILD INTERACTIVE BEHAVIORS

High Demand/Low Support

Children attempt to read all or part of the text. They will:

> read words and name letters and follow print conventions from top to bottom and from left to right

Support Strategies

Cognitive structuring Help children make distinctions and comparisons of relevant features of letters and sounds.

> That letter looks a lot like a d. It has a circle and a stick. Look where the stick is on this letter. See how it comes first? A stick and a ball. That's a b.

| | Providing feedback | Encourage children's attempts by accepting their rendition of the message. Then read the message back to them, and fingerpoint words as you read it aloud. |

Providing feedback
Encourage children's attempts by accepting their rendition of the message. Then read the message back to them, and fingerpoint words as you read it aloud.

Holding in memory
Remind children about the directionality of print.
> Remember, we start to read at the top of the page, and we read from left to right.

Task regulation
Have children select and circle individual words and letters that they choose to read to isolate them from the rest of the text.

Instructing
Provide a model.
> Tyler circled a t. Can you find another t?

Medium Demand/Medium Support

Children identify key words, such as children's or teachers' names, destinations or trips, or letters in their names. They will:
> recognize memorized words and identify letters and letter sounds

Support Strategies

Providing feedback
Point out words that children recognized correctly.
> Yes, there's Barney, just like you read.

Holding in memory
Remind children of the task.
> Remember, we're looking for all the s words.

Task regulation
Have children choose a word and circle or highlight it with a color marker before reading it.

Instructing
Ask the child to identify a specific word.
> Show me your name.

Model reading the word.
> Joshua circled his name. We wrote his name twice. Can you find his name?

Low Demand/High Support

Children identify key words, such as children's or teachers' names, destinations or trips, or letters in their names. They will:
> recognize memorized words and identify letters and letter sounds

Support Strategies

	Providing feedback	Encourage children's attempts by showing them parts that are correct.

> Tyler does start with t. Do we have another t name in our class?

	Holding in memory	Provide a model for children to match.

> Here's a g. I'll highlight it. Can you find another g?

	Instructing	Orient child's attention to the drawings and other contextual cues.

> Look, there's a cloud here.
> What do you think this word says?

Comments/Adaptations

Comments   Alternative activities for smaller groups—Make sure that each child contributed at least one sentence to the previous day's message. Break down the message in sentence strips. Give each child a strip, and have children put the strips together to re-create the entire message. As each child places the strip, help him or her read his or her news.

Adaptations   Use colors to help differentiate words and letters. Use color to highlight a special letter throughout the message. Discuss the sound of the letter and how the sound is used in words.

More Ideas   Send home a copy of the message for children to share with their parents.

Home Link   Parent Activities: Magnetic Letters; That's My Name!; Writing Messages

CLASSROOM POST OFFICE

Main Purpose	To use written messages as a communication tool

Children learn to use words to construct a written message that others will read. They use words and pictures to describe events and experiences in their lives and share them with others.

Materials	Paper; crayons; markers; pencils
Description of the Activity	Gather the children together to decide on a message that they would like to send to their peers in another classroom. Let the children choose the content of the message. If needed, offer suggestions (e.g., descriptions of an activity conducted during school; questions about peers; comments about the weather, seasons, animals, books, television shows). Have the children dictate a short message and draw pictures to illustrate. Select one or two children to serve as mail carriers to deliver the message to the other class. The teacher in the receiving classroom should show and read the message to the children and display the message prominently. Encourage children to comment and ask questions about the messages. Children may also send individual messages and drawings to special pen pals. Use special occasions, such as Valentine's Day, Halloween, birthdays, and other holidays to encourage writing to friends.

This activity develops the following behaviors and concepts that are related to early literacy:

Print Awareness	Print—awareness of graphic symbols, writing; letter–sound correspondence—single sounds and letters, words
Phonological Awareness	Perception and memory for sounds—phrases; phonological skills—blending, segmentation
Oral Language	Vocabulary—words and sentences; narrative skills—narrations of real events; literate discourse—conversations

ADULT–CHILD INTERACTIVE BEHAVIORS

High Demand/Low Support

Children will:

    draw a picture to communicate a message, label the picture with letters and words, and sign their names

Support Strategies

?	Open-ended questioning	Help children choose and plan their message.

> To whom would you like to write?
> What would you like to say?

Draw children's attention to the importance of taking into account the receiver's perspective with respect to both the content of the message and its form; help children place themselves in the other person's perspective.

> What do you think they would be interested to know about from among the things we did today?

↻	Providing feedback	Praise children's attempts at writing, and make supportive comments about the message conveyed. Request clarifications when messages are unclear.

> What does this mean?

⬛	Cognitive structuring	Show children how to sound out words.

> Dad. /D/ /a/ /d/. /D/ is the letter d, /a/ is the letter a, and /d/ is the letter d again.

Help children sequence sounds and letters.

> Love. Which sound comes first?

👤	Instructing	Demonstrate conventions in letter writing, such as the salutation and the closing.

> You've written a great letter. How will Takesha know that you wrote it?

◖	Task regulation	Encourage children to segment the words that they want to write to help them spell phonetically.

Medium Demand/Medium Support

Children will:

> draw a picture to communicate a message, label the picture, and sign their names

Support Strategies

?	Open-ended questioning	Help the children focus on a specific message.

> What would you like to tell your friend next door about what you did at grandma's house?

↻	Providing feedback	Praise children's attempts at writing, and make supportive comments about the message conveyed.

Rodi and Justin were caught in a thunder storm.

	Instructing	Remind children of the message they told you they were writing. Name words and sound out letters that children have written to help them complete words.

Fun. You wrote /f/. What else is in fun?

	Cognitive structuring	Help children use segmenting to sequence letters correctly.

Mom. Listen to the first sound. /M/.

	Task regulation	Provide a specific purpose for the message, such as making a Valentine's Day card for peers and family. Encourage children to make use of environmental print in the classroom.

You want to write about a dinosaur. Is that word in our classroom? Can you copy the word from the poster?

	Instructing	Print models of words that children request so that they can copy them. Pair children with more advanced peers.

Low Demand/High Support

Children will:

draw a picture to communicate a message, label the picture, and sign their names

Support Strategies

? | Open-ended questioning | Help children decide on what to draw by asking them questions.
> Which animals did you see at the zoo?

Providing feedback | Praise children's attempts at drawing, and make supportive comments.

Task regulation | Provide choices.
> Would you like to draw something that you saw on our field trip to the train station yesterday or that you brought to school today?

Provide objects for children to use as models.

Instructing | Provide a model of their names for children to copy. Help children sequence sounds and letters in words. Prepare pictures for children to paste and add a label to the picture.

Comments/Adaptations

Adaptations | Have children with visual or motor impairments dictate messages and record them on a cassette tape. Children can also generate their messages using the computer.

More Ideas | Have children design cards for their parents for special school events and other occasions. Mail cards and letters to children's homes.

Home Link | Parent Activities: Diaries; Magnetic Letters; Writing Messages

FILL IN THE BLANKS

Main Purpose

To use print as a communication tool

The structure of repetitive language encourages success when children start to read. In this activity, the teacher provides the repetitive format, and children practice writing and reading their own compositions.

Materials

Writing supplies; a phrase to be completed by children, in large type

Description of the Activity

Ask children questions that fit into a simple format ["My name is (blank). I like (blank)"]. Children take turns answering the questions while you write their responses. The group then reads the children's responses together while you fingerpoint to the words. Children take turns reading the responses of other students.

Sample Activities

I Like . . . : My name is (blank). I like (blank); A Pet . . . : I have a pet. You bet! I have a (blank); My Friend: My name is (blank). My friend's name is (blank). We like to (blank); I Can Name: I can name words that start with (blank): (blank, blank, blank).

This activity develops the following behaviors and concepts that are related to early literacy:

Print Awareness

Print—awareness of graphic symbols, letter identification, writing

Phonological Awareness

Phonological skills—blending, segmentation

Oral Language

Vocabulary—words and sentences; literate discourse—decontextualization

ADULT–CHILD INTERACTIVE BEHAVIORS

High Demand/Low Support

Children dictate their responses to an adult, who fills in the blanks. Children read back their responses. They will:

>   recognize a few familiar letters and words

Support Strategies

Providing feedback

Encourage and praise children's attempts at writing and invented spelling. Ask questions to help children clarify their writing.

	Cognitive structuring	Show children how to sound out words.

Pet. /P/ /e/ /t/. /P/ is the letter p, /e/ is the letter e, and /t/ is the letter t.

Help children sound out and sequence individual letters to form words.

Task regulation

Encourage children to segment the words that they want to write in order to help them spell phonetically.

Instructing

Demonstrate how to fill in the blanks.

I'll do the first one. My name is Joanna. I'll write Joanna in the first blank.
I like cupcakes, so I'll write cupcakes here.

Provide models of words for children to copy.

Medium Demand/Medium Support

Children write their own responses. They will:

use invented spelling and letter sounds to write words

Support Strategies

Holding in memory

Remind children of the question.

Remember, here we write what your favorite food is.

Task regulation

Assist by reading the initial text, and have the child complete the sentence.

We like to play with the (blank).

Instructing

Read the first part of the word.

Ma . . . ? (Maria)

Fill in the blanks with the child, and provide models.

This says, "My favorite color is red." We wrote red here. What did we write here?

Demonstrate segmenting short words and representing sounds with letters.

Red. /R/ /e/ /d/. How shall we write /R/?

Low Demand/High Support

Children and adults fill in the blanks together. Children will:

read back their responses and read the repetitive parts of other children's work

What do you like to do?

I _____.

I _____.

I _____.

Support Strategies

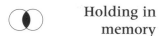

Holding in memory	Remind children of the task.
	Remember, we write your name here.

Task regulation	Assist by reading the initial text, and have the child complete the sentence.
	My name is (blank).

Instructing	Read the repeated phrase, and lead children through the phrase with you. Help children decide on the word to write in the blank.

Comments/Adaptations

Adaptations   For children who are nonverbal, prepare pictures for them to choose from. This activity can also be done on a computer.

More Ideas   Send home copies of their compositions for children to share with their parents. Compile all of the children's compositions into a classroom book.

Home Link   Parent Activity: My Very Own Book

MAKING BOOKS

Main Purpose

To use print as a communication tool

Children learn to link oral language and print. The translation of oral language into print enables the transmission of ideas beyond the immediate context. Making books of children's writing also reinforces the value of print as a tool for preserving thoughts and sharing ideas.

Materials

Paper; paint; paintbrushes; crayons; markers; pictures; glue

Description of the Activity

Have children write and illustrate their own books. Big books for the classroom library can be made as a group project. Children select a theme, and the adults assist in developing a storyline, identifying specific illustrations, and assigning tasks. Puppets or felt board figures can be used to act out a story. This activity can be used to create books that address culturally sensitive topics and issues related to children with disabilities (e.g., children in wheelchairs) that are difficult to find in the commercial literature. Choose subjects of interest to the class (e.g., families; favorite foods, animals, or toys; emotional reactions to birth of a sibling or to neighborhood violence). Children can paint, draw, or paste pictures. The Fill in the Blanks activity provides a good source for classroom books. Gather a classroom set of responses to one prompt (e.g., A Pet . . . , I Like . . .), and make a class cover for the book (Pets in Room 18). Read the book with the class during storytime, and add it to the classroom library for children to read to each other or alone. Children can also work in small groups or individually to make books.

This activity develops the following behaviors and concepts that are related to early literacy:

Print Awareness

Print—book conventions, awareness of graphic symbols, letter identification, writing; letter–sound correspondence—single sounds and letters, words

Phonological Awareness

Perception and memory—words; phonological skills—rhyming, blending, segmentation

Oral Language

Vocabulary—words and sentences; narrative skills—narrations of real events, narrations of fictional story

ADULT–CHILD INTERACTIVE BEHAVIORS

High Demand/Low Support

Children write or dictate text and read completed books independently. They will:

name letters and corresponding sounds and use invented spelling and letter sounds to write words

Support Strategies

? Open-ended questioning	Help children elaborate ideas and plan a story.

> What do you want to write about?
> What will happen?

Help children plan formats and the use of graphics and print (e.g., drawings, photographs, dictated text, own words, letters). Help children select specific words and letters that they can attempt to write themselves.

Providing feedback	Encourage and praise children's attempts at writing and invented spellings. Have children read aloud words and identify letters and sounds of letters that they wrote themselves.
Cognitive structuring	Help children break down words into individual letters and sounds.

> What's the first letter in tiger?

Holding in memory	Summarize events that children have dictated to help them continue the story. Spell or read aloud parts of words or letters that children have written.

> Remember here how you wrote m.
> Dog. You wrote d, o.

Task regulation	Propose a story that relates to an event familiar to the child.

> Let's write a story about your visit to the doctor.

Emphasize the sound of the letter in words by stretching ["ssspider"] or iterating ["b-b-b-bear"] the sound.

Instructing	Model writing words and letters for the child to copy or imitate.

Medium Demand/Medium Support

Children participate with the adult and peers in identifying topics, dictating events, and adding drawings and letters. Later, they look at completed books independently. They will:

name letters and corresponding sounds and use invented spelling and letter sounds to write words

Support Strategies

? Open-ended questioning	Help children identify a topic for the book or an idea about which to dictate or draw.

> What should we write here about the frog?

Cognitive structuring	Have children identify one letter or sound at a time.
	How do we write cat? What's the first letter?
	Help children make distinctions and comparisons of relevant features of letters and sounds.
	How do we write a b? On which side of the circle is the stick? And what about the d?
	While writing children's dictations, emphasize the link between words the children say and the printed text; read back dictations aloud and point to corresponding words.
Holding in memory	Remind children of the directionality of print.
Task regulation	Provide choices.
	Does cat start with a c or an s?
Instructing	Pair children with peers who have more skills. Model writing words and letters for the child to copy or imitate. Help children to listen for a letter sound they can use to begin writing a message.
	You said, "We went to the park." Do you hear any letter sounds in "we" that could help us write that down?

Low Demand/High Support

Children participate with the adult and peers in making the book by drawing and naming figures and words. Later, they look at completed books with an adult or a more capable peer. They will:

name letters and corresponding sounds and use invented spelling and letter sounds to write words

Support Strategies

?

Open-ended questioning

Ask children what they would like to draw or tell about.

Providing feedback

Encourage children's attempts at labeling. Help them interpret their drawings.

> That looks like a sun to me. What do you think?

Task regulation

After children draw their pictures, ask them to explain what they drew. Suggest they write the name of their picture.

> I see your lion. How shall we write lion? Can you add some letters to label your picture?

Show children where to write their name or other short responses.

> This line says, "My name is (blank)." What will you write in this space?

Instructing

Show children how to write a letter to label a picture.

> You've drawn a lion, and lion starts with an l. Do you see an l on the wall? It looks like this.

Show children an l, and encourage them to write an l by their picture. Model reading each child's contribution from a Fill in the Blanks activity. Fingerpoint to the words, and encourage the entire group to read the page together.

> Whose page is this? Yes, there's Brittany's name. She wrote, "I have a pet. You bet. I have a dog."

After several of the children's pages have been read and the model has been clearly established, ask the child who needs high support to read a page independently after the whole class has read it.

Comments/Adaptations

Adaptations

Songbooks with pictures and culturally diverse tunes can be made for musical instrument activities. Make a recipe book of foods made in class or described by children. Include recipes of ethnic meals children eat at home.

Home Link

Parent Activity: My Very Own Book

PHOTOGRAPHY

Main Purpose	To use familiar images and symbols as tools of thought
	Children learn that two-dimensional images can document events that happened in the past. They use photographic records to stimulate reflective thinking and language.
Materials	Camera; paper; binder
Description of the Activity	Take photographs of children engaged in various activities or of interesting objects seen in the classroom or during a field trip. Later, show the photographs to the children. Encourage them to identify objects and to remember and describe events. Create albums by mounting the photographs on paper and writing brief descriptions of the pictures. Laminate them, and put them in a binder to which the children can have easy access.
	This activity develops the following behaviors and concepts that are related to early literacy:
Print Awareness	Print—writing
Phonological Awareness	Perception and memory—words; phonological skills—segmentation
Oral Language	Vocabulary—words and sentences; narrative skills—narrations of real events; literate discourse—conversations, decontextualization

ADULT–CHILD INTERACTIVE BEHAVIORS

High Demand/Low Support

Children make comments and relate events about objects and events in photographs. They will:

> use invented spelling and letter sounds to write words and messages

Support Strategies

?	Open-ended questioning	Ask children questions about events represented in the photographs to help them choose what to write.
		What were you doing here?
		Why was Susan laughing?
		Was it fun?
		Was it big enough?

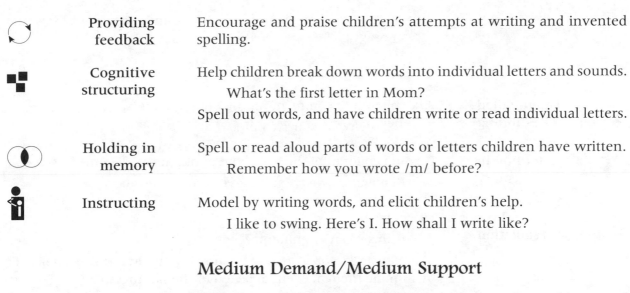

| | Providing feedback | Encourage and praise children's attempts at writing and invented spelling. |

Cognitive structuring

Help children break down words into individual letters and sounds.

> What's the first letter in Mom?

Spell out words, and have children write or read individual letters.

Holding in memory

Spell or read aloud parts of words or letters children have written.

> Remember how you wrote /m/ before?

Instructing

Model by writing words, and elicit children's help.

> I like to swing. Here's I. How shall I write like?

Medium Demand/Medium Support

Children make comments and relate events about objects and events in photographs. They will:

> use invented spelling and letter sounds to write words and messages

Support Strategies

Open-ended questioning

Encourage children to formulate a message.

> What happened here?
> Why were you laughing in this picture?

Providing feedback

Encourage and praise children's attempts to write. Ask children to read back their writing.

Instructing

Describe some aspect of objects or actions in the photograph, and encourage children to add their comments.

> You're counting apples. What else are you doing?

Begin writing, and then ask children to continue.

> Your turn to write.

Orient children's attention by pointing to specific objects or actions in the photograph.

> What's this?
> Look!
> What are you doing here?

Write letters and words for children to copy.

Low Demand/High Support

Children make comments and relate events about objects and events in photographs. They will:

use invented spelling and letter sounds to write words and messages

Support Strategies

?

Open-ended questioning

Ask children to comment on the photographs.

Tell me what you see here.

Holding in memory

Remind children of the event the photographs document.

Remember, we went here yesterday afternoon.

Task regulation

Offer choices.

Is this mom or grandma?

Make the task more concrete by showing children the real object or by miming the real event depicted in the photograph.

Instructing

Ask direct questions.

What's this?

Provide a model, and have children repeat.

House starts with /h/. Which letter makes /h/? We'll write h to start house.

Comments/Adaptations

Comment

This activity is best conducted with small groups of children as it requires individualized attention.

Adaptations

Use a tape recorder to record sounds during field trips (e.g., animal noises at the zoo) for children with visual impairments.

More Ideas

Use family photograph albums to encourage children to relate events in the past. Ask children to evaluate experiences ["What was the most fun that day?" "Where shall we go first next time we go to the zoo?"] and to consider relations and sequences among events ["How old were you then?" "Which one of these photos came first?"].

Home Link

Parent Activity: Art Portfolios

SORTING OBJECTS

Main Purpose	To use print as a tool of thought
	Children learn that print can be used to organize experiences and categorize objects and events.
Materials	Interesting objects such as shells, seeds, nuts, rocks, toy dinosaurs and other animals, foreign coins, and so forth; different colored containers, trays, bags, jars, and so forth; crayons; markers; paper/sticker labels; glue
Description of the Activity	Gather an assortment of objects. Talk to children about how they might put them in groups. Ask children which categories they want to use to sort the objects ["How are you going to put together the seeds that belong together?"]. Provide hints ["Do we have a lot of colored seeds?" "Do we have a lot of seeds that have different shapes?" "Which shells are you going to put in this box?"]. Have children look for similarities in objects (e.g., shells, seeds, toy dinosaurs); and put those that they think belong together into groups by color, size, or texture. Children should be encouraged to use their own criteria for grouping (e.g., favorite and nonfavorite objects). Ask children to provide reasons for their classifications ["Why did you put these shells together?"]. Have the children put the objects in colorful boxes or other containers. Children can print labels with the names of categories, criteria for classification, and other characteristics of the objects. Pictures and other symbols may also be prepared. Diversify the activity by introducing pretend play. Have children draw houses and yards for different groups of animals or garages and hangars for cars and airplanes, respectively. Draw children's attention to the function of the label ["What does this tell us?"]. Integrate classification and labeling into daily classroom routines. For example, have children sort classroom objects (e.g., different types of objects that go on different shelves or in different boxes or drawers) and prepare labels.
	This activity develops the following behaviors and concepts that are related to early literacy:
Print Awareness	Print—awareness of graphic symbols, writing; letter–sound correspondence—single sounds and letters, words
Phonological Awareness	Perception and memory—words; phonological skills—segmentation
Oral Language	Vocabulary—words and sentences; literate discourse—categorical organization, interpretive/analytical discourse

ADULT–CHILD INTERACTIVE BEHAVIORS

High Demand/Low Support

Children sort objects into categories. They will:

> use invented spelling and knowledge of letter sounds to write words.

Support Strategies

?   Open-ended questioning

Have children identify categories and write labels, and help them determine categories by asking them to provide reasons for their classification.

> Why did you put these rocks together?

Providing feedback

Encourage and praise children's attempts at writing and invented spelling. Encourage children to think aloud as they sort objects and write labels.

> Big, medium, and large. Big. B-b-b.

Cognitive structuring

Assist children in grouping objects and determining labels by drawing their attention to similarities and differences between objects.

> How are these seeds alike?

Help children break down words into individual letters and sounds.

> Look at the first letter. Which sound does it make?

Spell out words, and have children write or read individual letters.

Holding in memory

Spell or read aloud parts of words or letters children have written.

> Big. You wrote b. What comes next?

Instructing

Model the alphabetic principle by saying the word, segmenting the word into constituent sounds, and representing sounds with letters.

> Brown. /B/ /r/ /ow/ /n/. I need a b for /B/. . . .

Medium Demand/Medium Support

Children sort objects into categories. They will:

> use invented spelling and knowledge of letter sounds to write words

Support Strategies

Cognitive structuring

Assist children in grouping objects by drawing their attention to similarities among objects and reading the written label to identify the group.

> How are these rocks alike? We wrote it here.

Holding in memory

Help children recognize written words on labels by reminding them of their definitions and categories.

> Remember, you said these go together because they are big rocks.

Task regulation

Give children a reason to read the labels by asking them to group additional objects.

> Here's another green seed. In which box does it go?
> On which shelf does the rhino go?

Add visual contextual cues and drawings to written labels (e.g., place a banana by a yellow color card and an apple by a red color card; place a picture of a seed and a rock by the corresponding labels. Provide choices.

> Does this word say "big" or "little"?

Instructing

Ask direct questions to help children define categories to write on the labels.

> Which color is this?

Assist children in grouping objects by giving them directions.

> Let's put all of the red bears together and write the word red on this jar. Put this red bear in the correct jar. Can you find more red bears?

Say the first sound of the word to help children guess what the label says. Model reading the label, and have children repeat. Provide models of words for children to copy.

Low Demand/High Support

Children sort objects into categories. They will:

> use invented spelling and knowledge of letter sounds to write words

Support Strategies

Task regulation

Draw pictures of objects, or give children photographs.

Have children sort objects by matching them with pictures or other visual representations (e.g., place all leaves on a picture of a leaf, place all rocks on a picture of a rock).

 Instructing   Ask children to repeat labels provided by peers and to segment the label's first sound as the adult writes the label.

Comments/Adaptations

Adaptations   Use braille and relief pictures for children with visual impairments.

More Ideas   Have children take home containers (e.g., cups, boxes) with labels to sort and classify objects (e.g., color crayons) they have at home.

Home Link   Parent Activity: Going Places—The Zoo

SCIENCE PROJECTS

Main Purpose   To use print as a tool of thought

Literacy skills are fundamental in scientific activities. Children must read and write to gain and communicate knowledge. Labeling objects and events and recording observations and data are important aspects of scientific experimentation.

Materials   Materials for specific science project; notebooks; markers; pencils; posters; paper; books; charts

Description of the Activity   When planning science projects (e.g., planting seeds, studying animals), systematically integrate literacy activities into the project. For example, introduce the project by reading books about the topic. Show relevant pictures, and hang related posters in the science area. Have children make and label drawings. Prepare big charts on which children can record relevant daily data (e.g., colors, heights, lengths, weights, shapes). Use notebooks and bulletin boards on which children can write or draw observations and exchange messages on the progress of the project or experiment. Encourage children to categorize objects and events at both basic (e.g., bean, carrot) and superordinate (e.g., vegetable) levels. Expose children to simple scientific terms, and encourage them to seek definitions of new words. Involve children in planning the project. Before and during the project, facilitate a discussion about the project. Have children make predictions, formulate hypotheses, relate events, evaluate, and provide explanations and clarifications. Guide children to note relevant features and to notice similarities and differences and changes over time. If necessary, ask them direct questions ["Which color was it before?"]. At the end of the project, have the children use the data and observations recorded to summarize and evaluate the experiment. Have the children dictate a brief report based on their observations to go in a notebook. Make a poster or design an exhibit to share information with classmates, the children's families, and children in other classrooms.

This activity develops the following behaviors and concepts that are related to early literacy:

Print Awareness   Print—book conventions, awareness of graphic symbols, letter identification, writing; letter–sound correspondence—words

Phonological Awareness   Perception and memory—words; phonological skills—segmentation

Oral Language   Vocabulary—words and sentences; narrative skills—narrations of real events; literate discourse—decontextualization

ADULT–CHILD INTERACTIVE BEHAVIORS

High Demand/Low Support

Children prepare lists of things needed to grow plants; make labels; write the names of different plants they are growing; record numbers; mark dates and heights; and record events, such as rain or snow. Children will:

> use letter sounds to write and read simple words

Support Strategies

? Open-ended questioning

Ask children to identify relevant information to record.

> What should we write on the list?
> What do we need to know about this?
> How can we keep track of how it's growing?

Ask children to describe objects and events by referring to written information.

> How much taller is our sunflower?

Providing feedback

Encourage and praise children's attempts at writing or invented spelling. Comment on the explanations and predictions they make.

Cognitive structuring

Help children read and write words by having them sound out letters one at a time or segment a spoken word into sounds.

> What's the first sound in sun?

Show children how an object might fit into two different categories.

Holding in memory

Remind children of the purpose of recording information.

> Remember, we need to write down how many cups of water it took to fill up this can so that we can decide whether the bottle is bigger or smaller than the can.

Instructing

Sound out words, and point to each letter as you say the sound. Model reading and writing new words and letters. Demonstrate the recording system.

> Here are all of the days of the week.
> We measured the rainfall on Monday and wrote it here. Where shall we write today's measurement?

Medium Demand/Medium Support

Children prepare lists of things needed to grow plants; make labels; write the names of different plants they are growing; record numbers; mark dates and heights; and record events, such as rain or snow. Children will:

use letter sounds to write and read simple words

Support Strategies

? **Open-ended questioning**

Ask children to identify relevant objects or events to draw and label.

Which pictures will we need if we want to record the weather?

Providing feedback

Encourage and praise children's attempts at drawing, writing, and reading. Help children evaluate their drawings.

Did you draw all of the parts, or is something missing?

Cognitive structuring

Help children identify relevant features to record by pointing out categories and relations.

We'll need to know which are sunflower seeds and which are corn seeds.
The green jar is bigger.

Explain how pictures and signs are used to record and report information.

Every day we write our names on the attendance chart so we know who came to school each day. Tell me the name of someone who is here today.

Holding in memory

Remind children of the purpose of recording objects and events.

We need to draw what the tadpole looks like now to help us remember what it looked like before it became a frog.

Task regulation

Provide choices.

Look at my ruler. Is that 2 inches or 6 inches?

Instructing

Give children suggestions for drawings.

Let's draw a sun, a cloud, and rain.

Say the first sound in words to help children guess the label.

This word starts with /sss/.

Write labels, and have children copy letters and words. Model reading the words on the labels.

Low Demand/High Support

Children prepare lists of things needed to grow plants; make labels; write the names of different plants they are growing; record num-

bers; mark dates and heights; and record events, such as rain or snow. Children will:

> use letter sounds to write and read simple words

Support Strategies

Cognitive structuring

Explain how pictures and signs are used to record and report information.

> Every day we record the weather on our calendar. Look outside the window. Choose the picture that tells us what the weather is like.

Task regulation

Have children choose from drawings and pictures.

> Here's a picture of the sun, and here's a picture of a cloud. What is the weather like today?

Instructing

Ask children to find out specific information.

> In which pot did we plant the sunflower?
> What was the weather like yesterday?

Orient the children to relevant information.

> Look. These lines show us how far the turtle walked.

Comments/Adaptations

Comments

Prepare sequence cards before the activity. Have children draw before-and-after sketches (e.g., melting ice, growing seeds in potato heads). Use different colors to differentiate states. Photograph or videotape the results. The computer can be used to generate graphs and bar charts.

Adaptations

Children with visual impairments can record observations on an audiotape.

More Ideas

Planting seeds and charting growth; recording weather observations with weather chart; making potato heads with grass-seed hair; melting ice with salt and adding paint to fill cracks; measuring amount of liquid in containers of different shapes and sizes (use measuring cups with colored tape to mark levels); freezing objects in water; measuring shadows; looking with a magnifying glass or through a prism

Home Link

Parent Activity: Measuring

LONG JUMP

Main Purpose   To use print as a tool of thought

Children learn that printed symbols can be used to plan and organize events, make measurements, and serve as a record for making decisions.

Materials   Sand pit; paper; masking tape; markers

Description of the Activity   Have children take turns running from a starting point and jumping into a sand pit. Involve children in planning the event. Help children develop rules for deciding on the order of participation and for measuring and recording the jump. Use tape to mark the starting line. Use another piece of tape that you mark with measurement symbols. Place the measurement tape along the sand pit to measure the length of the jump. On a large sheet of paper, list children's names in the order in which each child will jump. Record by each child's name the length of the jumps. Make a bar graph of the results, and encourage children to compare the length of their jumps. Use a variety of symbols (e.g., numbers, letters, pictures, signs). For example, write the word start and place a picture of an arrow at the starting line in the direction of the runway. Use clear visual markers to indicate the track and the starting points for running and jumping. Let children have practice jumps. If necessary, provide verbal cues ["Run! Run! Run! Jump now!"] or accompany the child by running along for part of the way. Children can be assigned different responsibilities: jumping, measuring the jump, recording the measurements, or monitoring the order of participation.

This activity develops the following behaviors and concepts that are related to early literacy:

Print Awareness   Print—awareness of graphic symbols, letter identification, writing

Phonological Awareness   Perception and memory for sounds—words; phonological skills—segmentation

Oral Language   Vocabulary—words and sentences

From Forman, G. (1993). Multiple symbolization in the Long Jump Project. In C. Edwards, L. Gandini, & G. Forman (Eds.), *The hundred languages of children* (pp. 171–188). Norwood, NJ: Ablex; adapted by permission.

ADULT–CHILD INTERACTIVE BEHAVIORS

High Demand/Low Support

Children participate in the event at various levels in the planning, competition, measuring, and scoring. They read and write names, numbers, and other words related to the event. They will:

read simple words and use letter sounds to write words

Support Strategies

? Open-ended questioning

Encourage children to participate in the planning process and identify reasons and methods for recording events.

What are the important things we will need to write down?
How will we know whose turn it is to jump?
How will we decide who jumped the farthest?

Cognitive structuring

Encourage children to refer to the written information to establish categories and sequences and to examine relationships.

Let's group jumpers into long jumpers and short jumpers.
In which order are we jumping?
Whose jump was the longest?
Does running fast help to jump longer? Let's look at the results to find out.

Show how the letters in the printed word correspond to the sounds in the spoken word. Touch under each letter as you sound out the word.

Start. Here's how I know this word is start. It starts with s, and that says /sss/. Here's t, and it says /t/. Ssst.

Help children sequence sounds and letters as they write.

Andy. What's the first sound? /Aaa/. Which letter is that? Which sound comes next?

Task regulation

Have children touch under individual letters as they sound out the word. Highlight or circle specific words for children to read.

Instructing

Say the first sound to help children guess the word.

This word starts with /sss/.

Medium Demand/Medium Support

Children participate in the event at various levels in the planning, competition, measuring, and scoring. They read and write names, numbers, and other words related to the event. They will:

read simple words and use letter sounds to write words

Support Strategies

Cognitive structuring

Show children how to use a list of names to determine fair turns.

> Let's find your name in this list. Look. You jump after Brian. See, Brian's name is just before yours, and your name is right after Brian's.

Task regulation

Ask meaningful questions that encourage children to refer to written words and symbols for answers.

> Whose turn is it next?
> How long was Mara's jump?

Ask children to read their own name when it's their turn and to read the length of their own jump. Ask children to identify letters in familiar words and in the context of meaningful tasks.

> Whose turn is next? Andy's. Can you find the letter d in the name Andy?
> Can you find the letter f in the word finish?

Instructing

Say the first letter to help children guess the word.

> This name starts with a b.

Model reading names, numbers, and letters; and ask children to repeat.

Low Demand/High Support

Children participate in the event at various levels in the planning, competition, measuring, and scoring. They read and write names, numbers, and other words related to the event. They will:

> read simple words and use letter sounds to write words

Support Strategies

Instructing

Ask children to interpret the signs before they act.

> What does this sign tell you to do?

Provide verbal cues.

> You have to run to the sand pit from here.

Model appropriate behaviors (e.g., running, jumping, waiting).

Comments/Adaptations

Comment

This activity is best conducted with small groups, as young children have difficulty waiting a long time for a turn.

Adaptations

Children with motor impairments can assume a major role in the planning and in the scoring.

Home Link

Parent Activity: Measuring

MY FIRST JOURNAL

Main Purpose	To use print as a tool of thought

Children learn to express, understand, and organize their emotions and thoughts by creating a graphic and written record of their own thoughts, ideas, and experiences.

Materials   Individual notebooks; crayons; pencils; markers; pictures; photographs

Description of the Activity   Provide each child with his or her own notebook to record experiences, ideas, and feelings during the school year. Set aside specific times during the day for children to write or draw in their notebooks. Children may choose to share their journal with their classmates during the group times.

This activity develops the following behaviors and concepts that are related to early literacy:

Print Awareness   Print—book conventions, awareness of graphic symbols, letter identification, writing; letter–sound correspondence—single sounds and letters

Phonological Awareness   Perception and memory—words; phonological skills—blending, segmentation

Oral Language   Vocabulary—words and sentences; narrative skills—narrations of real events, narrations of fictional story; literate discourse—conversations, decontextualization, interpretive/analytic discourse

ADULT–CHILD INTERACTIVE BEHAVIORS

High Demand/Low Support

Children draw pictures, dictate a structured narrative, and write words and messages. They will:

> write messages, label pictures, and use invented spelling and letter sounds to write words

Support Strategies

Open-ended questioning   Assist children in organizing their text.
> What do you want to write about?

Providing feedback   Encourage and praise children's attempts at writing or invented spelling. Have children talk aloud as they draw and write messages, words, and letters.
> I'm writing shaggy . . .

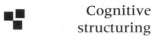

Cognitive structuring — Help children read and write words by having them segment words into sounds and sound out letters one at a time.

Instructing — Sound out words, and point to each letter as you say the sound. Model reading and writing new words and letters by sounding them out first if needed.

Medium Demand/Medium Support

Children draw pictures, dictate a structured narrative, and write words and messages. They will:

> write messages, label pictures, and use invented spelling and letter sounds to write words

Support Strategies

Open-ended questioning — Encourage children to draw pictures and dictate sentences by helping them identify a topic.

> How about writing about your favorite science project?
> Tell us about what you saw today on your way to school.

Ask open-ended questions about children's drawings.

> What's happening here?

Providing feedback — Encourage and praise children's attempts at drawing and writing. Have children talk aloud as they draw and write words and letters.

> I'm drawing two circles for the eyes, then a mouth . . .
> I'm writing "shaggy" . . .

Comment on children's drawings to help them elaborate their drawings.

> You're drawing a face. A face has eyes, a nose, and a mouth.
> You're drawing a bus, but it looks like it's sitting on the street. What else do you need to add?

Point out the children's appropriate choices for letters to represent words.

Task regulation — After children draw their pictures, ask them to tell you what they drew, and suggest they write the name of their picture.

> I see your lion. Can you add some letters to label your picture?

Suggest choices for letters.

> Bus. Which letter starts bus: a, b, or f?

Instructing — Show children how to write a word or letter to label a drawing.

> You've drawn a lion, and lion starts with l. Do you see an l on the wall? It looks like this.

Use children's dictations as labels, and model how to write the words.

Low Demand/High Support

Children draw pictures, dictate a structured narrative, and write words and messages. They will:

write messages, label pictures, and use invented spelling and letter sounds to write words

Support Strategies

? **Open-ended questioning**

Encourage children to draw pictures by helping them identify a topic.

Tell us about your favorite pet.

Ask open-ended questions about children's drawings.

What's happening here?

Providing feedback

Encourage and praise children's attempts at writing. Have children talk aloud about their drawing and the word(s) they are writing.

Instructing

Ask children what they would like for you to write on their drawings, and encourage them to read the words with you and to their classmates.

Comments/Adaptations

Adaptations Children with visual impairments may keep a journal in the form of a personal audiotape.

Home Link Parent Activity: Diaries

LANDSCAPES AND MAPS

Main Purpose   To use print as a tool to acquire knowledge

Children learn how graphic symbols, drawings, words, and signs can be used to represent space, the classroom, familiar landscapes, towns, countries, or the world.

Materials   Large or small blocks; paper; crayons; paint; boxes; cloth; sandbox

Description of the Activity   Have children work as a group to create familiar large-scale landscapes such as mountains, lakes, rivers, bridges, or buildings. Use large blocks to build houses, blue cloth or paper to form rivers and lakes, or a box to represent a mountain. Landscapes can also be created by playing with sand in the sandbox. For smaller-scale landscapes, have children draw maps or build playdough models of the classroom, school, home, or neighborhood. Use print to label various landmarks (e.g., a lake, the zoo, streets, a school, traffic signs, directions). Representations can be three dimensional (using boxes), can be drawn on large sheets of paper, or can be cutouts pasted as a mural on the wall. Encourage children to enact pretend play scenes using the landscapes as contexts (e.g., adventures at sea, animals in the jungle). Have children re-create landscapes and maps of places they visited on field trips (e.g., the port, train station, library, market, zoo). Encourage the children to recall events related to the outing. Other themes include "My Dream House" or "My Dream City." Encourage children to collaborate on the same project, and facilitate peer interaction. This activity may require adult guidance and advance preparation of materials (e.g., maps, objects representing various landmarks). A project can be implemented over multiple sessions. For example, during the first session, children can paint a big lake, then during following sessions, they can add islands and lakeside buildings, labels, and signs as well as build bridges and boats.

This activity develops the following behaviors and concepts that are related to early literacy:

Print Awareness   Print—awareness of graphic symbols, writing

Phonological Awareness   Perception and memory—words; phonological skills—segmentation

Oral Language   Vocabulary—words and sentences; narrative skills—narrations of real events

ADULT–CHILD INTERACTIVE BEHAVIORS

High Demand/Low Support

Children use specific themes, build landscapes, and enact imaginary stories. They write words to label buildings, roads, and other aspects of the landscape. They will:

> use invented spelling and letter sounds to write words and messages

Support Strategies

? Open-ended
questioning

Help children in planning.

> Which areas of the zoo do you want to draw in your model?
> Who will build what? Where? Let's make a list.

Encourage them to label areas and constructions.

> How will you know which door is the entrance?

Providing
feedback

Encourage and praise children's attempts at drawing, writing, or invented spelling. Have children evaluate the correctness of their model or map and the need for additional labels.

> Is the duck pond that close to the alligator river? How do we
> know which is which?

Cognitive
structuring

Help children write words by having them sound out letters one at a time.

Task
regulation

Sound out and dictate letters individually.

Instructing

Model writing new words and letters.

Medium Demand/Medium Support

Children use specific themes, build landscapes, and enact imaginary stories. They write words to label buildings, roads, and other aspects of the landscape. They will:

> use invented spelling and letter sounds to write words and messages

Support Strategies

? Open-ended
questioning

Ask children what they would like to draw on the map.

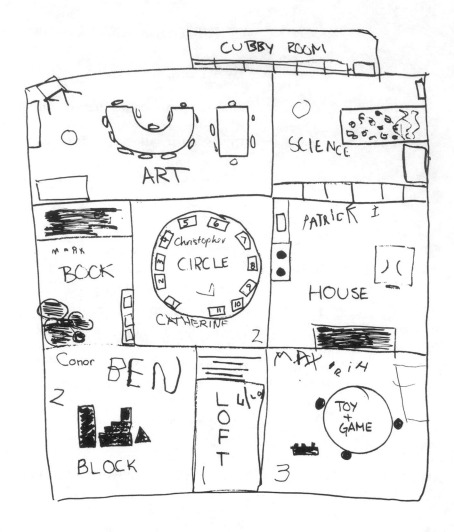

 Providing feedback   Encourage and praise children's attempts at drawing and writing. Have children describe their drawings to help them identify ways to make the drawing more accurate and to select appropriate labels or signs.

 Task regulation   Have children draw models or maps of their immediate environment (e.g., the classroom, the playground).

Instructing   Pair children with peers who have more advanced skills. Draw children's attention to relevant features.

   Look at how big the lake is and how small the boat is.

Offer verbal suggestions to help children make the drawing more recognizable.

   Can you make the river longer?

Provide models of words for children to copy.

Low Demand/High Support

Children use specific themes, build landscapes, and enact imaginary stories. They write words to label buildings, roads, and other aspects of the landscape. They will:

> use invented spelling and letter sounds to write words and messages

Support Strategies

Task regulation   Ask children to identify objects represented in pictures that are in their immediate environment (e.g., in the classroom).

Instructing   Prepare a model of the larger landscape ahead of time (e.g., a big sheet of paper representing the school building and grounds), and have children locate specific areas (e.g., classrooms, gym, library).

> Where's the gym?
> Show me the library.

Model responses, and have children imitate. Help children select words for labels, and provide the word for children to copy.

Comments/Adaptations

Comments   This project can be extended over a long period of time. Completed projects can be the subject of a museum exhibit.

More Ideas   Send home a copy or photograph of the child's project.

Home Link   Parent Activity: Mapping the Territory

THE TRANSITION TO READING WORDS

Main Purpose   To understand the relation between spoken and printed words

When children are ready to read words, they will benefit from the integration of sound play and phonological awareness, story context, and the printed form of new words. By demonstrating how writing captures speech, you will help children understand the alphabetic principle.

Materials   Easy-to-read books or big books; three frequently used, decodable words printed on cards for each book

Description of the Activity   Choose a book that has a few words that are used repeatedly throughout the story (e.g., *Ten Apples up on Top* [LeSieg, 1961], *Great Day for Up* [Dr. Seuss, 1974], *Green Eggs and Ham* [Geisel & Geisel, 1960]). You can facilitate word reading by encouraging children to recognize the relations among the sounds in spoken words ["Which sounds do you hear in top?"], the letters that make those sounds ["Which letter makes /t/?"], and the function of the word in the story ["Where are those apples?"].

Choose three short, decodable words to introduce during your story reading, and try the following sequence of activities with children who are interested in reading printed words.

Teaching Sequence

1. Read the book aloud to children. Encourage children to comment on pictures or story features as you read. Pay special attention to the function of the three words you want children to learn.
2. When you come to a special word in the story, show the word on a card to your group, and ask a child to find the same word on the page ["Here's cat. Can you find cat on this page?"]. Allow children to use the card as a model as they look for the word on the page.
3. Using the word cards as your list, have children blend the sounds, segment the sounds of the word, and then read the word. For each word, do the following:
    *   Play Guess the Word ["/T/ /o/ /p/. Which word is that?"].
    *   Segment the word ["Say all of the sounds in top"].
    *   Decode and blend the word ["Sound it out"].
    *   Read the word.
4. Show children the word cards again, and encourage children to use letter cues (i.e., first sound or sounding out all letters) to read the words.
5. Now read the story again, pausing when you come to a word from the set of cards. Show children the word in print, and encourage them to read it.

6. Give children a printed list of the three words, and encourage them to write about the story. They may write a phrase, a sentence, or several sentences. Encourage children to read their writing to other children. Examples of books with decodable words include *Green Eggs and Ham,* by Dr. Seuss (e.g., Sam, ham, not); *Abiyoyo,* by Pete Seeger (e.g., up, sit, grab); and *Snug House, Bug House,* by Susan Schade and Jon Buller (e.g., snug, bug, mix, stop).

This activity develops the following behaviors and concepts that are related to early literacy:

Print Awareness

Print—book conventions, awareness of graphic symbols, letter identification, writing; letter–sound correspondence—single sounds and letters, words

Phonological Awareness

Phonological skills—rhyming, segmentation, blending

Oral Language

Vocabulary—words and sentences

INTEGRATING SPELLING AND READING

Main Purpose   To establish an understanding of the alphabetic principle

Children learn to segment spoken words, represent sounds with letters, and sequence letters to spell short words. They learn to read what they spell by generating sounds for letters and blending the sounds.

Materials   Sets of five to eight letters for which children know the most common sounds; the same letters printed on transparency film; overhead projector

Description of the Activity   Provide each child with a set of five to eight letters for which children know the most common sounds. Tell the children a decodable word that can be spelled with the letters in their set; and ask children to repeat the word, segment the word into sounds, and spell the word by arranging letters from their set on their desk. Have them check their spelling by modeling the same activity on the overhead projector. Encourage children to help each other with this activity. When children have spelled the word correctly, model sounding out and blending the word with the overhead model. Examples for beginning lessons include the following: sample set of letters (a, c, f, n, t) to be used to spell and read (at, cat, fat, an, can, fan, tan) and sample set of letters (a, i, f, n, s, t) to be used to spell and read (at, sat, fat, an, fan, tan, in, fin, tin, it, fit, sit).

Teaching Sequence

1. ["Cat. Say cat"]
2. ["Say all of the sounds in cat"]
3. ["Cat. What's the first sound?"]
4. ["Spell cat on your table with your letters. It's okay to help each other"]
5. ["Now look up here. Did you spell it this way? Spell cat with me: c-a-t. Did you spell it c-a-t? Change it if you want to"]
6. ["Watch me read cat"] Touch under each letter, and say the sounds. ["Read it with me"] Touch under each letter, and encourage children to read along with you.
7. ["What did we spell?"]

This activity develops the following behaviors and concepts that are related to literacy:

Print Awareness   Letter–sound correspondence—single sounds and letters, words

Phonological Awareness   Phonological skills—blending, segmentation

Oral Language   Literate discourse—interpretive/analytic discourse

SECTION III

Phonological Awareness

Phonological awareness enables one to reflect on and manipulate the structural features of spoken language, such as sounds within words and words within sentences (Tunmer, Herriman, & Nesdale, 1988). Studies have powerfully demonstrated the connection between the ability to manipulate sounds in spoken words and learning to read (Blachman, 1994; Cunningham, 1990; Hatcher, Hulme, & Ellis, 1994; Maclean et al., 1987; O'Connor et al., 1995; Share, Jorm, Maclean, & Matthews, 1984). Moreover, one of the best predictors of success in literacy in the first grade is phonological segmentation (Felton, 1992; Juel, 1988; Leather & Henry, 1994; Share et al., 1984). This knowledge about and ability to manipulate sounds develops naturally for many children but is often a missing element in the repertoire of children with disabilities and others at risk for reading difficulties. Since the early 1990s, instructional studies with preschool and kindergarten children with or at risk for language delays (Ben-Dror, Bentin, & Frost, 1995; Blachman et al., 1994; O'Connor et al., 1995; O'Connor et al., 1993; Rubin & Eberhardt, 1996; Slocum et al., 1993; Torgesen, Morgan, & Davis, 1992) have demonstrated that we can teach these fundamental abilities to children not expected to acquire them independently. The link between improved phonological awareness in kindergarten and improved reading in first grade has also been established (Blachman, 1994; Byrne & Fielding-Barnsley, 1993; Byrne, Freebody, & Gates, 1992; O'Connor et al., 1998). Children's ability to understand and manipulate the structural features of language develops gradually (Brady, Gipstein, & Fowler, 1992; Rubin & Eberhardt, 1996; Vandervelden & Siegel, 1995). Word play activities explicitly teach phonological processes by making children increasingly aware of the sounds in spoken words. The *Ladders to Literacy* activities guide children, through games and small-group lessons, to be able to rhyme, segment, and blend sounds together. Because these skills are taught through multiple game formats, the activities are fun for children with and without learning difficulties and, thus, are appropriate for inclusive kindergarten settings.

- **Rhyming words**—Phonological awareness often begins with a child's knowledge of nursery rhymes—the first experience with literacy for many children and also the first opportunity to analyze sounds in words. The rhyme (i.e., the match between the ending sounds of two or more words) is a salient clue that makes it easier for children to remember and recite poems. Children who can recite rhymes at the age of 3 tend to become better readers than 3-year-old children who cannot, and the ability to recite rhymes is not dependent on intelligence or cultural background (Maclean et al., 1987). Later in school, when reading instruction begins, children who understand that two words share a common feature—the ending sound—may have an advantage for decoding words within word families (Goswami & Bryant, 1992;

Haskell, Foorman, & Swank, 1992; Treiman, 1992). Activities with rhymes are developmentally appropriate for children with varying ability levels, from about 3 years of age through the primary grades. Early in the kindergarten year, most children can rhyme with 60%–75% accuracy (Lundberg, Frost, & Petersen, 1988; O'Connor et al., 1995). Rhyming activities can be conducted in whole-class settings; in small groups; and/or individually by trained teachers, teacher assistants, and parents. Children can rhyme with the names of foods they eat during snacktime or recite rhymes while waiting for the bus. Rhymes can also initiate conversation, build vocabulary, or be incorporated into art activities. Because the lessons and games provide a variety of rhyming formats and a range of children's responses for each activity, they can be adapted readily for heterogeneous kindergarten classrooms.

- **Discriminating syllables**—Separating spoken words into syllables provides an early opportunity to identify speech units smaller than whole words. In *Ladders to Literacy*, syllable discrimination is treated as an oral game: Children listen and/or say the word and count its syllables without seeing the word in print (banana = ba-na-na = three syllables). Breaking words into syllables is an easier task than splitting individual syllables into phonemes (Fox & Routh, 1975; Treiman & Zukowski, 1996), and children are developmentally able to do this task with spoken words much earlier than they can learn to read, often by the age of 4. The ability to hear and see the syllables in words makes decoding longer words easier for beginning readers and is a strategy that continues to be useful through adulthood (Adams, 1990). The approach to syllable discrimination in *Ladders to Literacy* accommodates a range of abilities within a group of young children and begins with small- and large-group clapping games, with procedures for individual practice as necessary. While some children clap to the syllables in a word, other children may hold up fingers, may say the number, or may write the number of syllables they hear. Research suggests syllable games may provide the necessary foundation for isolating phonemes during segmentation (Lundberg et al., 1988). Because syllable counting only requires a one-word stimulus, it is integrated into other activities throughout the kindergarten day by using the names of objects around the room, favorite animals, children's names, and longer words in the stories teachers read to children.

- **Alliteration**—Alliterating, or recognizing or producing words with common initial sounds, requires a sensitivity to speech units smaller than words and syllables (Ball, 1993). Children as young as 3 years of age are able to recognize words that start with a same sound, and measures of alliteration are related to early reading (MacLean et al., 1987).

- **Sound blending**—Sound blending is an oral activity; however, it is also an essential part of early reading instruction. To decode a word independently, a child must be able to say the sound of each letter in a word and blend those sounds together (S + a + m = Sam). Oral blending of two sounds (/m/ + /at/ = /mat/) has been easily taught to 4-year-old children in a Head Start pre-school (Slocum et al., 1993), to 5- and 6-year-old children with disabilities (O'Connor et al., 1993), and to kindergarten children at risk (O'Connor et al., 1995). Some kindergarten children are able to blend sounds without explicit instruction (Bentin & Leshem, 1993; Torgesen, Wagner, & Rashotte, 1994; Yopp, 1988); however, most second-grade children with reading disabilities still have difficulty with oral blending (Vellutino & Scanlon, 1987). Researchers have suggested that instruction in oral blending before children begin reading instruction could make the difficult task of decoding words easier (Haddock, 1976; Lewkowicz, 1980). All of these experiences are introduced in *Ladders to Literacy* through play. For example, the teacher may use puppets (e.g., the teacher talks through a turtle, which only knows how to say words slowly; the children become turtle interpreters) or guessing games ["Let's see if I can fool you. Who knows what I'm trying to say? Mmmaaasssk"].
- **Segmenting phonemes**—Segmenting, or saying all of the sounds in spoken words separately, is a compound skill because a child must hold the word in memory *and* isolate a portion of the word in order to correctly segment it. A child who can segment words finds it easier to use orthographic codes in reading and to acquire spelling rules (Ball & Blachman, 1991; Hatcher et al., 1994; Juel, 1988; O'Connor & Jenkins, 1995; Tangel & Blachman, 1992). Because of the importance of segmenting in later reading and spelling experiences, we have considered ways to break this complex skill into simpler parts. By the time most children are midway through kindergarten, they have learned to say the first sound in spoken words (Warrick & Rubin, 1992). Teachers can then use this ability as the foundation for more difficult segmenting tasks.

EARLY LITERACY SKILLS

The phonological awareness concepts included in this section are described in the following sections. To assist in teaching these skills, we have listed the activities that target each concept.

Perception and Memory

- **Words**—Child will repeat multisyllabic words.
  Activity: Musical Instruments
- **Phrases**—Child will repeat phrases (e.g., repetitive lines in familiar songs, nursery rhymes and stories).

Activity: Listening to Songs

- **Phonemes**—Child will repeat single phonemes after a short delay. Child will repeat two or three phonemes after a short delay. Child will discriminate between two phonemes (same/different).
Activity: Sound Isolation

Word Awareness

- **Words**—Child will identify a word from a spoken sentence. Child will identify the longer word of two spoken words. Child will play with the pronunciation of a word.
Activity: Rhythmic activities

Phonological Skills

- **Rhyming**—Child will say common rhymes along with the teacher or peers. Child will fill in the last word in rhymes. Child will recite common rhymes independently. Child will recognize that pairs of words do or do not rhyme. Child will say a rhyming word to a target.
Activities: Nursery Rhymes; Rhyming Pictures; Rhyming Triplets
- **Alliteration**—Child recognizes words that start with a same sound. Child will tell a word that starts with the same sound as another word.
Activities: Letter Sound of the Week; First Sound Song
- **Blending**—Child will blend syllables into words. Child will blend words pronounced in onset-rime format (e.g., m-ake). Child will blend three to four phonemes into words (e.g., s-a-t, m-a-n).
Activities: Guess the Word (Blending); I'm Thinking of a . . . (Blending by Category)
- **Segmentation**—Child will segment words into syllables. Child will identify the first sound in words. Child will separate words into onset-rime (e.g., c-at). Child will segment one-syllable words into three to four phonemes (e.g., d-o-g).
Activities: Clap the Syllables; Pretend Play with Miniature Toys; Word to Word Matching Game: First Sound; Sing a First Sound; First Sound Bingo; Segmenting with Onset-Rime Boxes; Segmenting into Three Phonemes; Onset-Rime with First Letter

MUSICAL INSTRUMENTS

Main Purpose   To use music to discriminate sounds and segment words

Children learn to produce, discriminate, and manipulate sounds of objects and words.

Materials   Drums; cymbals; bells; xylophone; tambourine; triangle; songbooks

Description of the Activity   Let the children choose instruments and make sounds with them. This activity helps children discriminate contrasting sounds (e.g., high, low; loud, soft). If necessary, help the children to produce loud and soft sounds as well as to notice which instruments make high and low sounds. Encourage children to make comments about the music and instruments.

Select songbooks with pictures, and encourage children to sing and chant. Show the children how to segment multisyllable words by using the instruments to emphasize each syllable (e.g., by producing one drumbeat for each syllable). Select or make pictures and written labels for instruments. Introduce children to instruments and songs from a variety of cultures (e.g., balalaika, sitar). If instruments are too complicated for the children to play, then the adult can play and the children can sing along and comment on sounds, melody, tempo, rhythm, and pitch. Have children learn or create verses to go with the music.

This activity develops the following behaviors and concepts that are related to early literacy:

Print Awareness   Print—awareness of graphic symbols, letter identification

Phonological Awareness   Perception and memory—words, phrases; word awareness—words

Oral Language   Vocabulary—words and sentences

ADULT–CHILD INTERACTIVE BEHAVIORS

High Demand/Low Support

Children play instruments, sing songs, and discuss sounds and instruments. They will:

discriminate between different phonemes and segment words into syllables and phonemes

Support Strategies

?	Open-ended questioning	Encourage children to segment words of their choice.

Adagio means we sing and play the music slowly. Which word would you like to sing slowly?

■	Cognitive structuring	Highlight the relationships among instruments, actions, and sounds.

The harder you hit the drum, the louder you made the sound. How did the big bell sound compared with the little bell?

Have children group together instruments that make similar sounds. As children segment a word, have them count the number of separate syllables or phonemes.

How many parts are there in the word butterfly?

◖	Task regulation	Have children segment words into syllables or phonemes while playing an instrument (e.g., beating a drum). Begin with segmenting familiar words such as children's own names.

i	Instructing	Provide a model (e.g., beat the drum five times and segment ["hi-ppo-po-ta-mus"], and have children repeat or say along. Model using visual cues (e.g., raise a finger for each phoneme).

Medium Demand/Medium Support

Children play instruments, sing songs, and discuss sounds and instruments. They will:

identify the source of sounds; repeat unusual, multisyllable words; and segment words into syllables

Support Strategies

?	Open-ended questioning	Encourage discussion about instruments, music, and related cultural aspects by using new and unusual words.

Some Native Americans play drums at their powwows. Has anyone been to a powwow?

Encourage children to plan together which kind of song or melody they want to play (e.g., happy, sad, slow, fast, loud, soft), and have them make predictions.

How should we play to make the song sound happy?

■	Cognitive structuring	Discuss the names of instruments and the sounds they make. Point out that their sounds may be quite different from their names.

i	Instructing	Show children a few instruments along with their names and sounds, and then ask children direct questions.

What's the name of this instrument?
Which instrument made this sound?

Model unusual names, and have children imitate.

Can you say balalaika? Now say it this way: ba-la-lai-ka.

Low Demand/High Support

Children play instruments, sing songs, and discuss sounds and instruments. They will:

repeat multisyllable and segmented words

Support Strategies

Task regulation   Ask children to select instruments with long or short names.

Balalaika. Drum. Which name is longer?

Instructing   Model names of instruments, and have children imitate.

Can you say trumpet?

Ask children direct questions.

What's this?

Model syllabification, and lead children to say words in syllables.

Say accordion. Listen to this way: a-ccor-di-on. Say it with me. A-ccor-di-on. Now you say it.

Comments/Adaptations

Comments   Use songbooks made by the class. Incorporate words from other languages. Use rhyming activities that go with music. Use instruments from different cultures such as maracas, gongs, gourds, drums, flutes, conch shells, and Tibetan bells.

Adaptations   For children with hearing impairments, use amplified vibrating musical instruments (e.g., big drums).

Home Link   Parent Activity: Let's Dance!

RHYTHMIC ACTIVITIES

Main Purpose

To develop awareness of sounds and the ability to separate sounds from their meanings

Children learn to explore rhythm by moving their bodies to music. Exploration of rhythm helps children become sensitive to the temporal quality or duration of sounds. Children also learn to manipulate sounds in words independent of their meanings.

Materials

Drum; sticks; pictures; piano; books; other rhythm instruments

Description of the Activity

Have children move their bodies to different rhythms and music. Beat a drum, clap hands, or play the piano to different beats (e.g., even, uneven), tempos (e.g., fast, slow), intensities (e.g., soft, loud), frequencies (e.g., high, low), and durations (e.g., long, short). Begin with slow, regular, even beats to which children can clap their hands. Introduce uneven beats later, with variations in intensity and tempo. Encourage children to sing and chant along. Introduce blending and segmenting of sentences and multisyllable words by clapping hands, banging the drum, or hopping or jumping to individual syllables. Relate movement to children's personal experiences ["Let's move slowly and pretend we are walking in heavy snow"]. Propose a theme or an imaginary story for the children to mime. Pretend, for example, that the children are slowly climbing up a mountain and then running down fast. Pretend that children are different animals (e.g., a heavy, slow elephant; a light butterfly). Use pictures or books to help children focus on the theme. Encourage children to plan ahead ["Which animal will you be when the music gets real loud?"]. Discuss how different music can affect feelings (e.g., sad, happy, sleepy). During and after the activities, ask the children to explain what they thought the music was about, how the music made them feel, and why they moved in a certain way. Encourage imaginative thinking and dramatic play.

This activity develops the following behaviors and concepts that are related to early literacy:

Phonological Awareness

Perception and memory—words, phrases; word awareness—words; phonological skills—blending, segmentation

Oral Language

Literate discourse—conversations, decontextualization, interpretive/ analytic discourse

ADULT–CHILD INTERACTIVE BEHAVIORS

High Demand/Low Support

Children move to the different rhythms of the music, playing imaginary roles and developing pretend play scenes. They will:

> segment words into syllables and blend syllables into words

Support Strategies

?	Open-ended questioning	Have children choose to be an object or an animal that moves slowly or in a fragmented manner, and have them segment words into syllables.

> Think of an animal that hops on one foot or that jumps on two feet and can say words in little bits. Which animal would you like to be?

✿	Task regulation	Have children segment words into syllables and hop or clap to each syllable. Begin with segmenting familiar words such as children's own names.
👤	Instructing	Model word segmentation, and have the children repeat or say word segmentation along with you.

> How many parts are there to the word butterfly?

Use visual and auditory cues while modeling (e.g., hop, clap hands).

Medium Demand/Medium Support

Children move to the different rhythms of the music, playing imaginary roles and developing pretend play scenes. They will:

> segment words into syllables and blend syllables into words

Support Strategies

?	Open-ended questioning	Ask children to choose an animal or object that moves fast, and have children say words fast.
✿	Task regulation	Play slow music when presenting the segmented word and fast music when asking children to blend the word

> Ba-na-na (to slow music).
> Banana, banana (to fast music).

👤	Instructing	Draw children's attention to what to listen for.

Is this music fast or slow?
Raise your hands when the music changes.

Say words segmented into syllables, and ask children to say the word fast. Model the blended word, and have children repeat.

Low Demand/High Support

Children move to the different rhythms of the music, playing imaginary roles and developing pretend play scenes. They will:

segment words into syllables and blend syllables into words

Support Strategies

?	Open-ended questioning	Ask children how the music makes them feel like moving.
↻	Providing feedback	Describe the music and children's actions and movements.
		The music is fast, and you are hopping up and down just like a little rabbit! Say rabbit fast. Now the music is slow. Say rabbit slowly.
♦	Task regulation	Provide choices.
		This music is fast and soft. Do you want to run or walk? Can you be a but-ter-fly?
		Ask children to repeat words and sentences to a peer.
		Tell Jamal to be an el-e-phant.
		Tell Josie, "I'm jumping up and down like a jumping bean!"
🛈	Instructing	Give directions.
		When Nathan plays the drum quickly, everyone run fast!
		Ask direct questions.
		How are you going to run?
		Ask children to imitate words and sentences.
		Let's see how slowly we can say "I'm walking slowly. III'mmm wwwaaalking ssslllllooowlllyyy."

Comments/Adaptations

Comments	Introduce this activity after children have become familiar with the musical instruments, as they will tend to focus first on the instruments rather than on the beat and rhythms. The Clap the Syllables activity can be incorporated within this activity.
Home Link	Parent Activity: Let's Dance!

LISTENING TO SONGS

Main Purpose

To develop listening skills and memory for sounds

Children develop listening skills by attending to verbal and non-verbal sounds. Children need to listen in order to learn and produce words and sounds. Especially important is the ability to focus on relevant sounds and words and screen out other auditory stimuli.

Materials

Tapes of songs (e.g., "Can You Sound Just Like Me?" "Finger Play," and "Ready Set" by Red Grammer; "Letter Sounds" by Hap Palmer; multicultural children's songs sung by Ella Jenkins); tape recorder

Description of the Activity

Have children listen to songs that require them to imitate sounds (e.g., "Can You Sound Just Like Me?"), to make gestures with their hands (e.g., "Finger Play"), and to move their whole bodies. Show children the cover of the tape, with the name of the song and the singer. After listening to the songs, encourage children to talk about the content and actions. Ask them to describe what they like and dislike about the music, movements, and other aspects of the activity. Include photographs and props, such as pictures representing other cultures or musical instruments used in the songs. Expose children to music and songs from different cultures. Talk about the background of the song and music. Have children bring favorite recordings from home. Include nursery rhymes and rhyming songs, and draw attention to words that rhyme.

This activity develops the following behaviors and concepts that are related to early literacy:

Print Awareness

Print—awareness of graphic symbols, letter identification

Phonological Awareness

Perception and memory—words, phrases, phonemes; phonological skills—rhyming

Oral Language

Literate discourse—conversations, decontextualization, interpretive/analytic discourse

ADULT–CHILD INTERACTIVE BEHAVIORS

High Demand/Low Support

Children listen to the songs and actively participate by making gestures and moving their bodies. They will:

> recite familiar rhymes and rhyming songs independently and identify words and phrases from the songs or rhymes

Support Strategies

?	Open-ended questioning	Ask children to volunteer to say a rhyme or song of their choice.

Which song would you like to sing?

Have children tell just one word from the song or rhyme.

	Task regulation	Display posters and pictures representing characters and events in the song or rhyme for children to refer to while reciting. Recite parts of the rhyme or song, and have children fill in the rest.

Medium Demand/Medium Support

Children listen to the songs and actively participate by making gestures and moving their bodies. They will:

> say common rhymes along with peers and repeat phrases and lines in songs and rhymes

Support Strategies

?	Open-ended questioning	Ask children to choose phrases to repeat from the song or rhyme.

What does this song say?

	Providing feedback	Show children how the lyric and action go together.

When we said "up the water spout," we climbed up the water spout with our fingers.

	Task regulation	Focus children's attention to the activity by telling them they will need to "put on their listening ears" and listen carefully to the words in the songs. Ask them to tell you when they feel ready, and provide the initial words.

The itsy bitsy spider . . .

	Instructing	Highlight and model parts of songs and rhymes for them to repeat.

Low Demand/High Support

Children listen to the songs and actively participate by making gestures and moving their bodies. They will:

> repeat common words

Support Strategies

	Holding in memory	Repeat the phrase with the action as children are learning the gestures.

Task regulation   Have children repeat words in fingerplay songs that are associated with gestures, and practice each phrase with gestures several times until children can do them easily.

Instructing   Ask children direct questions.

> The itsy bitsy spider went up the water spout. Who went up the water spout?

Use cumulative introduction to rehearse just one phrase of the song at a time. Provide a peer model ["Follow Jaime"] or adult model ["Do what I do"]. Assist children by exaggerating movements, slowing them down, or gently guiding their hands or bodies.

Comments/Adaptations

Comments   Encourage children to change words to familiar songs and make up their own verses.

Adaptations   Use sign language, pictures, and props to assist children with hearing impairments.

More Ideas   Ask parents to send to school cassette tapes of songs they enjoy at home, especially those from different cultures. Tape songs in school, and send them home to parents.

Home Link   Parent Activity: Sing a Song

CLAP THE SYLLABLES

Main Purpose

To understand that words can be conceptualized as a collection of parts

Children recognize that words can be subdivided at the syllable level. Children begin to view words as collections of sounds that can be differentiated apart from their meaning.

Materials

None

Description of the Activity

Begin the activity by modeling the clapping behavior and encouraging taking turns. Go around the circle. Say each child's name, then say the name in syllables, clapping for each beat. Encourage children to clap the beats with you ["Andrew! An-drew"]. Lead children in clapping several times. After the first few times, children should join you in clapping syllables. You can extend the activity in several ways. Call out the names of objects in the classroom ["Table"]. Have the children repeat the word and then clap the syllables along with you. Encourage children to take turns calling out the name of an object in the classroom. Then have all of the children repeat the child's word, clapping the syllables. Pictures and labels with names can be used as support.

This activity develops the following behaviors and concepts that are related to early literacy:

Print Awareness

Print—awareness of graphic symbols

Phonological Awareness

Perception and memory—words; phonological skills—blending, segmentation

Oral Language

Vocabulary—words and sentences

ADULT–CHILD INTERACTIVE BEHAVIORS

High Demand/Low Support

Children will:

 segment words into syllables by clapping and saying words in syllables

Support Strategies

Cognitive structuring

Explain how to segment words.

Table has two beats. Ta-ble. Do you hear the two beats in table? Ta-ble.

Task regulation

Have children segment familiar words such as their names or objects present in their classroom.

Say Kelly in two parts.
Say banana in little parts.

Have children choose words to segment. Have children segment compound words (e.g., caterpillar, spaceship). Say the first one or two syllables, and then have children add the syllables that follow.

Elephant. I say el-e-. You say -phant.

Instructing

Model saying words in syllables, and have children count the number of syllables before clapping themselves.

Hippopotamus. Count the parts. Hip-po-pot-a-mus! How many parts did you count?

As you model saying words in syllables, have children clap to the syllables. Model saying words in syllables, and have children repeat the word in syllables.

Vol-ca-no. Say volcano like that.

Medium Support/Medium Demand

Children will:

segment words into syllables by clapping and saying words in syllables.

Support Strategies

Task regulation

Have children segment familiar words such as their names or objects present in their classroom. Use two-syllable words.

Window. Say it slowly. Wwwiinnndooow. Win-dow.

To elicit children's interest, say unusually long words that are likely to be novel and unfamiliar to them (e.g., kookaburra, extraordinary, enormous). Enunciate words slowly.

Instructing

Model segmenting the word, and ask children to repeat it. Then repeat the task with a new word. Say a word segmented into syllables, and have children repeat.

Pump-kin. Say these two sounds: pump-kin.

Low Demand/High Support

Children will:

segment words into syllables by clapping and saying words in syllables

Support Strategies

Task regulation
Use a set of four or five objects, such as fruit in a basket. Model, and lead children through segmenting the words (e.g., apple, pear, banana, strawberry) into syllables several times.

Instructing
Have children repeat words that peers have blended or segmented.

> Which word did Ly say?

Physically guide children by holding them in your lap and taking their hands and gently clapping to the syllables.

Comments/Adaptations

Comments
This activity can be incorporated into the rhythmic activities. This activity can also be used for segmenting sentences into words and segmenting compound words. Children can use movements and actions other than clapping (e.g., jumping, placing a block in a container for each segment, tapping the table with their hand).

More Ideas
Audiotape activity, and send tape to parents.

Home Link
Parent Activity: Let's Dance!

NURSERY RHYMES

Main Purpose	To develop awareness of the sounds of words

Nursery rhymes give children the opportunity to become aware of the sounds in words. By learning to recite nursery rhymes, children develop listening and auditory memory skills and learn about rhyme.

Materials	Picture sequence of story in nursery rhyme; text with rhyming words highlighted; crayons

Description of the Activity	Show children pictures that illustrate well-known nursery rhymes, accompanied by text. Use different pictures that illustrate the sequence of events in the rhyme. Recite the rhyme; and proceed to sequence the pictures, eliciting the participation of the children. Encourage each child to learn to recite lines of the nursery rhyme. Draw the children's attention to the words that rhyme, and write words that share spelling patterns on the chalkboard. Focus the children's attention on the match between the ending sounds and letter sequences of two or more words that rhyme (e.g., write wall and fall, but not men and again.). Toward the end of the activity, have each child color and keep one of the pictures. You can also encourage discussion about the content or story of the nursery rhyme.

This activity develops the following behaviors and concepts that are related to early literacy:

Print Awareness	Print—awareness of graphic symbols
Phonological Awareness	Perception and memory—words, phrases, phonemes; phonological skills—rhyming
Oral Language	Vocabulary—words and sentences; narrative skills—narrations of fictional story; literate discourse—decontextualization

ADULT–CHILD INTERACTIVE BEHAVIORS

High Demand/Low Support

Children will:

> recite the whole nursery rhyme independently and produce new rhyming words

Support Strategies

?	Open-ended questioning	Have children choose a rhyme to recite to their peers. Encourage children to talk about the story told by the rhyme and to comment about related personal experiences.

> What's this rhyme about?
> Do you look at stars at night? Can we see stars during the day?

Ask children to choose two rhyming words from the rhyme and to add a new one of their own.

	Providing feedback	Have children repeat their rhyming words or repeat back to them their answers, and ask children to reevaluate whether they rhyme.

> Wall. Horse. Do these two words sound the same?

	Cognitive structuring	Explain the concept of rhyme.

> Words that rhyme end with the same sound. Funny. Bunny. Both end with -unny. They rhyme.

	Holding in memory	Provide visual cues in the form of posters, pictures, or books that illustrate the nursery rhyme story.

	Task regulation	Say two words that rhyme, and emphasize the parts of the words that sound alike, asking children to identify the parts that sound the same. Have children pick the odd word or the two words that sound the same from three words of which only two rhyme.

> High, sky, star. Which is the odd word? Which two sound the same?

Medium Demand/Medium Support

Children will:

> recite the whole nursery rhyme along with peers and recognize pairs of words that do or do not rhyme

Support Strategies

?	Open-ended questioning	Have children choose a rhyme to recite with their peers. Ask children questions about the story.

> What did the spider do?

	Holding in memory	Provide visual cues in the form of posters, pictures, or books that illustrate the nursery rhyme story.

	Task regulation	Pair a word chosen by the children from the rhyme with another word, and ask children to identify whether the words rhyme.

> Mouse, house. Do these words sound the same?

Pair nonrhyming words that sound very different.

> Clock, rhinoceros. Do these words rhyme?

Provide pictures for rhyming and nonrhyming words (e.g., a pear and a bear, a cat and a house).

Instructing

Model, and have children repeat pairs of words that rhyme.

> Fox, box. Say fox, box. Do you hear -ox in fox? How about in box? They rhyme.

Low Demand/High Support

Children will:

> recite nursery rhymes along with peers and fill in last words of rhymes

Support Strategies

Task regulation

Give children choices of rhymes.

> Shall we say "Hickory Dickory Dock" or "Hey Diddle Diddle"?

Have children fill in the final rhyme in a familiar rhyming couplet.

> Humpty-Dumpty sat on a wall. Humpty-Dumpty had a great . . .

Instructing

Draw children's attention to specific illustrations related to lines or words in the rhyme. For example, point to a picture of the wall when saying ["Humpty-Dumpty sat on a . . ."]. Call on children individually to ensure their participation in the recital.

> Andy, say it along with us.

Model, and have children repeat lines.

Comments/Adaptations

Comments

Flannel board figures and props can be used as well as pictures.

Adaptations

Use sign language, pictures, and props to assist children with hearing impairments.

Home Link

Ask a librarian to help select picture books with rhymes, and enjoy these books with children. Send home copies of rhymes with pictures for children to learn with their parents. Tape record children as they recite the rhymes. Let children borrow the tape to play at home.

RHYMING PICTURES

Main Purpose

To recognize that some words share common sounds

Children learn that words are made up of sounds that can be disassociated from the entire word. Rhyming has been identified as one of the earliest competencies that demonstrate phonological awareness. It is a skill that may help children to isolate the smaller sounds in words and to use analogy as a reading strategy in first grade.

Materials

Laminated pictures of rhyming word pairs; rhyming puzzles; rhyming mazes

Description of the Activity

Take some laminated pictures displaying rhyming words and spread them out on the floor, beginning with one pair of pictures, and then gradually expanding the set. Each pair of pictures should have a jagged (puzzle-like) edge that can be used to help children find rhyming mates. Ask the children to match the rhyming pair, say the rhyming words represented by the pictures, and fit the pairs together. As children become competent with picture rhymes, add labels to the pictures. Rhyming mazes can also be prepared to help children match rhyming words. For example, a maze may have a snake trying to find its way to eat a cake or a mouse going to its house. Encourage children to ask questions and talk about the pictures.

This activity develops the following behaviors and concepts that are related to early literacy:

Print Awareness

Print—awareness of graphic symbols, letter identification; letter–sound correspondence—words

Phonological Awareness

Perception and memory—words, phonemes; phonological skills—rhyming

Oral Language

Vocabulary—words and sentences

ADULT–CHILD INTERACTIVE BEHAVIORS

High Demand/Low Support

Children independently match rhyming pictures and identify rhyming word pairs. They will:

    generate a word that rhymes with a pictured word

Support Strategies

| ? | Open-ended questioning | Ask children to produce new rhymes by using either real or nonsense words. |

> You put the boy with the toy. What else goes with these two words?

| ◯ | Providing feedback | Repeat back to children their answers, and ask children to reevaluate whether words rhyme. |

> You put box with chair. Do these two words sound the same?

Encourage children to repeat aloud names of objects to determine whether words rhyme.

| ◆ | Task regulation | Select three pictures of objects, two of which rhyme. Then have children pick the odd word or the two words that rhyme. |

> Cat, truck, hat. Which two pictures go together? Which one doesn't rhyme?

Medium Demand/Medium Support

Children independently match rhyming pictures and identify rhyming word pairs. They will:

> generate a word that rhymes with a pictured word

Support Strategies

| ◆ | Cognitive structuring | Explain the concept of rhyme. |

> Words that rhyme end with the same sound. Snake. Cake. Both end with -ake. They rhyme.

| ◆ | Task regulation | Pair a picture chosen by the children with another picture, and ask children to identify whether the words rhyme. |

> Pear, bear. Do these words sound the same?

Pair pictures of nonrhyming words that sound very different.

> Cat, table. Do these pictures rhyme?

Instructing   Model by matching correct pictures, draw children's attention to the reason for matching, and have them repeat pairs of words that rhyme.

> Cat. Hat. They go together because they rhyme. Say cat, hat. Do they rhyme?

Low Demand/High Support

Children independently match small sets of rhyming puzzle pieces. They will:

> match rhyming pictures and identify rhyming word pairs

Support Strategies

 Cognitive structuring   Demonstrate self-checking of rhyming accuracy with a perfect puzzle fit.

 Task regulation   Begin with only two pairs of rhyming pictures. Provide multiple opportunities to match these pairs. As children become more adept at discriminating rhyming words, gradually increase the number of rhyming pairs in the game.

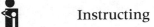 Instructing   Provide a model, and have children name pictures to peers.

> You have a cake and a snake. Tell José what you have.

Model matching correct pictures, and have children repeat the pairs of words that rhyme.

> The fox goes with the box. Say fox, box.

Comments/Adaptations

Adaptations   Use paste or glue to create relief mazes for children with visual impairments. Write the words or outline them in the paste.

Home Link   Parent Activity: Tell Me a Word that Rhymes with . . . !

RHYMING TRIPLETS

Main Purpose

To recognize that some words share common sounds

The child learns that words are made up of sounds that can be disassociated from the entire word. Rhyming has been identified as one of the earliest competencies that demonstrates phonological awareness and as a skill that may help children to isolate the smaller sounds in words.

Materials

A few pairs of rhyming pictures for the first time; no materials needed following times

Description of the Activity

Show the children a pair of rhyming pictures, and say the picture names in rhythm: cake, snake. Encourage children to say the pair of words with you, and then call on a child to add a third rhyming word. Nonsense words are fine. Use the first rhyme for several individual turns, and then switch to a new rhyming pair ["cake, snake; cake, snake, take!; cake, snake; cake, snake, make!; cake, snake; cake, snake, dake!"].

This activity develops the following behaviors and concepts that are related to early literacy:

Print Awareness

Letter–sound correspondence—words

Phonological Awareness

Phonological skills—rhyming, blending

Oral Language

Vocabulary—words and sentences

ADULT–CHILD INTERACTIVE BEHAVIORS

High Demand/Low Support

Children repeat and generate new trios of rhyming words. They will:

> repeat the teacher's pair and add a new word or nonsense word to rhyme with the first two

Support Strategies

Providing feedback

Use a child's incorrect response to demonstrate how a child can make a rhyme.

Thanks to Judy Hasselmann for this activity.

Cake, shake, mmmilk don't rhyme; try cake, shake, mmm-make.

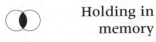

Holding in memory

Repeat the rhyming pairs softly while children are thinking of a new rhyming word.

Mark, shark . . . Mark, shark . . .

Task regulation

If a child cannot generate a rhyme, then provide a first sound for the child.

Cake, shake, l . . . (lake).

Instructing

Tell children how to make a rhyme.

You need to say a word that has the same ending as the other two words. Cake and shake both end with -ake. Can you find a word that ends with -ake?

Medium Demand/Medium Support

Children repeat and generate new trios of rhyming words. They will:

repeat the teacher's pair and add a new word or nonsense word to rhyme with the first two

Support Strategies

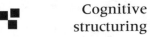

Cognitive structuring

Provide an explanation and many models before starting the game.

We're saying words that rhyme. Words that sound the same at the end rhyme. Here are some words that rhyme: make, cake, take; feet, wheat, sweet; mine, brine, sign; kit, fit, lit; Yertle, turtle, murtle.

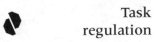

Task regulation

Use only two or three rhymes each session (e.g., words that end in the -at sound and words that end with the -eet sound).

Instructing

Rhyming is more easily taught through examples and repetition. Use pictures of trios of rhyming words to make it easier for children to rehearse rhymes. Mount pictures of pairs or trios of rhyming words around the classroom or activity area.

Low Demand/Low Support

Children repeat trios of rhyming words generated by their peers. They will:

repeat the teacher's pair and add a new word or nonsense word to rhyme with the first two

Support Strategies

 Holding in
memory

Point to the pictured words while saying rhyming words.

> Phone, bone. Phone, bone.

Task
regulation

Use only one rhyming sound for each session, and provide multiple opportunities to generate and repeat rhymes that share that sound.

Instructing

Model sets of rhyming words.

> Joe said, "Make, cake, take." Everyone say, "Make, cake, take. Make, cake, take." They rhyme. They sound the same.

SOUND ISOLATION

Main Purpose

To encourage children to learn that sounds can be isolated from words

Phonological activities require children to attend to sounds of language, yet many children have little experience uttering sounds in isolation. This activity develops familiarity with the phonemes and smaller-than-word units.

Materials

A collection of songs familiar to children ("Apples and Bananas" by Raffi; "Letter Sounds" by Hap Palmer; and so forth).

Description of the Activity

Use any tunes (e.g., "Happy Birthday," "I'm a Little Teapot") or rhythms (e.g., knocking patterns) with which children are familiar. Instead of words and beats, substitute isolated phonemes. Using the tune of "Happy Birthday," sing Lala, lala, la, la . . . for the entire song, and then substitute Beebee, beebee, bee, bee . . . and Tata, tata, ta, ta. . . . When children are able to articulate and enjoy tunes with meaningless phonemes, try starting all of the words in a familiar song with the same phoneme (e.g., Bappy Birthday bo bou . . .). Integrate the tasks within a play context. For example, introduce the B puppet bear who only says words that start with b. Or ask the children to select a sound of the hour. During that time, start all children's names with that sound (e.g., if /p/ is the sound, then Susan becomes Pusan, Tom becomes Pom, etc.). The traditional song "Apples and Bananas" by Raffi is good for children to listen to and sing along. Each lyric of the song substitutes a new long vowel sound in the words (e.g., apples becomes oples).

This activity develops the following behaviors and concepts that are related to early literacy:

Print Awareness

Letter–sound correspondence—single sounds and letters

Phonological Awareness

Perception and memory—words, phonemes; word awareness—words; phonological skills—rhyming, alliteration, segmentation

Oral Language

Vocabulary—words and sentences

ADULT–CHILD INTERACTIVE BEHAVIORS

High Demand/Low Support

Children participate in modifying sounds and words and make suggestions for new words and games. They will:

play with the pronunciation of words and identify the first sound in words

Support Strategies

?	Open-ended questioning	Ask children to select a sound of the hour and modify words of their choice by starting them with the selected sound. The sound of the hour is /g/. Daniel, change the word soccer. Right, now it's goccer!
	Providing feedback	Praise children. You made the Barney song really funny when you started all of the words with /h/.
	Cognitive structuring	Make rules explicit to the children. We change the first sound only. We start all of the words with the same sound.
	Task regulation	Emphasize first sounds by stretching ["Sssssusan"] or iterating ["T-t-t-tom"]. Have children begin by modifying their own names. Have children modify familiar songs.

Medium Demand/Medium Support

Children participate in modifying sounds and words and make suggestions for new words and games. They will:

play with the pronunciation of words and identify the first sound in words

Support Strategies

	Task regulation	Ask children to choose a favorite syllable, and practice saying the syllable before beginning the song. Fo! Let's all say Fo! Now we'll sing.
	Instructing	Draw children's attention to the changes in pronunciation of words in the songs and rhymes by telling them they will need to "put on their listening ears" and listen carefully to the new words in the songs, and then ask them to tell you when they feel ready. Highlight and model phonemes, words, and parts of songs and rhymes for them to repeat. Ask children to imitate. You say, "Bappy birthday bo bou." You say, "The itsy mitsy mider."

Low Demand/High Support

Children participate in modifying sounds and words and make suggestions for new words and games. They will:

> play with the pronunciation of words and identify the first sound in words

Support Strategies

Task regulation	Have children repeat words in favorite and familiar songs. Exaggerate the pronunciation of the new sounds. Begin with having children imitate repetitive sequences of the same syllable. Dadadada . . .
Instructing	Tell children the new sound ["Instead of words we'll say Kay"], model the first line of the song with the new sound ["Here's what 'If You're Happy and You Know It' sounds like: Kay Kay Kay . . ."], and invite children to sing with you ["Let's all sing with Kay"]. Highlight and model phonemes, words, and parts of songs and rhymes for them to repeat. Ask children to imitate. Banini. Can you say Banini?

Comments/Adaptations

Link with Print Awareness	Post a menu of songs the children know. Encourage children to choose a song from the list, and provide the sound to substitute for words.
Home Link	Parent Activity: What Did You Hear?

PRETEND PLAY WITH MINIATURE TOYS

Main Purpose

To develop phonological segmentation of the first sound and word manipulation skills

Children learn how words are composed of individual sounds.

Materials

A box of small toys for the first several sessions (Expand the activity by using objects in the classroom, children's names, and pictures in books.)

Description of the Activity

Organize the children to engage in pretend play with miniature animals and characters. Encourage children to enact pretend play themes (e.g., a visit to the zoo, a night in the jungle) and to talk about the animals and other toys. As children play, seize opportunities to practice identifying first sounds of animals with which children choose to play, blending animal names pronounced in an onset-rime manner, and repeating new words. For example, hold up an object and stress the first sound ["B-b-b-bear. Say it with me. B-b-b-bear. /B/ is the first sound in bear. Say the first sound /b/. Bear starts like /b/," "What's this?" (Hold up the boy doll.) "Yes! B-b-b-boy. Say it with me. B-b-b-boy. Say the first sound /b/. Boy starts like /b/," "What's this?" (Hold up a ball, and repeat pattern.)]. Call attention to objects in the classroom that start with /b/ ["What's this?" (Hold up a baby.) Yes! B-b-b-bottle. Say it with me. B-b-b-bottle. What's the first sound?"]. Focus on one initial sound until a few of the children are consistently accurate. Then switch to a new initial sound. If a child suggests correct letter names, along with letter sounds, then write the letter on paper for the child to copy. To continue play, encourage children to select an object. Ask the child to name the object, and then stretch or iterate the first sound in the object's name while encouraging the child to do the same. Use the same set of toys for children to guess your word when you say the names in onset-rime ["C-ow"] or segmented ["T-i-ger"] formats. Throughout the activity, encourage the child to select objects from the box or around the room.

This activity develops the following behaviors and concepts that are related to early literacy:

Print Awareness

Print—letter identification; letter–sound correspondence—single sounds and letters

Phonological Awareness

Perception and memory—words, phonemes; phonological skills—alliteration, blending, segmentation

Oral Language

Literate discourse—categorical organization

ADULT–CHILD INTERACTIVE BEHAVIORS

High Demand/Low Support

Children engage in complex dramatic play. They will:

> identify the first sound in words and blend sounds into words

Support Strategies

Cognitive structuring

Define the concept of *first sound*.

> Listen to the very first sound you say when you pronounce the word. The first sound is how you start the word.

Task regulation

Ask children to identify first sounds of words or objects of their choice. Stretch or iterate the first sound.

> Mmmmonkey. B-b-b-bear.

Limit toys to two or three categories of objects that have names that start with similar first sounds (e.g., monkey, moose, mouse; cow, cat, kangaroo).

Instructing

Provide models.

> Bear starts with /b/. What's the first sound in bear?

Ask children to repeat first sounds identified by peers.

> What did Marco say the first sound in bear was?

Demonstrate how you have broken words into parts that can be blended back together.

> See the tiger? Now I'll say tiger. Now I'll say tiger in little bits: t-i-ger. Say it with me!

Medium Demand/Medium Support

Children engage in pretend play. They will:

> identify the first sound in words and blend sounds into words

Support Strategies

Task regulation

Provide four to five toys and multiple opportunities to name the first sound of these toys or to blend sounds into the names of the toys.

Instructing

Encourage children to repeat the segmented word before guessing. Provide a model, and have the child repeat the task.

> C-ow. That's a cow. C-ow. What's that?

Low Demand/High Support

Children engage in simple symbolic play actions with objects and toys. They will:

> identify the first sound in words and blend sounds into words

Support Strategies

? Open-ended questioning

Encourage children to name toys ["What is this?"] and to talk about them ["What does a lion say?" "What is it doing now?"] before beginning the sound play games.

Holding in memory

The adult says the name of the toy with the first sound stretched or iterated while children think about and then tell the sound.

Task regulation

Introduce only two to three toys. Provide multiple opportunities to blend the sounds of the toys' names (b-at, wi-tch) or to practice identifying the first sound.

> Bat starts with /b/. Say /b/. Tell me the first sound in bat.

Instructing

Provide a model, and ask children to repeat.

> Giraffe. Say it with me: giraffe. Now we'll say the first sound: /g/. Say it with me: g-g-g-iraffe. Now you say it. (Children respond.) What's the first sound in giraffe?

Comments/Adaptations

Comments

Print words, and highlight first sounds on word cards by coloring them or cutting them apart from the rest of the word.

Home Link

Parent Activity: First Sound

LETTER SOUND OF THE WEEK

Main Purpose   To isolate and identify first sounds in words

Children develop awareness of the first sound in words and the letter that accompanies that sound. Children also develop familiarity with phonemes and smaller-than-word units.

Materials   Pictures; individual letters; drawing materials

Description of the Activity   This activity takes place over several days. Select a letter to study for each week. Focus on the sound of the letter rather than on its name. Day 1: Introduce a letter, and say its most common sound ["Here's s. It says /s/. Let's think of things that start with /s/"]. Begin by identifying children's names that begin with /s/. Then encourage children to find things in the classroom that start with /s/. Day 2: Review s and /s/; invite children to name things that start with /s/. Then use pictures to demonstrate objects and actions that start like /s/. Include some pictures of objects that do not start with /s/, and encourage children to listen for and discriminate /s/ words. Day 3: Review s and /s/; invite children to name things that start with /s/. Start a list of /s/ pictures and words, and post this list prominently. Encourage children to expand the list with their own drawings or pictures from the Home Link activity. Encourage children to generate alliterative phrases or sentences.

This activity develops the following behaviors and concepts that are related to early literacy:

Print Awareness   Print—letter identification, writing; letter–sound correspondence—single sounds and letters, words

Phonological Awareness   Perception and memory—words, phonemes; phonological skills—alliteration, segmentation

Oral Language   Vocabulary—words and sentences

ADULT–CHILD INTERACTIVE BEHAVIORS

High Demand/Low Support

Children will:

identify the first sound in words and tell a word that starts the same as another

Support Strategies

◧	Cognitive structuring	Make sure children differentiate the letter name (i.e., s) from its sound (i.e., /s/).

> Which letter is this? Which sound does it make?

◖	Task regulation	Stress the first sound of several word examples beginning with the letter sound by stretching ["Ssssnake, Ssssally, ssssalad"] or iterating ["T-t-t-turtle, T-t-t-tommy, t-t-t-tiger"], and have children add words.

> What else starts like /s/?

Provide visual cues in the form of alphabet letters and pictures of one or more words that start with the letter sound.

ⓘ	Instructing	Tell children to listen for a particular sound before you say words.

> Listen for the /k/-/k/-/k/ at the beginning of this word: cat. Do you hear the /k/ at the beginning?

Ask children direct questions after teaching.

> Which sound does apple start with?
> Does sssssnack start with /s/?

Make the first sound obvious by stretching or iterating it, have children repeat, and then elicit identification of the first sound.

> M-m-m-monday. /M/ is the first sound you say in Mmmmonday. Say Mmmmonday. Say the first sound in Monday.

Model lists of words that start with a same sound, and ask children to add a new word.

> Tell me a word that starts the same as these: bear, ball, bell.

Medium Demand/Medium Support

Children will:

> identify the first sound in words and tell a word that starts the same as another

Support Strategies

◧	Cognitive structuring	Make sure that children understand the concept of same and different by asking them to identify similarities and differences among concrete objects and pictures.

◖	Task regulation	Use words and sounds that are taken from meaningful contexts such as cards, pictures in books, or objects in the classroom.

> Sack and silly. /S/ and /s/. Do they start the same?
> Dog and doll. Do they start the same?

Instructing

Model sounds that are similar and sounds that are different by stretching or iterating sounds, and then repeat the question.

> B-b-b-bug and p-p-p-puppy. /B/ and /p/. They sound different. /B/ and /p/. Are they the same or different?
> S-s-s-sock and s-s-s-sun. They start with the same sound. Sock and sun. Do they start the same?

Low Demand/High Support

Children will:

> identify the first sound in words and tell a word that starts the same as another

Support Strategies

Cognitive structuring

Make the first sound obvious by stretching it.

> Mmmmonday. /Mmm/ is the first sound in Mmmmonday.

Task regulation

Present the task within meaningful contexts. For example, ask children to repeat a word or sound to a peer who was not present or attentive. Present words that are familiar to children and phonemes that are easy to pronounce. Provide visual cues (e.g., signs, pictures) to help children recall sounds and words. For example, use a picture of a snake to help remember the sound /s/. Have children discriminate between phonemes that are distinctly different (e.g., /s-s-s/ versus /t-t-t/). Present sounds in the context of words that are clearly similar or different.

> Here's a boat, and here's another boat. This boat starts with /b/, and this boat starts with /b/. Are they the same or different?
> Cat, /k/, and salamander, /s/. /K/ and /s/. Are they the same or different?

Provide visual cues by accompanying words and sounds with pictures of objects or letters of the alphabet. Have children select the odd word from three words, two of which share a common initial sound.

> Book, hand, hat. Which starts differently?
> Sea, lake, sun. Which is the odd word?

Instructing

Ask children to repeat first sounds identified by peers.

> Which sound did Laura say?

Model, and ask direct questions.

> This is a tadpole. What is this?

Model sounds and words, and ask children to repeat.

Right, Rena. Monday starts with /M/. Doug, can you say /m/? Lisa, can you say Monday?

Ask children directly to repeat sounds.

Moon. Can you say /m/?

Comments/Adaptations

Comments   Decorate the classroom with graphics of the letter, objects, and pictures of objects with names beginning with the letter sound of the week. Midway through the school year, introduce letters and sounds in the first and last position in words. Begin to use vowel letter sounds in the medial position in words.

Home Link   In your newsletter to parents, add a paragraph about the letter the class is learning about at the present time ["We are learning about the letter *S* and the sound it usually makes at the beginning of words. Please take a few minutes over the next few days to look through pictures or magazines with your child to find at least one picture of a word that starts with *S*. Encourage your child to cut out the picture(s) and bring it to school. We will mount the picture(s) and add it to our *S* list"].

FIRST SOUND SONG

Main Purpose	To develop phonological segmentation and sound manipulation
	Children learn to remember words, phrases, and sounds and to identify the first sound in words.
Materials	Trios of pictures to illustrate verses; First Sound Song booklet (see the end of this activity for an example of a First Sound Song)
Description of the Activity	The following song encourages children to think about the sounds in words. Sing the First Sound Song to the tune of "Old MacDonald Had a Farm." Have the children learn the verses. Then encourage them to change and propose new words. At the end of a verse, repeat the words, and ask children to identify the first sound ["We sang tiger, tree, and train. Which sound do these words begin with?"]. A single sound may be emphasized throughout the whole song, or each verse may focus on a different sound, as in the following example.
	This activity develops the following behaviors and concepts that are related to early literacy:
Print Awareness	Print—book conventions, awareness of graphic symbols, letter identification; letter–sound correspondence—single sounds and letters
Phonological Awareness	Perception and memory—words, phonemes; phonological skills—alliteration, segmentation
Oral Language	Vocabulary—words and sentences

ADULT–CHILD INTERACTIVE BEHAVIORS

High Demand/Low Support

Children draw pictures and label words that begin with the same first sound to use in verses of the song. They will:

> identify the first sound in words and tell a word that starts the same as another

---

This activity was developed from a recommendation in Yopp, H. (1992). Developing phonemic awareness in young children. *The Reading Teacher, 45*(9), 696–703.

Support Strategies

?	Open-ended questioning	Ask children to identify words that begin with a particular first sound, and incorporate children's suggestions into the verses of the song.

What words begin with /t/?

⬛	Cognitive structuring	Make sure children differentiate the letter name (i.e., t) from its sound (i.e., /t/).

/T/ is the sound of t.

◐	Task regulation	Stress the first sound of words by stretching ["Ssssilly, Ssssam, and ssssick"] or iterating ["D-d-d-daddy, d-d-d-duck, and d-d-d-deep"]. Repeat the trio of words several times, emphasizing the first sound.

👤	Instructing	Tell children to listen for a particular sound in words before beginning the song.

Listen for the /t/ at the beginning of the words in the song.

Have a more advanced peer identify the correct first sound. Model, and elicit a response.

Betty, bear, and bat. /B/, /b/, /b/. What's the sound that starts Betty, bear, and bat?

Model lists of words that start with the same sound, and ask children to add a new word.

Candy, cat, and can. What's another word that starts the same?

Medium Demand/Medium Support

Children sing along with peers. They will:

identify the first sound in a trio of words that share the same onset

Support Strategies

⬛	Cognitive structuring	Make sure that children understand the concept of same and different by asking them to identify similarities and differences among concrete objects and pictures.

◉	Holding in memory	Make a picture board of the three words for the verse, and label pictures with the letter that starts all three.

◐	Task regulation	Repeat the trio of words several times before singing the song.

👤	Instructing	Model sounds, and repeat the question.

Mommy, man, and milk. /M/, /m/, /m/. They all start with /m/. What's the sound that starts these words: Mommy, man, and milk?

Low Demand/High Support

Children sing along with peers. They will:

identify the first sound in a trio of words that share the same onset

Support Strategies

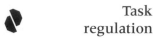

Task regulation   Provide visual cues by drawing children's attention to the pictures in the book or concrete trios of objects (e.g., miniature toys, props). Use the same trio of words several times until children sing the verse along with peers.

Instructing   Ask children to repeat first sounds following a peer model. Model sounds, words, and sentences in the verse; and ask children to repeat before leading the song.

Comments/Adaptations

Comments   Initially, the teacher will lead the song. As children learn to classify pictures by first sound or to name objects by first sound, they can "create" a trio of words to use in verses. These words can be posted and identified by several class members before beginning the song. This activity can be extended later in the school year by having children identify the *last* sound in words. When most children can identify the last sound, try identification of medial sounds, which is the most difficult level (e.g., cot, lot, boss).

First Sound Song Example   These lyrics are sung to the tune of "Old MacDonald Had a Farm."

First verse: ["What's the sound that starts these words: turtle, time, and teeth?" (Wait for a response from the children.) "/T/ is the sound that starts these words: turtle, time, and teeth. With a /t/, /t/ here and a /t/, /t/ there, here a /t/, there a /t/, everywhere a /t/, /t/. /T/ is the sound that starts these words: turtle, time, and teeth."]

Second verse: ["What's the sound that starts these words: chicken, chin, and cheek?" (Wait for a response from the children.) "/Ch/ is the sound that starts these words: chicken, chin, and cheek. With a /ch/, /ch/ here, and a /ch/, /ch/ there, here a /ch/, there a /ch/, everywhere a /ch/, /ch/. /Ch/ is the sound that starts these words: chicken, chin, and cheek"].

Third verse: ["What's the sound that starts these words: daddy, duck, and deep?" (Wait for a response from the children.) "/D/ is

tiger

tree

train

the sound that starts these words: daddy, duck, and deep. With a /d/, /d/ here and a /d/, /d/ there, here a /d/, there a /d/, everywhere a /d/, /d/. /D/ is the sound that starts these words: daddy, duck, and deep"].

Link with Print Awareness	Post the trio of words to use in the verse for the day. Show children the words, call their attention to the similarity among them (e.g., first letter, first sound), and encourage children to read the words along with you before and during the song.
Adaptations	Use sign language with children who have hearing impairments.
Home Link	Send home First Sound Song booklets of illustrated, labeled trios generated by the children.

GUESS THE WORD (BLENDING)

Main Purpose	To demonstrate how sounds can be blended into spoken words
	Children learn how to blend initial sounds to form words.
Materials	Simple pictures of concrete words. (Include words that begin with stretched sounds [e.g., s, m, l, r] as well as stop sounds [e.g., c, k, t, d].)
Description of the Activity	Spread four pictures across the floor or table. Begin by saying to the children ["Guess the word I'm saying. It's one of these pictures"]. Pronounce words segmented into onset-rime ["m-oon"], phonemes ["b-a-t"], and syllables ["tur-tle"]. Begin with words that start with stretched sounds ["sssnnnaaaake"]. When the children guess snake, call on a child to show the picture of a snake with the word snake printed at the bottom. Repeat the game with other pictured words. Next time you play, use the same cards but add two words beginning with stop sounds (e.g., c-ake, k-ey, t-ear). Children may have more difficulty with words that cannot be stretched out. Vary the skill level required for correct responding by the way you pronounce the word that children are to blend. Syllables are easiest, then stretched sounds (e.g., mmmoussse), and then words with one break (e.g., c-at, d-og). The most difficult are words with all sounds separated (e.g., h-a-t, t-r-ea-t). This game can also be played with objects and miniature toys.
	This activity develops the following behaviors and concepts that are related to early literacy:
Print Awareness	Letter–sound correspondence—single sounds and letters, words
Phonological Awareness	Phonological skills—blending
Oral Langauge	Vocabulary—words and sentences

ADULT–CHILD INTERACTIVE BEHAVIORS

High Demand/Low Support

Children will guess words correctly. They will:

- blend words with sounds pronounced as two, three, or four phonemes

Support Strategies

Task regulation   Use pictures and objects to represent the words to be blended. Ask children to name the objects or pictures before guessing the words from separated phonemes.

Instructing   Have children repeat the segmented word before blending it.

Medium Demand/Medium Support

Children guess words correctly. They will:

> blend words with sounds pronounced in onset-rime format

Support Strategies

Task regulation   Reduce choices of pictures and objects to three or four. Ask children to name the objects or pictures before guessing the words pronounced in onset-rime format. Use words with stretchable sounds (e.g., ssssail, mmmmoon, shshshsheet, fffffly) rather than stop sounds (e.g., b-oy, c-up, t-op, h-at, p-encil), so that words can be stretched without breaking between sounds.

Instructing   Have children repeat the segmented word before blending it. Model blending the word. Then repeat the segmented form, and ask children to blend the sound.

> M-ap is mmmmaap. Map. You try it. Guess this word: m-ap.

Low Demand/High Support

Children will guess small sets of pictured words correctly. They will:

> blend words with sounds pronounced in onset-rime format

Support Strategies

Cognitive structuring   Name the pictures with children, and explain that you will say the words in little bits.

> Let's name these pictures: cat, pig, bike. Now I'll say the little bits of a word. It's one of these, but you have to listen and guess: /p/-/i/-/g/.

Task regulation   Limit choices of pictures and objects to two or three. Begin with stretched words.

> Sssaaailll, mmmaaannn.

 Instructing   Model, and then repeat the task.

Comments/Adaptations

Extension   When most children can blend the pictured word correctly, add word cards to the stack to use as a "match the picture with the word" activity. Children will write a word (e.g., carrot) and find the picture to match it.

Adaptations   Use objects and props that children with visual impairments can explore.

Home Link   Parent Activity: Say it Fast!

I'M THINKING OF A . . .
(BLENDING BY CATEGORY)

Main Purpose

To facilitate blending of sounds into words

This activity introduces blending of sounds into words by providing categories to facilitate children's answers.

Materials

None (may use pictures or objects)

Description of the Activity

Encourage children to blend isolated sounds into words by providing categories for children's responses. For this activity, teachers provide a category for children to search (e.g., animals, things with which to write, children in the class, birds, things on which to sit). If letters and their sounds are taught concurrently, then teachers can also use first sound categories to reinforce beginning sounds and particular letters. Begin by stating the category, perhaps linked to a current theme in the classroom ["I'm thinking of an animal. Here's the clue: c-at," "I'm thinking of a flying thing that is not a bird. Can you tell me what this word is: pl-ane?"]. The first several times you play the game, present words in an onset-rime format (e.g., /c/ /at/, /l/ /ion/, /m/ /onkey/), and have children repeat the segmented words. As children become better at guessing, present short words with all phonemes separated ["/D/ /o/ /g/"], and ask children to repeat the segmented version before they guess an answer. Provide one longer word each session as a challenge to students who are more advanced. To sustain motivation over several days, vary the activity by putting objects into a bag for the children to guess or by using picture cards, which you turn to show the children when they correctly guess the words ["/F/ /l/ /y/, /b/ /ee/, /bu/ /tter/ /fly/"].

This activity develops the following behaviors and concepts that are related to early literacy:

Print Awareness

Letter–sound correspondence—single sounds and letters

Phonological Awareness

Phonological skills—blending

Oral Language

Literate discourse—categorical organization

ADULT–CHILD INTERACTIVE BEHAVIORS

High Demand/Low Support

Children guess words correctly. They will:

blend three to four phonemes into words

Support Strategies

	Cognitive structuring	Provide additional clues.
		    It's a bug. It flies. It stings. It's a w-a-s-p.
		Point out contradictions.
		    The first sound is /p/, so it can't be train.

	Instructing	Encourage children to repeat the segmented word before blending the sounds.

Medium Demand/Medium Support

Children guess words correctly. They will:
>   blend three to four phonemes into words

Support Strategies

	Cognitive structuring	Review names that go into a category before having children guess words. Let's think of words that are names of food, such as carrot, jam, and milk.
	Task regulation	Begin with two- to three-phoneme words. Use words with initial sounds (onsets) that can be stretched easily (e.g., seal, not teal). Provide visual cues by letting children choose pictures or objects: bear, tiger, and cat. Which word am I thinking of? /C/ /at/?
	Instructing	Encourage children to repeat the segmented word before guessing. Have children repeat words modeled correctly by peers.

Low Demand/High Support

Children guess words correctly. They will:
>   blend three phonemes into words

Support Strategies

	Holding in memory	Provide children three objects or pictures of the words from which to select.
	Task regulation	Give children a choice of two objects or pictures from which to select (e.g., milk and juice). Which word am I thinking of? J-uice.

Pronounce words in onset-rime format.

L-unch. M-ilk.

Instructing   Begin with two objects, their names pronounced in onset-rime format (see Task Regulation, above). When children correctly guess these words, add one additional picture of an object, gradually increasing the set to four or five as children learn how to combine sounds.

Comments/Adaptations

Adaptations   Use objects and props that children with visual impairments can explore.

Home Link   Parent Activity: Say it Fast!

WORD TO WORD
MATCHING GAME: FIRST SOUND

Main Purpose	To develop categorization and segmentation of sounds
	Children learn to discriminate and identify sounds and words based on their onset sounds.
Materials	A deck of laminated picture cards with several examples of words beginning with each sound represented in the deck
Description of the Activity	To play this game, children need a stack of cards that have simple pictures of common objects on them. Lay out one card (e.g., a card on which there is a picture of a table) for all children to see. Ask the children to name the picture and identify the onset sound (e.g., table, /t/). Let each child draw a card and name the new picture (turtle), then the shared word (table), and decide whether they share the same onset ["Table, turtle. Yes, they start the same"]. Let children take turns drawing cards, and continue the game until all of the cards have been drawn. For the next round of play, the teacher (or a child) picks a new picture card for the others to match. This game can also be played with objects.
	This activity develops the following behaviors and concepts that are related to early literacy:
Print Awareness	Print—letter identification; letter–sound correspondence—single sounds and letters
Phonological Awareness	Perception and memory—words, phonemes; phonological skills—alliteration, segmentation
Oral Language	Vocabulary—words and sentences

ADULT–CHILD INTERACTIVE BEHAVIORS

High Demand/Low Support

Children will:

> identify the first sound in words and tell a word that starts with the same sound as another

Support Strategies

Cognitive structuring	Tell children the name of the letter.
	Pig starts with the letter p. Which sound does a p make?

134

Show children other cards with words that begin with the same sound.

> Snake. That goes with these pictures of a seal and a sailboat.

Associate words with those that start with the same onset.

> Turtle. Table, turtle. They start the same. Which sound do they start with?

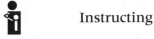

Holding in memory

Remind children of specific onset sounds.

> We are looking for a match for table. /T/, /t/, /t/.

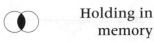

Instructing

Participate in the game, draw cards, and model. Ask children direct questions.

> Does tiger start with /t/?

Stretch ["sssslug"] or iterate ["t-t-t-turtle"] the first sound, and have children imitate the stretched or iterated words. Model words that start with the same sound, and have children repeat.

> Box and book. They start with the same sound. Box. Tell me a word that starts the same as box.

Model lists of words that share a common initial sound, and have children add new words.

> Pet, pig, pop. What else?

Medium Demand/Medium Support

Children will:

> discriminate between phonemes (same or different) and recognize two words that start with the same sound

Support Strategies

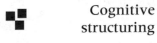

Cognitive structuring

Make sure that children understand the concept of same and different by asking them to identify similarities and differences among concrete objects and pictures.

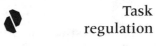

Task regulation

Select cards for the deck that represent phonemes that are clearly different (e.g., /d/ versus /k/). Limit the number of initial sounds represented in the deck to two or three sounds. Have children select the odd word of three words, two of which share a common initial sound.

> Wig, wasp, and mug. Which is the odd word?

Instructing

Model words and sounds that are similar and sounds that are different, and repeat the question.

> Bug and squirrel. Bug starts with /b/, and squirrel starts with /s/. Are they the same or different?

Put together two cards with pictures of objects that have names beginning with the same sound, and have children name the pictures.

Low Demand/High Support

Children will:

discriminate between two phonemes (same or different) and recognize two words that start with the same sound

Support Strategies

Cognitive structuring

Intensify the salience of the onsets of words as you emphasize same and different.

Ssssunflower. Ssssalt. They start the same. They start with /sss/. Say sssunflower.

Holding in memory

Provide visual cues (e.g., signs, pictures) to help children recall sounds and words, such as a picture of a snake to help remember the sound /s/.

Task regulation

Select cards for the deck that represent only two onsets (e.g., /s/ words and /t/ words). Repeat picture names to children, and stress the first sound by stretching ["Ssssnake, sssssalad"] or iterating ["T-t-t-turtle, t-t-t-table"]. Provide choices.

Which word starts with /s/: silly or tile?

Instructing

Use a small set of concrete objects representing two onsets.

Here's man, moose, monkey, doll, dog, dime.

Assist children in arranging objects in piles based on onsets. Mix objects, and encourage children to categorize them again by first sound. Repeat with new objects and sounds.

Comments/Adaptations

Comments

As children become competent in matching the first sound in words, extend the activity and have them match the last sound in words and, once they master that, the medial vowel sound among words.

Adaptations

Use objects and props so that children with visual impairments can feel them. Use sign language and color code letters to assist children with hearing impairments.

Home Link

Parent Activity: First Sound

SING A FIRST SOUND

Main Purpose	To practice matching isolated sounds to the first sound in words

Children listen to a sound provided by the teacher, analyze words for their first sound, and select words that match the teacher's sound.

Materials None

Description of the Activity The teacher begins the song sung to the tune of "Jimmy Cracked Corn" (song lyrics by Hallie Yopp) as follows: ["Who knows a word that starts with /s/? Who knows a word that starts with /s/? Who knows a word that starts with /s/? It must start with /s/"].

Be sure to use the most common sound for the letter rather than its name. If children do not call out appropriate examples for the next verse, then the teacher can supply one ["Snake! Snake is a word that starts with /s/. Snake is a word that starts with /s/. Snake is a word that starts with /s/. Snake starts with /s/]. Repeat the first verse to elicit more /s/ words from the children. Vary the sound for the day to highlight particular sounds of interest to the children, or match sounds to go with the first sound of the name of a particular child. The song can be incorporated into circle activities (children hold hands and walk in a circle as they sing) or sung as children sit at desks or wait for lining up. If also teaching letter names, then post the letter prominently prior to beginning the song to help children associate the sound with the letter. Write the words chosen by the children on the board or on paper, lining up the first sound in the children's choices to demonstrate the sameness among the words. The list can be used later as a copying or drawing activity.

This activity develops the following behaviors and concepts that are related to early literacy:

Print Awareness Print—letter identification; letter–sound correspondence

Phonological Awareness Perception and memory—words; phonological skills—segmentation

Oral Langauge Vocabulary—words and sentences

This activity was developed from a recommendation in Yopp, H. (1992). Developing phonemic awareness in young children. *The Reading Teacher, 45*(9), 696–703.

ADULT–CHILD INTERACTIVE BEHAVIORS

High Demand/Low Support

Children take turns supplying appropriate words for the verses. They will:

> sing the song, supply appropriate words for verses, and generate sounds and words for new verses

? Open-ended questioning

Before singing the song, brainstorm words that start with the target letter sounds.

Providing feedback

Tell children they were correct by immediately beginning the second part of the song.

> Cat is a word that starts with /k/ . . .

If children name an inappropriate word, then tell them what their choice began with, repeat the direction, and repeat the question.

> Lion starts with /l/. What starts with /k/?

Instructing

Provide a clear direction for the task.

> It must start with /sssss/. What starts with /sssss/?

Medium Demand/Medium Support

Children take turns supplying appropriate words for the verse. They will:

> sing the song, supply appropriate words for verses, and generate sounds and words for new verses

Support Strategies

Cognitive structuring

Be sure children understand the concept of first sound. Review other first sound games.

Holding in memory

Softly say the target sound while children are thinking of appropriate words.

> /P/-/p/-/p/.

Task regulation

Offer a choice while emphasizing the first sound.

> /Sssss/ Sssssilly. Mmmmarble. Say those words. (Children respond.) Which starts with /ssss/?

Use the same letter sound for several verses to provide more opportunity to practice.

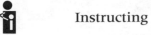 Instructing   Clarify directions, and provide a model.

> We're thinking of /ssss/ words. Ssssign. Sign starts with /sss/. Let's sing our verse with ssssign.

Low Demand/High Support

Children will sing the song using the picture names to generate appropriate words. They will:

> sing the song and supply appropriate words for verses

Support Strategies

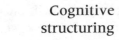 Cognitive structuring   Show children a poster that has many easy-to-name pictures that begin with the target sound. Guide children to repeat these words as you point to the pictures.

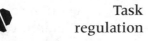 Task regulation   Using the poster (see Cognitive Structuring above) or a choice of two pictures that both start with the appropriate sound, ask children to pick one of the picture names when it is time to generate a word that matches the sound.

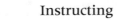 Instructing   Stretch or iterate the first sound in appropriate pictures, and encourage children to say the words and sounds in stretched or iterated fashion.

> C-c-c-cat; c-c-c-can; c-c-c-colt; c-c-c-corn. Tell me a word that starts with /k/.

Comments/Adaptations

Comments   Midway through kindergarten, extend the activity by singing "Who knows a word that ends with /t/?" Add other known letter sounds.

Home Link   Parent Activity: First Sound

FIRST SOUND BINGO

Main Purpose

To identify first sounds and match sounds and letters

The child gains practice in recognizing the first sound in words and in making sound–symbol correspondences.

Materials

Bingo cards with 16 randomly arranged pictures; letter cards with s, t, p, and m (eight of each, shuffled), or any set of four letters and sounds to be learned. (This game is designed as a practice activity for children who already know the first sounds of a few words and the sounds of the four letters: s, t, p, and m.)

Description of the Activity

Let each child select a bingo card, with the following pictures randomly arranged in a 4 x 4 array: popcorn, puppy, pencil, pie, tiger, tack, ten, tie, milk, mouth, man, mountain, snake, sock, six, and seal. Shuffle the letter cards and place them face down. In turn, have each child draw one letter and look for a picture of an object that starts with the letter. Have the child place the letter on the picture, and then let the next child take a turn. (*Note:* Children can also use blank markers to cover a picture that starts with the letter drawn. Increase the variety of pictures and first sounds as children learn more letter sounds.)

This activity develops the following behaviors and concepts that are related to early literacy:

Print Awareness

Print—letter identification; letter–sound correspondence—single sounds and letters

Phonological Awareness

Phonological skills—alliteration, segmentation

Oral Language

Vocabulary—words and sentences

ADULT–CHILD INTERACTIVE BEHAVIORS

High Demand/Low Support

Children will:
   play the game independently

Support Strategies

Providing feedback

Confirm correct choices as a model for other children.

Yes, telephone starts with /t/, so you put the t on the telephone.

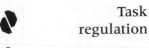 **Holding in memory** Repeat the letter sound, as needed, as children decide whether it matches the target word.

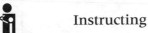 **Task regulation** Use only letter sounds that children know thoroughly.

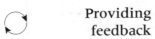 **Instructing** Tell children the sound of the letter, and ask them to repeat it along with words that begin with that sound.

Medium Demand/Medium Support

Children may need assistance with the sound–symbol correspondences for the letters they draw. They will:

    play the game with limited numbers of letters

Support Strategies

Open-ended questioning Ask children who cover their pictures appropriately to explain their choice.

    Why did you put the s on the seal?

Providing feedback Praise children who correctly cover their pictures.

    Yes, you put the s on the seal because seal starts with /sss/.

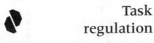 **Task regulation** Use only the four letters that children know most thoroughly and the same 16 pictures, arranged in random order, so that all children can place a letter on a picture with each new letter drawn.

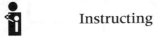 **Instructing** After providing feedback, allow children who have difficulty to take another turn with the same letter sound.

    John put his s on the star. Sssstar starts with /sss/. Where would you like to put your s?

Low Demand/High Support

If some children do not know letter sounds or how to identify the first sound in words, then adults can use this game as a teaching tool. Children will:

    learn one letter–sound correspondence and select pictures of words that begin with that sound

First Sound Bingo—Demonstration page

Pie	Smile	Truck	Snake
Tree	Star	Man	Puppy
Moon	Pencil	Sun	Train
Snail	Tooth	Mouse	Pen

First Sound Bingo Letter Chips

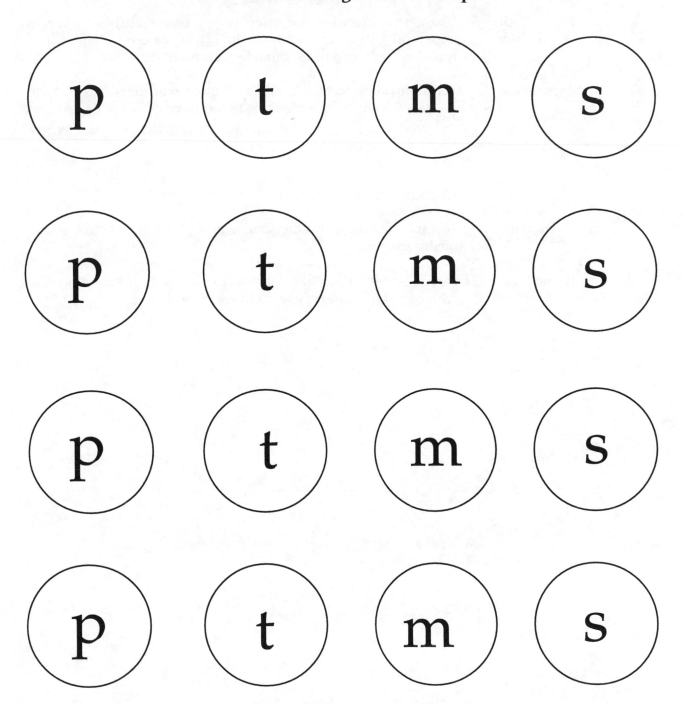

Support Strategies

Task
regulation

Use only two very familiar letters (e.g., s, t) and pictures that begin with those two letter sounds on the playing card (e.g., eight s pictures and eight t pictures, randomly arranged).

Instructing

After providing feedback, allow children who have difficulty to take another turn with the same letter sound

> John put his s on the star. Sssstar starts with /ssss/. Where would you like to put your s?

Comments/Adaptations

Comments

Toward the end of kindergarten, play the game with last and medial sounds.

Home Link

Parent Activity: Encourage parents to make a First Sound booklet with one of the letters targeted by the game board.

SEGMENTING WITH ONSET-RIME BOXES

Main Purpose

To practice auditory segmentation and facilitate children's awareness of the sounds in words

Segmentation of spoken words stimulates word analysis and is strongly associated with successful acquisition of reading and spelling. Separating words after the onset (initial consonant or consonant blend) is the easiest level of phonological segmentation for one-syllable words (e.g., c-at, sn-ake, p-ig, br-own). Learning to segment also encourages children to attempt to write words and to use invented spellings during other class activities.

Materials

Onset-rime box for the teacher and each child

Description of the Activity

Children listen to a word provided by the teacher and practice saying the word in two parts: the onset (first sound or blend) and the rime (the part of the word that remains, beginning with the first vowel after the onset). Following is a suggested way to introduce the onset-rime boxes to a group of children ["Here's a new way to say parts in words: Magic Squares! Here's how they work." (Show the large two-rectangle form.) "When I want to say *sail* in two parts, I touch the squares like this." (Touch the first box: /s/.) (Touch the next box: -ail. Repeat twice.) "Do it with me." (Repeat demonstration as children segment the word.) "Who can say the parts in sail with the magic squares?"]. Give individual turns to two children. The children may make errors the first time this activity is introduced. Encourage participation, even if children are incorrect. Gently model once more for the children during individual turns, and praise engagement. ["Good! You're saying the parts!" (Model with two to three more words during the first session.) "C-at, d-og"]. Do this activity for several consecutive days, repeating a few of the same words and adding new ones. If the group is also learning letters and sounds, then use words that begin with the sounds being taught. ["When I want to say hat in two parts, I touch the squares like this." (Touch the first box and say the sound for the letter h. Touch the next box while saying -at. Repeat two times.) "Who can say the parts in hat with the magic squares?" (Give individual turns to two children.) "Let's try some more words with the Magic Squares"]. After a few days of children saying short words in onset-rime format with you, give children their own onset-rime boxes to touch. In small groups, children enjoy touching their own squares. In large groups, teachers can direct children by holding up one finger for each segmented sound or tapping a table. Children might also suggest appropriate words for their classmates to segment using the boxes. If you are teaching letter names, then prominently post the letters that will be used prior to beginning the activity, and practice associating the names with the most common sound for each letter. Use words that begin with the letter sounds you are teaching. To work on /s/ and /h/, for example, use hope, sign, hot, high, and say.

You may wish to follow up this activity with a writing activity in which children listen to words that begin with sounds they have practiced (try the same words used for the box activity) and then write a letter to represent the word's first sound on the board or on paper. This list can be used later as a copying or drawing activity. For children who perform this task easily, encourage them to add letters for other sounds they hear in the word. (*Note:* Children find it easier to segment words with single-consonant onsets [e.g., h-am; s-it; f-arm] than words that start with consonant blends [e.g., cl-ock; gr-een; str-eet].)

This activity develops the following behaviors and concepts that are related to early literacy:

Print Awareness	Print—writing; letter–sound correspondence—single sounds and letters, words
Phonological Awareness	Phonological skills—segmentation
Oral Language	Vocabulary—words and sentences

ADULT–CHILD INTERACTIVE BEHAVIORS

High Demand/Low Support

Children will:

> take turns supplying short words to segment with the onset-rime boxes

Support Strategies

Open-ended questioning

This activity should begin in a structured manner with extensive modeling; however, as children suggest words that begin with available letter sounds, incorporate their suggestions.

> Can you think of a short word we can play with today?

Encourage the children to segment the word, correct if necessary, and have the group repeat the correct model.

> Yes, Beth is B-eth. Everybody segment Beth.

Providing feedback

> Put just the first sound in the first box. What's the first sound? (Children respond /b/.) Yes, touch the first box and say /b/.

Holding in memory

Remind children of the first sound while they are thinking of the rest of the word.

/B/. . . .

 Task regulation

Use only five to seven words each session until children segment easily.

 Instructing

Model segmenting while touching the boxes, and have children repeat.

Watch me say Beth. B-eth. Now you say Beth.

Medium Demand/Medium Support

Children will:

take turns supplying short words to segment with the onset-rime boxes

Support Strategies

Task regulation

Limit the first sound choices to two (e.g., use words starting with /m/ and /p/), and have children say the first sounds for words prior to beginning the activity. Use only three to four words each session until children segment easily, and provide several opportunities to segment these three to four words.

Instructing

Model, lead segmenting while touching the boxes, and have children repeat several times after you,

Watch me say Beth. B-eth. B-eth. Do it with me.

Segment the word several times before you ask children to do it independently. Review the words that were segmented correctly the last time you played the game.

Low Demand/High Support

Children will:

practice segmenting words with the onset-rime boxes following teacher and peer models

Support Strategies

Cognitive structuring

Ask children to say the word slowly before they try to segment it. Touch the first box while stretching or iterating the first sound ["Milk. Mmmmilk. Mmm"], and then say ["-ilk"] while touching the second box.

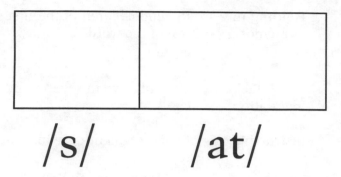

/s/   /at/

| **Task regulation** | Limit the words to a small set of pictures used successfully in a first sound or blending game. |
| Instructing | Give the children a set of words that begin with just one letter sound for the first few days (a different letter sound each day), then go to two letter sounds in one day that review sounds used previously. Encourage the child to repeat the word and say its first sound after you. Model segmenting while touching the boxes, and have children repeat several times after you. If necessary for a particular child, then gently hold the child's hand and touch the boxes with the child until confidence grows. |

Comments/Adaptations

| Home Link | Parent Activity: Writing Messages |

SEGMENTING INTO THREE PHONEMES

Main Purpose   To practice segmenting words into their constituent sounds

Segmenting all the sounds in words is a prerequisite to spelling and also highly related to later reading achievement.

Materials   Three-square form for the teacher and a form for each child

Description of the Activity   The child listens to a three-phoneme word (e.g., cat, dog, cake) provided by the teacher and learns to say the word in three parts: each phoneme separated from the others (e.g., /c/-/a/-/t/). Following is a suggested manner for introducing the three-square forms to a group of children ["Let's say all of the sounds in a word. Watch me." (Show the three-square form.) "When I want to say all the parts in sail, I touch the squares like this." (Say /s/, and touch the first box; say /ai/, and touch the next box; and say /l/, and touch the last box. Repeat twice.) "Do it with me." (Encourage children to say the sounds as you touch the boxes.) "Who can say all of the parts in sail with the magic squares?"] Give individual turns to two children. Model with two to three more words during the first session. Do this activity for several consecutive days, repeating a few of the same words and adding new ones. If the group is also learning letters and sounds, then use words that include the letter sounds being taught. When working with small groups of children, give them their own three-square form, and have them touch the squares while saying each separate sound in three-phoneme words. ["When I want to say all of the sounds in hat, I touch the squares like this." (Say /h/, and touch the first box; say /a/, and touch the next box; and say /t/, and touch the last box. Repeat twice.) "Who can say all of the parts in hat with the magic squares?"] Give individual turns to two children. Children might also suggest appropriate words for their classmates to segment using the boxes.

If also teaching letter names, then post the letters that will be used prominently prior to beginning the activity, and practice associating the names with the most common sound for each letter. To work on s and h, say, "Let's try some more words with the magic squares." Use hope, sign, hip, hot, and sat one at a time, as examples.

This activity develops the following behaviors and concepts that are related to early literacy:

Print Awareness   Letter–sound correspondence—single sounds and letters

Phonological Awareness   Phonological skills—segmentation

Oral Language   Vocabulary—words and sentences

ADULT–CHILD INTERACTIVE BEHAVIORS

High Demand/Low Support

Children will:

> take turns supplying short words to segment with the three-phoneme boxes

Support Strategies

? Open-ended questioning

Begin the activity in a structured manner with extensive modeling; however, as children suggest words that begin with available letter sounds, incorporate their suggestions.

> Can you think of a short word we can play with today?

Encourage the child to segment the word, correct if necessary, and have the group repeat the correct model.

> Yes. Pat is /P/-/a/-/t/. Everybody segment Pat.

Providing feedback

Correct errors by clarifying instruction.

> Put just the first sound in the first box. What's the first sound? (Children respond /b/.) Yes, touch the first box and say /b/.

Holding in memory

Remind children of the first sound while they are thinking of the rest of the word.

> /B/. . . .

Task regulation

Use only five to seven words each session until children segment easily.

Instructing

Model segmenting while touching the boxes, and have children repeat after you.

> Watch me do Beth. /B/-/e/-/th/. Now you do Beth.

Medium Demand/Medium Support

Children will:

> take turns supplying short words to segment with the three-phoneme boxes

Support Strategies

Task regulation

Limit the first sound choices to two, and have children say the first sounds for words prior to beginning the activity. Use only three to four words each session until children segment easily, and provide several opportunities to segment these three to four words.

Instructing

Model segmenting while touching the boxes, and have children repeat several times after you.

> Watch me do Sam. /S/-/a/-/m/. Sam. Do it with me.

Segment the word several times before you ask children to do it independently. Review the words that were segmented correctly the last time you played the game.

Low Demand/High Support

Children will:

> practice segmenting words with the three-phoneme boxes following teacher and peer models

Support Strategies

Cognitive structuring

Ask children to say the word slowly before they try to segment it. Touch the first box while stretching or iterating the first sound ["Mat. Mmmmat. Mmm"]. Touch the second box while stretching or iterating the second sound ["aaa"].

Task regulation

Give children a set of words that begin with just one letter sound for the first few days (a different letter sound each day), then go to two letter sounds in one day (which review sounds used previously). Encourage children to repeat the word and say its first sound after you. Limit the words to a small set of pictures used successfully in a first sound game.

Instructing

Model segmenting while touching the boxes, and have children repeat several times after you.

> Watch me do Mike. /M/-/i/-/ke/. /M/-/i/-/ke/. Do it with me.

Segment the word several times with children segmenting with you before you ask children to do it independently. If necessary, then gently hold the child's hand and touch the boxes with the child until confidence grows.

Comments/Adaptations

Comments

For segmenting with larger groups, the same activity can be conducted with other cues, such as holding up one finger for each phoneme as it is pronounced or tapping a tabletop for each phoneme in a word. It may be easier for the teacher to use these cues in a large group than to give children individual segmenting forms.

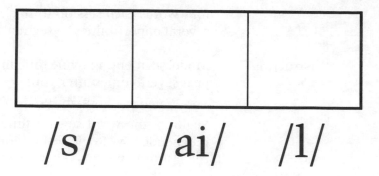

/s/   /ai/   /l/

Extension into Writing

You may want to follow up this activity with a writing activity in which children listen to words that they have practiced (begin with the same words used for the box activity) and then write a letter to represent each word sound on the board or on paper. For children who have learned first sounds, extend the writing by asking them to write all three sounds in the words you have practiced with the squares. This list can be used later as a copying or drawing activity. For children who perform this task easily, encourage them to write sounds they hear in longer words ["If this word is cat, write cats"].

Home Link

Parent Activity: Magnetic Letters (*Note:* Tell parents that when using magnetic letters, they should encourage their child to spell a short word. Show how the letters represent the sounds in the word. Suggest that parents use the Magnetic Letters to help their child listen for sounds in words and construct two- and three-letter words, such as am, at, sam, and sat.)

ONSET~RIME WITH FIRST LETTER

Main Purpose   To select a letter to represent a word's onset

This activity helps children develop an understanding of the alphabetic principle that the sounds in spoken words are represented by letters in words we read or spell.

Materials   Onset-rime box for each child; a small set of letter tiles (e.g., Scrabble-like tiles, laminated letters)

Description of the Activity   Children listen to a word provided by the adult and say the word's first sound. Children select from the collection provided a letter to represent that sound and place the letter in the box on the left. With the letter in place, the child says the onset-rime form of the word. Children might also suggest appropriate words for their classmates to segment using the boxes. If the word begins with one of the available letters, then children can place it in the first box. If also teaching letter names, then prominently post the letters that will be needed prior to beginning the activity, and practice associating the names with the most common sound for each letter. You may wish to follow up this activity with a writing activity. Beginning with words children have practiced (words used for the box activity), ask children to write a letter to represent the word's first sound on the board or on paper. This list can be used later as a copying or drawing activity. For children who perform this task easily, encourage them to add letters for other sounds they hear in the word.

This activity develops the following behaviors and concepts that are related to early literacy:

Print Awareness   Letter–sound correspondence—single sounds and letters, words

Phonological Awareness   Phonological skills—alliteration, blending, segmentation

Oral Language   Vocabulary—words and sentences

ADULT–CHILD INTERACTIVE BEHAVIORS

High Demand/Low Support

Children will:

    take turns supplying appropriate words using their set of letter sounds

Support Strategies

Begin the activity in a structured manner; however, as children suggest words that begin with available letter sounds, incorporate their suggestions. Remember to use the most common sound. Children should be encouraged to use probable letters to represent sounds, even if the words are actually spelled using different letters, such as f to spell photograph, k for can, or s for circus.

?	Open-ended questioning	Focus children on the available letter sounds.

We have 10 letters today. Can you think of a word that starts with one of these letters for our game?

	Holding in memory	Direct children to say the first sound in the word they are trying to segment, and then search for the letter that makes that sound. Repeat the sound as needed as children search for the first letter.

	Task regulation	Be sure to use letters that have sounds the children know thoroughly before you play the game.

	Instructing	Model how to play the game.

Charlie said fish. Ffffish. /Fff/ is the first sound. Now, where's /fff/? Where's f?]

The adult puts the f in the first box. The adult may need to encourage children to say the first sound of words, before searching for a letter to represent the sound.

Medium Demand/Medium Support

Children will:

take turns supplying appropriate words using their set of letter sounds

Support Strategies

?	Open-ended questioning	Direct children to brainstorm words beginning with the collected letters.

We have three letters today. Can you think of short words that start with these letter sounds?

	Cognitive structuring	Explain the steps children need follow.

First we need to say the first sound, and then we'll find the letter that makes that sound.

	Providing feedback	Demonstrate why responses are correct or incorrect.

Yes, cat starts with /k/, and c makes /k/. So you put the c in the first box.

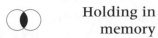

Holding in memory   Repeat the word as necessary until children identify the first sound. Encourage children to say the first sound as they search for the letter that makes that sound. Repeat the sound as needed as children search for the first letter.

Low Demand/High Support

Children will:

match a letter to the sound provided by the teacher

Support Strategies

Cognitive structuring   Stretch or iterate the first sound of words to be segmented.

Holding in memory   Provide a picture of the word for children to refer to as they search for a letter.

Task regulation   Use only two familiar letters and two to three words for each letter sound. Provide children with a choice.

Mouse. Mmmmouse. Does mmmmouse start with /mmmm/ or /t/?

Instructing   Model, and lead several familiar words.

Bat. Say bat. /B/-/b/-/at/. What's the first sound? Watch me. (Touch the boxes.) /B/-/at/.

When children segment correctly, use b and another known letter to continue the activity by selecting which letter sounds like /b/.

Comments/Adaptations

Comment   To encourage left–right progression, put a dot in the box on the left so that children know where to put the letter.

Extension   After children participate successfully in this activity for several days, encourage them to add the last sound they hear by selecting letters for first and last sounds using the three-phoneme forms.

Home Link   Parent Activity: Print in the World

SECTION IV

Oral Language

Ladders to Literacy also develops oral language with a constant interplay among meaning, language, and representation. Children need something to talk about in order for language development to occur, and this grist for the mill teaches children to use print to get information. *Ladders to Literacy* uses many kinds of literate events as opportunities for children to develop their oral language skills. Because of its clearly delineated structure and semantically restricted context (Bruner, 1983), story reading constitutes an ideal language learning situation for children with disabilities and children at risk for reading difficulties (Kirchner, 1991). Story reading also engages children in literate types of oral discourse, an experience that may be limited for some children from different ethnic and lower socioeconomic groups (Heath, 1982; Snow, 1983). Story reading with parents and teachers, along with other media such as songs and videotapes, provides conversational topics to facilitate children's language development (Lemish & Rice, 1986). An important aspect of these activities is their adaptability for children of different ability levels within the same classroom. Research suggests that children focus on different aspects of story reading at different points of development. Suggestions are provided for parents and teachers to adapt their questions and comments to each child's interests and developmental level.

- **Vocabulary and syntactic knowledge**—At the earliest developmental levels (ages 1–2 years), children learn labels for objects through story reading (Ninio & Bruner, 1978). Using an interactive style of story reading and asking questions ["What's this a picture of?"] facilitates this development. As children become older (2–5 years and beyond for complex or archaic language), they begin to listen to and remember syntactic constructions from stories. Snow and Goldfield (1983) found that children then would reuse these patterns in their speech. Appropriate teaching strategies include asking children to tell ["What does that mean?"] and providing alternative ways of expressing complex ideas.
- **Narrative skills: Story structure and genre**—Children learn story structure and narrative form by listening to stories (Heath et al., 1986; Sulzby, 1985). This knowledge progresses at more advanced levels to familiarity with genre, such as distinguishing fiction from historical text. Examples of teaching strategies include asking children to talk about this aspect of stories ["Is this a real story or a make-believe story?"] and calling children's attention to story structure, motivation, and goals ["Why did the princess do that?"].
- **Literate discourse: Decontextualization**—Literate language is characterized by a removal from the here and now and by a separation of writer from reader or speaker from listener. This kind of decontextualized language is used in school settings.

These activities provide suggestions for teachers and parents on how to engage with children in literate types of oral discourse by having children reconstruct past events through open-ended questioning and asking for explanations. Learning to read and write requires the child to reconceptualize his or her language. Early oral language takes place in face-to-face social interactions and is highly dependent on the immediate context (Snow, 1983); written language is decontextualized, the writer and the reader being removed from one another in time and in space. The acquisition of literacy involves making the transition from oral to written language (Cook-Gumperz & Gumperz, 1981; Share & Stanovich, 1995). Storybook reading, which includes aspects of oral *and* written language, may facilitate this transition.

EARLY LITERACY SKILLS

Vocabulary

- **Words and sentences**—Child will use one-word utterances to label a variety of objects, qualities, people, and events. Child will use longer utterances to express a variety of semantic intentions. Child will use a variety of adult-form sentences (e.g., declarative, interrogative, negatives).
  Activities: Show and Tell; Food Talk

Narrative Skills

- **Narrations of real events**—Child will relate events with a beginning, a middle, and an end. Child will make explicit causal and temporal sequences among events.
  Activities: Portraits; Interviews
- **Books**—Child will attend to and label pictures in book. Child will make comments and ask questions about individual pictures. Child will tell a story and link events based on pictures using conversational language. Child will form a written story based on pictures using reading intonation and wording.
  Activity: Book Review/Story Grammar
- **Narrations of fictional story**—Child will attend to story. Child will add comments and ask questions. Child will relate elements of story structure (e.g., setting, theme, plot, episodes, and resolution in correct sequence).
  Activities: Enacting Storybooks; Book Buddy

Literate Discourse

- **Conversations**—Child will maintain social interaction over two or more turns. Child will initiate and maintain a topic.
  Activities: Treasure Boxes; Movie Reviews; My Dream

- **Categorical organization**—Child will use superordinate labels to indicate general categories (e.g., food, animals, people).
  Activity: Special Words
- **Decontextualization**—Child will generalize experience to other settings. Child will provide explanations. Child will make predictions. Child will make interpretations/judgments. Child will distinguish fiction from real events.
  Activities: What Did You Hear?; Foreign Languages: Let's Say it Another Way!
- **Interpretive/analytical discourse**—Child will use internal state words to express feelings and motivations. Child will use cognitive words to refer to mental states. Child will use phonological words to refer to the use of language. Child will seek definitions of words.
  Activities: Feeling Objects; From This to That; Brainstorming; Let's Find Out!

SHOW AND TELL

Main Purpose   To expand vocabulary and conversational skills

Children learn they can communicate with others through speaking, writing, and reading. This activity develops pragmatic skills of sharing information among children. It also prepares children for literate discourse through learning to answer questions, describing objects and events, and providing explanations. The teacher facilitates appropriate communication among children and elicits language features that characterize literate discourse.

Materials   Objects chosen by children; pictures of objects; written label of objects

Description of the Activity   This activity can be implemented during opening circle time or in smaller groups. Let children take turns showing and telling the other children about an object that they have brought from home. Ask each child to label and describe the object and to explain why he or she chose the object for the presentation. Encourage the other children to ask questions about the object that require literate discourse. When more than one show-and-tell item has been shared, ask children to make nonjudgmental comparisons ["Would you play with these objects differently?" "How are they the same?" "How do they differ?"]. Draw a picture, and write the name of each object to demonstrate the connection between language and print. Direct children's attention to the relationship among the name of each object, the picture, and the written label.

This activity develops the following behaviors and concepts that are related to early literacy:

Print Awareness   Print—awareness of graphic symbols, writing; letter–sound correspondence—single sounds and letters, words

Phonological Awareness   Perception and memory—words

Oral Language   Vocabulary—words and sentences; narrative skills—narrations of real events; literate discourse—conversations, categorical organization, decontextualization

161

ADULT–CHILD INTERACTIVE BEHAVIORS

High Demand/Low Support

Children will:

> relate events organized in causal and temporal sequences, provide explanations, and adapt information to the level of the listener

Support Strategies

? **Open-ended questioning**

Invite children to ask questions about objects and to comment about personal experiences with similar objects.

> What else would you like to know about this?
> Is this like anything you have at home?

Ask questions that require children to provide explanations.

> Why is this your favorite stuffed toy?
> How does it work?

Encourage children to express temporal notions.

> When did this happen?

Providing feedback

Praise and encourage children's presentations.

> That's very interesting. I like that, too.

Request children to clarify information, if necessary.

> Did you go before or after the puppet show?

Reinterpret information.

> Oh, you mean your cousin from Mexico gave you the doll.

Cognitive structuring

Point out contradictions in children's narrations.

> I'm not sure I understand. You said that these poppies grew from seeds, but the birds ate all of the seeds, and there were none left.

Help children sequence events.

> What happened after it rained?

Instructing

Provide models to encourage children to reword sentences.

Medium Demand/Medium Support

Children will:

> initiate and maintain the topic and describe and relate events related to the object

Support Strategies

| ? | Open-ended questioning | Encourage children to initiate and describe the object. |

Tell us about this beautiful necklace.
Where does it come from?

| ↻ | Providing feedback | Praise and encourage children's presentation. |

That's very interesting. I like that, too.

Help continue the conversation by adding information related to the object or topic.

It has very bright colors.

| ✎ | Task regulation | Encourage children to respond to a set of structured questions as they prepare to show their objects. |

What is it called?
What do you like to do with it?
What do you like best about it?

| 👤 | Instructing | Provide models to encourage children to repeat simple sentences. |

Low Demand/High Support

Children show and label the object when it is their turn. They will:

initiate and maintain the topic and describe and relate events related to the object

Support Strategies

| ↻ | Providing feedback | Praise and demonstrate interest in the object. |

That's very cute.
I'd like to know its name.

Help maintain the conversation by expanding on children's utterances.

Ball. A red ball.

| ✎ | Task regulation | Provide choices. |

Is it a cat or a lion?
Do you play with it inside or outside?

| 👤 | Instructing | Ask children to talk about their objects. |

Tell us what you brought to class.
Tell us the name of your favorite toy.

Encourage peers to provide models.

Claire, can you tell Kyle what that is?

Ask children to label features.

What's this?

Which color is that?

Model, and ask children to repeat.

Say, My dog is Snoopy.

Comments/Adaptations

Comments

This activity can also be done immediately after a classroom routine such as playtime or snacktime. Children can recall which toy they most liked to play with or what their favorite food is.

Adaptations

Children with hearing impairments can communicate with sign language, which the adult translates for the rest of the group. Teach other children basic signs.

Home Link

Parent Activity: Let's Use Words to Describe . . . ! Encourage children to bring objects that represent their cultural backgrounds (e.g., clothing, jewelry, foods) or class themes (e.g., autumn, stuffed animals).

FOOD TALK

Main Purpose   To develop expressive vocabulary and literate discourse

Children will develop descriptive vocabulary and a repertoire of attributes to describe a range of objects. They will also refer to situations beyond the immediate context.

Materials   Menu of snack items and foods children bring or are served by the school

Description of the Activity   Refer to the foods on the snack menu (see Snack/Lunch Treat Menu activity); foods that children bring for lunch, birthday, or holiday treats; or pictures of food. Ask children to talk about the foods, using descriptive words. Prompt reluctant students with questions ["Yes, here's a carrot. Which color is the carrot? Mmm. An orange carrot. What else could we say about it?"]. Encourage general discussion among children. When the topic seems exhausted, try going around the group asking each child to say one thing about the food being described. Accept and encourage all plausible responses, including repeating other students' descriptions. To expand the activity, ask children what they had for breakfast. Encourage children who had the same food (e.g., Cheerios, oatmeal) to describe what it was like (e.g., small, round, crunchy, rough, poured from a box, eaten with milk). Encourage children to describe a food across a range of attributes (e.g., size, shape, color, texture, smell). Children may want to associate the food with personal experiences, their feelings about the food, or other times they have eaten the food. Encourage all such verbal behavior, especially as it generates discussion among the children. Ask direct, simple questions of children reluctant to participate in group description. When possible, focus discussion on description. Questions can be used to stimulate discussion ["What does it taste like?" "What does it smell like?" "How does it make you feel?" "What does it make you think of?" "Where does it come from?" "How does it grow?" "What kind of package does it come in?" "What is your favorite way to eat it?"]. On other days, vary the activity by using classroom toys or figures or pictures for children to describe.

This activity develops the following behaviors and concepts that are related to early literacy:

Print Awareness   Print—awareness of graphic symbols

Phonological Awareness   Perception and memory—words, phrases

Oral Language   Vocabulary—words and sentences; narrative skills—narrations of real events; literate discourse—conversations, categorical organization, decontextualization

ADULT–CHILD INTERACTIVE BEHAVIORS

High Demand/Low Support

Children engage in conversation about foods and expand to related topics. They will:

> expand descriptive vocabulary, use complex sentences, draw from their own experiences, and use superordinate labels to categorize foods

Support Strategies

? Open-ended questioning — Encourage conversation by asking children questions about attributes, origins, and personal preferences of foods.

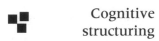 Cognitive structuring — Encourage children to categorize and compare foods according to taste, origins, culinary use, and so forth.

 Instructing — Generate a web or chart of children's descriptive words, and review them. Discuss what else these words describe.

Medium Demand/Medium Support

Children engage in conversation about foods and expand to related topics. They will:

> expand descriptive vocabulary, use complex sentences, draw from their own experiences, and use superordinate labels to categorize foods

Support Strategies

? Open-ended questioning — Encourage conversation by asking children questions about attributes and personal preferences of foods.

Cognitive structuring — Provide categories for children to use when describing foods.

> Tell us how it tastes, smells, and feels.

Instructing — Participate in the conversation, and provide models by rewording and expanding on children's sentences. Ask direct questions about foods.

> How does it taste?
> Do you like it?
> What's your favorite food?

Brainstorm, and record words related to particular attributes.

Let's talk about texture. Texture is what things feel like when you touch them. Touch the rug. What does it feel like? The texture of the rug is rough. Now touch the floor. What is its texture?

Low Demand/High Support

Children engage in conversations about foods. They will:

expand descriptive vocabulary, use simple sentences to describe attributes, and make judgments about personal preferences

Support Strategies

Task regulation

Comment on foods children are eating. Provide choices.

Does the banana taste sweet or sour?

Instructing

Provide models by expanding on children's utterances. Ask direct questions.

What are you drinking?
Which color is it?

Model, and have children repeat.

This is a corn muffin. What's that?

Comments/Adaptations

Link with Print Awareness

Write the children's responses, and categorize the attributes. For example, you might ask the children to describe cats by using the following attributes: names for cats (e.g., cat, kitten, Sparky); what cats do (e.g., eat, bite, purr, scratch); what cats feel like (e.g., soft, furry, rough, smooth); and colors for cats (e.g., black, brown, white, orange, grey). Show several pictures of cats, and ask a child to describe one cat, while other children guess which cat was chosen by using the description.

Adaptations

Children with hearing impairments can communicate using sign language, which the adult translates for the rest of the group.

More Ideas

Have children talk about ethnically diverse foods that they eat at home.

Home Link

Parent Activity: Let's Use Words to Describe . . . !

ENACTING STORYBOOKS

Main Purpose	To develop literate discourse and awareness of the link between oral and written language
	Through reading stories, children learn about objects, people, and events in the real world. By enacting the stories, children learn to relate print to narrative sequences and to oral language. They also learn to play different roles and to communicate with others.
Materials	Books; costumes; puppets; toys; flannel board and figures
Description of the Activity	Read books, and have children mime simple actions or implement activities related to the stories. For example, after reading *Brown Bear, Brown Bear, What Do You See?* (Martin, 1970), have the children pretend to be the animals. After reading *The Very Hungry Caterpillar* (Carle, 1969), go with the children to the grocery store and buy the foods the caterpillar ate, or have the children paint or model them. Create paper bag prop stories. Put a familiar book into a paper bag with props (e.g., puppets, toy animals, dolls, objects, pictures) representing the characters and setting of the story. Have the children enact the stories. For example, present toy animals with *Brown Bear, Brown Bear, What Do You See?* Include stuffed animals, a troll, blue paper, and a toy bridge with *The Three Billy Goats Gruff* (Brown, 1957). Have children dramatize the stories with miniature toys, flannel board figures, or puppets or by dressing in costumes. Have children practice a favorite story and present it to the public (e.g., parents, other classrooms) as a play at the theater.
	This activity develops the following behaviors and concepts that are related to early literacy:
Print Awareness	Print—book conventions
Phonological Awareness	Perception and memory—words, phrases
Oral Language	Vocabulary—words and sentences; narrative skills—narrations of fictional story; literate discourse—conversations, decontextualization

ADULT–CHILD INTERACTIVE BEHAVIORS

High Demand/Low Support

Children collaborate in planning actions and assigning roles. They will:

relate and organize elements of story structure in a coherent sequence, make predictions and interpretations, distinguish fiction from real events, and use words that refer to mental states and use of language

Support Strategies

Open-ended questioning

Ask questions to help children plan actions and assign roles.

> Who is in this story?
> What important things happened?
> What will Sara do?
> How can we make a stream?
> Can this happen for real?

Ask children about mental states and use of language.

> Did the goat know?
> What did the troll say?

Cognitive structuring

Help children sequence events.

> Who speaks first?

Define the notion of pretend, and explain differences between fictional and real events.

Holding in memory

Remind children of major characters and events of the story. Summarize what children have organized so far.

> We decided that Nick was going to pretend to be the caterpillar and Lara was going to be the butterfly.

Instructing

Help children focus on specific elements of the story.

> Tell Mike who this story is about.
> How does the story end?

Medium Demand/Medium Support

Children actively participate in enacting the story and playing imaginary roles. They will:

> provide explanations, draw from personal experiences, and use words to describe their feelings and desires (e.g., want, like, happy, sad)

Support Strategies

Open-ended questioning

Encourage children to express feelings and draw from their own personal experiences.

> Who do you want to be?
> Who do you like the most?

How does the princess feel?
Have you ever seen a castle?

Ask questions that help children coordinate their actions and roles.

Which role are you going to play?
What do you do after he leaves?
How will you know when to clap your hands?
When do you jump across the stream?

Ask children for explanations.

Why did she do that?
Why was he sad?

	Providing feedback	Request children to clarify information, if necessary.

What do you mean?
Did he forget?

	Cognitive structuring	Help children sequence events.

The wolf speaks first, then it's the pig's turn.

	Holding in memory	Summarize events that children enacted.

The caterpillar ate one apple, two pears, and three plums.

Provide reminders.

It's the boa constrictor's turn now.

	Task regulation	Provide visual cues (e.g., display pictures of major events to be enacted).

Low Demand/High Support

Children actively participate in enacting the story and playing imaginary roles. They will:

provide explanations, draw from personal experiences, and use words to describe their feelings and desires (e.g., want, like, happy, sad)

Support Strategies

	Holding in memory	Provide reminders.

The polar bear hears the lion roaring in his ear. Aaron, you're the lion.

	Task regulation	Provide visual cues. For example, hold up a puppet or mask of a pig when it's the pig's turn to say something.

Instructing   Provide directions.

John, you speak now.
Maria, run around this circle.

Model, and have children repeat.

The pigs say, not by the hair of my chinny chin chin. You say it.

If we were caterpillars, Patty would eat through a strawberry. Lonnie would eat through a pear. Ashanti would eat through a sandwich. Dordi would eat through an apple. Gilmar would eat through a banana.

Comments/Adaptations

Comments   Stories can also be created by the children. Have them dictate a story, read it back to them, and have them enact it.

Adaptations   Use sign language, visual props, and gestures to enhance the participation of children with hearing impairments.

Home Link   Invite families to come to the performance, or videotape it and lend it to parents to view at home.

WHAT DID YOU HEAR?

Main Purpose To develop narrative skills and literate discourse

Children use language to describe sounds they hear and make inferences and generalize experiences beyond the immediate context.

Materials Objects that produce sounds; paper; crayons

Description of the Activity Have children close their eyes and listen to the sounds around them. After approximately 1 minute, have them open their eyes and describe what they think happened while their eyes were closed. Children can also draw pictures, mime, or write words to describe their thoughts. While their eyes are closed, direct the children's attention to sounds that occur naturally in the classroom (e.g., water dripping, clock), sounds that occur naturally outdoors (e.g., birds, cars), or sounds that you produce intentionally (e.g., shoes stepping on the floor, musical instruments being played, paper being crumpled). You can also use records or audiotapes of common sounds (e.g., walking, running, clapping, laughing, sneezing) so that children do not need to close their eyes. After children have expressed their ideas, show them or have them identify the source of the sounds.

This activity develops the following behaviors and concepts that are related to early literacy:

Print Awareness Print—writing

Phonological Awareness Perception and memory—words, environmental sounds

Oral Language Vocabulary—words and sentences; literate discourse—categorical organization, decontextualization

ADULT–CHILD INTERACTIVE BEHAVIORS

High Demand/Low Support

Children will:

> make personal interpretations about what the sounds may represent, use cognitive words to refer to mental states, and use superordinate labels to indicate categories

Support Strategies

? **Open-ended questioning** Ask questions to encourage children to make interpretations and use cognitive words.

172

What do you suppose makes a sound like that?
What do you think happened?
What does this remind you of?

Providing feedback

Make encouraging comments about children's guesses.

> That's a good answer, but remember that crows make loud noises.

Ask for clarifications.

> Why do you think it's a drum?

Cognitive structuring

Help children categorize sounds and objects and make associations and distinctions between sounds and objects.

> This sound seemed like that of a vehicle.
> Did you notice that this bird made a louder sound than the one we heard before?

Point out contradictions.

> That's a good suggestion, but this sound is much louder. Snow doesn't make much noise.

Instructing

Provide models for interpretive and cognitive use of words and general category labels.

Medium Demand/Medium Support

Children will:

> describe objects, sounds, and events; generalize experiences to other settings; and provide explanations

Support Strategies

Open-ended questioning

Encourage children to describe objects and events, relate them to their personal experiences, and provide explanations.

> Have you ever heard a sound like that before?
> Why does the wind make such a loud noise?

Providing feedback

Make encouraging comments about children's guesses. Ask for clarifications.

> Why do you think it's a truck?

Cognitive structuring

Point out contradictions.

> It could be water, but waterfalls are very loud.

Task regulation

Provide children with clues that refer to concrete actions and personal experiences.

> This sound uses your hands.

Use sounds that are familiar to children or that are produced by objects that are present in the children's immediate environment.

 Instructing

Provide models by relating personal experiences and providing explanations, and then ask children to do the same.

> I hear lots of crows by my house. Have you heard crows before?
>
> My book made a very loud noise when it fell because it's big and heavy. Why did your book make a loud noise?

Low Demand/High Support

Children will:

> label and describe a variety of objects, sounds, and actions

Support Strategies

 Providing feedback

Encourage elaboration of children's responses.

> Yes, it sounded like rain to me, too. Do you think it was a rainstorm? Or was it a gentle rain?

 Task regulation

Reproduce the sound when the children have their eyes open. Have children reproduce the sound themselves. Provide choices.

> Do you think that's rain or wind? Was that loud or soft?

Provide verbal cues.

> I think it's the sound of someone who is happy.

 Instructing

Ask direct questions.

> What did you hear?
> What was that?

Provide a model, and then elicit another response.

> That's thunder. What sound was that?

Comments/Adaptations

Comments

Try tape recording children's as well as staff's voices. Ask the children to guess whose voice they hear on the audiotape. Ask them how they know whose voice is on the tape.

Home Link

Parent Activity: What Did You Hear?

PORTRAITS

Main Purpose	To develop expressive vocabulary and narrative skills

Children learn to expand their vocabulary and narrative skills by describing themselves (e.g., their bodies, feelings, ideas, lives).

Materials	Paper; crayons; markers

Description of the Activity	Have children draw their own portrait or work in pairs to draw a portrait of a peer. The portrait can be of the face only or of the entire body. Then have them label body parts and describe themselves (or the peer) and particular aspects of their lives (e.g., favorite activities, foods). Portraits can be made using a variety of methods including drawing, painting, making silhouettes by having children trace an outline of their body on large sheets of paper, and taking photographs. Portraits can also be cut apart, and then children can glue the parts back together. Children can also write or copy words or dictate ideas for adults to write.

This activity develops the following behaviors and concepts that are related to early literacy:

Print Awareness	Print—awareness of graphic symbols, letter identification, writing
Phonological Awareness	Perception and memory—words
Oral Language	Vocabulary—words and sentences; narrative skills—narrations of real events; literate discourse—conversations; decontextualization, interpretive/analytic discourse

ADULT–CHILD INTERACTIVE BEHAVIORS

High Demand/Low Support

Children will:

> relate information about themselves organized according to temporal and causal sequences, provide explanations, make interpretations and judgments, and use cognitive words to refer to mental states

Support Strategies

? **Open-ended questioning**	Ask general questions.

> What would you like to tell us about yourself?

Encourage children to provide explanations, make interpretations and judgments, and use cognitive words to refer to mental states.

> Why do you like the library?
> Does this look right?
> What do you think this is?

Providing feedback

Manifest interest in the information children provide. Request clarifications.

> Does Snowball live with you in your house or on your grandfather's farm?

Task regulation

Ask specific questions about topics of interest.

> What's your favorite place to go after school?
> What's your favorite pet?

Medium Demand/Medium Support

Children will:

> relate information, generalize experiences to other settings, and use internal state words to express feelings and motivations

Support Strategies

? Open-ended questioning

Ask children questions about their daily lives and likes and dislikes.

> What do you do on the weekends?
> What do you like to have for dinner?

Providing feedback

Show interest in the information children provide.

> That was a great story about your birthday.

Task regulation

Ask specific questions about topics of interest.

> What's your favorite food?
> What's your favorite color?

Instructing

Directly elicit peer interactions.

> Ask Leigh what her favorite color is.

Low Demand/High Support

Children will:

> label objects, answer questions about themselves, and engage in social interaction

Support Strategies

Task regulation

Provide a set of questions for children to answer.

> Do you have sisters or brothers?
> Do you have a pet?
> Which color are your eyes?

Provide choices.

> Do you want a crayon or a paintbrush?

Providing feedback

Comment on present objects and actions.

> Eyes. You are painting the eyes.
> Green. That's green paint.

Instructing

Have peers with more advanced skills provide models. Provide models by expanding on children's utterances. Ask direct questions.

> What are you drawing?
> Which color is it?

Use Fill in the Blanks activities (Print Awareness) to provide models for talking about physical attributes, likes, and dislikes. Model, and have children repeat.

> Say, "I have brown eyes."

Direct children to initiate or respond to social interaction.

Tell Shona what this is.

Comments/Adaptations

Comments

Portraits can be used as a topic for Show and Tell. Children can present themselves to their peers, or a child can introduce another child to their peers at circle time. Portraits can also be modeled in clay.

Adaptations

Tape-record verbal portraits by children with visual or motor impairments.

Home Link

Send home a copy of the portrait for the child's art portfolio.

FEELING OBJECTS

Main Purpose	To develop narrative skills and literate discourse

Children learn to express their ideas to communicate information to others as well as to use verbal information expressed by their peers. They also make inferences and judgments.

Materials	Familiar objects with interesting textures and shapes (e.g., shells, carrots, apples, cotton balls, mittens, Velcro strips); cardboard box or cloth bag; flipchart or chalkboard

Description of the Activity	Have children work together to guess the identity of an object that is hidden from their view and that they explore tactually. The objects can be placed in a cloth bag or in a cardboard box. Children take turns exploring the object with their hands. They describe shape, texture, and size. Encourage children to compare their discoveries with those of their peers and to share information and ideas about the identity of the object. Record children's descriptions of the object and guesses on a flipchart or a chalkboard. If multiple objects are used, then encourage comparisons of the different qualities of each object.

This activity develops the following behaviors and concepts that are related to early literacy:

Print Awareness	Print—awareness of graphic symbols
Phonological Awareness	Perception and memory—words
Oral Language	Vocabulary—words and sentences; literate discourse—conversations, categorical organization, decontextualization, interpretive/analytic discourse

ADULT–CHILD INTERACTIVE BEHAVIORS

High Demand/Low Support

Children describe and discuss the identity of the object. They will:
>make judgments and inferences about the attributes and identity of the object, use cognitive words to refer to mental states, and use superordinate labels

Support Strategies

? **Open-ended questioning**	Encourage children to formulate hypotheses and to explain inferences.

What do you think it could be?
What makes you think that?
How do you know?

	Providing feedback	Encourage children to talk aloud while they are feeling the object.
		Tell us how it feels now.

Cognitive structuring

Help children use systematic strategies to explore objects and make inferences about identity.

You might want to start at the top and feel your way down. What's a fruit that's long and shaped like a half moon?

Holding in memory

Summarize different characteristics.

You said it had two sharp points and a soft center.

Medium Demand/Medium Support

Children describe and discuss the identity of the object. They will:

make judgments and inferences about the attributes and identity of the object, use cognitive words to refer to mental states, and use superordinate labels

Support Strategies

Open-ended questioning

Encourage children to describe the object and what they think it might be.

Providing feedback

Encourage children to talk aloud while they are feeling the object.

What do you feel?

Cognitive structuring

Provide verbal clues.

It comes from a tree.

Point out contradictions.

It can't be a leaf because it feels hard.

Holding in memory

Summarize different characteristics.

You said it's cold and slippery.

Instructing

Model, and expand on children's utterances.

Low Demand/High Support

Children will:

use a variety of sentences to describe the attributes and name of the objects

Support Strategies

Cognitive structuring	Allow children to look at the object first, then conceal it, and ask them to feel and describe it.

Task regulation	Provide choices.

> Does it feel hard or soft?
> Is it a leaf or a nut?

Have similar objects or pictures visible to children. Have children explore and describe an object that is visible to them.

> Touch the leaf, and tell me how it feels.

Instructing	Ask direct questions.

> Which shape is it?

Model, and expand on children's utterances.

> A nut. A big walnut.

Comments/Adaptations

Comments	Use objects that are representative of diverse cultural backgrounds (e.g., tropical fruits, clothing, musical instruments).
Adaptations	Use pictures and sign language with children who have hearing impairments. Translate signs for peers. Teach basic signs to other children. Use easily recognizable objects that require little exploration with children who have motor impairments.
Home Link	Parent Activity: Let's Use Words to Describe . . . ! *(Note:* Tell the child's parent[s] to talk with the child about a favorite toy [e.g., colors, shapes, textures, smells] and to talk about good times with the toy, trips it has taken, and the adventures it might have.)

FROM THIS TO THAT

Main Purpose	To facilitate expressive vocabulary and the use of literate discourse

Children learn to use oral language to provide explanations, make predictions, and form judgments.

Materials	Related materials; paper; markers
Description of the Activity	Have children observe events during which a physical or visual change occurs. Encourage them to describe the different stages of the transformation. For example, have them observe natural events related to weather changes (e.g., the wind that makes branches of trees bend, the sun that melts the snow). Prepare particular experiments (e.g., melt butter, freeze water). Discuss the change. The transformation of foods during cooking and baking also provides excellent opportunities to observe changes. During this activity, have children shift positions to view the materials from different perspectives. For example, have the children look at the same object first when they are lying down and then when they are standing on top of a chair. Ask children to describe the difference.

This activity develops the following behaviors and concepts that are related to early literacy:

Print Awareness	Print—awareness of graphic symbols, letter identification, writing; letter–sound correspondence—single sounds and letters, words
Phonological Awareness	Perception and memory—words, phrases
Oral Language	Vocabulary—words and sentences; narrative skills—narrations of real events; literate discourse—decontextualization, interpretive/ analytic discourse

ADULT–CHILD INTERACTIVE BEHAVIORS

High Demand/Low Support

Children will:

provide explanations and make predictions

Support Strategies

? Open-ended questioning	Ask children to make predictions about events.

How did it change?

What do you think the vinegar will do to the egg?

What would happen if you added yellow paint to the blue paint?

Ask children to provide explanations.

Why did it melt?

What made the milk curdle?

Why does it look different under the magnifying glass?

Cognitive structuring   Emphasize relationships between events.

If you look at it closer, it looks bigger.

It was red before you added yellow.

Medium Demand/Medium Support

Children will:

provide explanations and make predictions

Support Strategies

Open-ended questioning   Ask general questions to encourage children to describe events.

What did we see?

What happened?

What's different?

Encourage children to relate events to their own experience.

Have you ever eaten ice cream in the sun?

Have you ever looked through a telescope?

Cognitive structuring   Help children sequence and organize events.

What happened first?

What happened after we boiled the eggs?

Holding in memory   Remind children of earlier events.

We poured water in the tray. We put it in the freezer, and it turned into hard frozen ice. Then we put the ice in the sun. What happened?

Task regulation   Provide visual cues such as charts and drawings of the sequence of events.

Instructing   Ask specific questions.

Which color was it before we started?

Which shape is it now?

Encourage generalization of causal events by observing several related occurrences (e.g., the effect of heat on ice, butter, and ice cream).

Low Demand/High Support

Children will:

provide explanations and make predictions

Support Strategies

?	**Open-ended questioning**	Ask children to describe an object or an event. What happened? What do you see?
	Task regulation	Provide visual cues. Here's some macaroni that hasn't been cooked. Provide choices. Are they hard or soft? Does it look bigger or smaller?
	Instructing	Model by describing objects and events. Ask direct questions. What's this? Which color is this now? Provide several related events. When we put the ice on the hot sidewalk, it melted. When we put the ice on the radiator, it melted. When we put ice in the skillet, it melted. What do you think makes ice melt?

Comments/Adaptations

Link with Print Awareness   Write some of the children's descriptions into short stories that can be read by the class and individual children at another time.

Adaptations   Draw pictures, diagrams, and flowcharts for children with hearing impairments or language delays.

Home Link   Encourage parents to discuss seasonal changes with their children. They can help children recognize signs of change by observing a familiar tree or garden during periods of rapid change, such as fall or spring.
Parent Activity: What Will Happen Next?

TREASURE BOXES

Main Purpose	To develop conversational skills and the use of literate discourse

Children learn to communicate personal feelings and facts to their peers and adults. They express likes, dislikes, judgments, and opinions.

Materials	Cardboard or metal boxes; crayons; paint materials
Description of the Activity	Have each child keep a personal treasure box for storing objects that have a special meaning. Children can create their own treasure box by decorating a cardboard shoebox. Throughout the year, encourage children to place special objects in their boxes. They may choose objects found during a field trip or on the school playground (e.g., rock, leaves, flowers) or objects from home (e.g., miniature toys, photographs). At regular times, have children take turns presenting their treasures to their peers. Encourage them to explain why they like the objects and what the objects mean to them.

This activity develops the following behaviors and concepts that are related to early literacy:

Print Awareness	Print—awareness of graphic symbols, writing
Phonological Awareness	Perception and memory—words
Oral Language	Narrative skills—narrations of real events; literate discourse—conversations, categorical organization, decontextualization, interpretive/analytic discourse.

ADULT–CHILD INTERACTIVE BEHAVIORS

High Demand/Low Support

Children will:

> relate events and use cognitive and metalinguistic verbs to explain personal meanings related to their objects

Support Strategies

? **Open-ended questioning**	Ask questions that encourage use of cognitive and metalinguistic words.

> What does this rock remind you of?
> What do you know about this ring?

What does this mean to you?
Who told you that it belonged to your grandfather?

Providing feedback

Offer encouragement and praise.

That's an interesting looking piece.

Instructing

Model use of cognitive and metalinguistic words.

I know that each nation has its own different stamps.
I read a story about a crab.

Medium Demand/Medium Support

Children will:

relate events and use cognitive and metalinguistic verbs to explain personal meanings related to their objects

Support Strategies

?   **Open-ended questioning**

Ask questions to encourage children to generalize their experiences to other settings.

How do you use this at home?
Where did you find this?

Providing feedback

Offer encouragement and praise.

That looks interesting.

Instructing

Ask direct questions.

This coin is from Mexico. Did you go to Mexico this summer?

Model associating objects with children's experiences.

We saw these shells yesterday when we went to the beach.

Low Demand/High Support

Children will:

relate information and use internal state words to express feelings and motivations regarding their objects

Support Strategies

?   **Open-ended questioning**

Ask children questions to encourage expression of feelings.

Why do you like this?
Why is this your favorite?

Providing feedback	Offer encouraging comments.

    That's beautiful.

Instructing   Model use of internal state words.

    I like this, too.
    This makes me happy.

Model relating information.

    I saw a rock like that at the beach yesterday. Tell us where you found your rock.

Comments/Adaptations

Home Link   Encourage children to bring from home objects that are part of their family's cultural background.

BOOK REVIEW/STORY GRAMMAR

Main Purpose To identify common elements of narrative structure

Children learn to translate information gained through print into oral language to communicate to others. This activity develops the pragmatic skills of sharing information among children and the narrative skills of telling a story.

Materials Books; magazines; newspapers

Description of the Activity After rereading a familiar story, ask children to describe the story. Help the children structure the story by asking questions about the setting ["Where does the story take place?" "When?" "Who is in the story?"], the theme ["What is it about?"], the episodes ["What happens?"], and the ending ["How does it end?"]. Invite children to ask questions about the story and to comment about personal experiences. Ask questions that require children to provide explanations and clarifications. Encourage the other children to ask questions about these explanations. Also, help children become aware of writing conventions (e.g., title page, ending, reading of text from top to bottom and from left to right). Facilitate appropriate communication among children, and assist children in reconstructing the story (e.g., correct sequencing of episodes and ending).

This activity develops the following behaviors and concepts that are related to early literacy:

Print Awareness Print—book conventions, awareness of graphic symbols; letter–sound correspondence—single sounds and letters, words

Phonological Awareness Perception and memory—words, phrases; phonological skills—segmentation

Oral Language Vocabulary—words and sentences; narrative skills—books, narrations of fictional story; literate discourse—conversations, categorical organization, decontextualization, interpretive/analytic discourse

ADULT–CHILD INTERACTIVE BEHAVIORS

High Demand/Low Support

Children will:

relate and organize elements of story structure in a coherent sequence, provide explanations, make predictions, and distinguish fiction from real events

Support Strategies

| ? | Open-ended questioning | Ask children general questions. |

Ask children general questions.

> What's the story about?
> What happened?

Encourage children to make inferences and predictions.

> How is she going to get to her mother's castle?
> What if there were a big storm?

Ask children to provide explanations.

> Why did the witch give him the magic plant?

Providing feedback

Request that children clarify information, if necessary.

> Did the monkey climb up or jump down the coconut tree?
> Who do you mean by he?

Reinterpret information.

> Oh, you mean he was very frightened and couldn't remember the magic word?

Cognitive structuring

Review the separate elements of story structure and how they are connected to each other. Point out contradictions in children's narrations.

> The monkey ran away? But, you said he was a good tiger.

Help children organize and sequence their story.

> Tell Zoe what happened after the bear ate all of the apples.

Task regulation

Provide visual cues, for example, outlines on the chalkboard or paper sheets with blanks to fill in for separate elements of story grammar.

Instructing

Help children focus on specific elements of the story.

> Where did it happen?
> Who is the story about?
> How does the story end?

Medium Demand/Medium Support

Children will:

> relate and organize elements of story structure in a coherent sequence, provide explanations, make predictions, and distinguish fiction from real events

Support Strategies

Open-ended questioning

Ask children general questions.

> What's the story about?
> What happened?

Ask children to provide explanations.

> Why did the witch give him the magic plant?

Encourage children to relate objects and events to their own personal experiences.

> Have you ever seen a person dressed like that?
> Has this ever happened to you?

Cognitive structuring

Help children sequence events.

> What happened first?
> What did she do after she left?
> How did it end?

Remind children to use book illustrations as a guide to the story.

> The pictures show us what happens in the story.

Holding in memory

Remind children of the events told so far.

> The father told his son he could make Abiyoyo disappear only if . . .

Instructing

Ask direct questions.

> What did the whale say to the shark?

Orient children to look at the pictures.

> What's in this picture?

Low Demand/High Support

Children will:

> relate events with a beginning, a middle, and an end and tell the story based on pictures

Support Strategies

Open-ended questioning

Encourage children to add comments and ask questions.

> Jamie, would you like to tell us something else about this picture?
> Is there anything more you want to know about Mr. Frog?

Cognitive structuring

Explain the features of the story grammar by using just one feature each day and reviewing the taught features.

> Here's the title. It's on the front of the book. Show me the title.

Task regulation

Provide choices.

> Did she go to Grandma's or go home?

Book Review
Title:
Author:
Characters:
Setting:
Problem:
Events:

Figure 1.   An example of a book review form that can be sent home for children to complete with their parents.

Ladders to Literacy: A Kindergarten Activity Book
by Rollanda E. O'Connor, Angela Notari-Syverson, and Patricia F. Vadasy
©1998 Paul H. Brookes Publishing Co., Baltimore

Instructing

Help children formulate questions to ask a peer.

> Mary, ask Ruth what the three little pigs said to the wolf.

Model, and have children repeat.

> The owl sat on the big chestnut tree. Who sat on the tree?

Comments/Adaptations

Comment

Introduce a daily private reading time for children to look at books in the library area.

Link with Print Awareness

Use a story grammar chart (e.g., title, author, setting, theme, characters, problem, events, ending) as children tell about books to demonstrate the structures commonly shared by all stories. Have children do book reviews.

Adaptations

Translate sign language used by children with hearing impairments. Teach basic signs to all children.

Home Link

Give parents the following instructions: After reading a book or story together, talk about it with your child, using questions such as Why?, When?, and What happened next? These questions help your child learn about the order and causes of events. Ask your child to describe where the events happened and to compare places and characters among favorite stories.

Parent Activity: Going Places—The Library; Storybook Reading Routines. (*Note:* Have parents help children complete a book review for the child to bring back to class and share with peers.)

BOOK BUDDY

Main Purpose   To develop conversational and narrative skills

Children learn to engage in sustained social interaction with peers within the context of joint book reading routines. They learn to retell familiar, predictable stories and organize story elements in a coherent, logical sequence.

Materials   Familiar books

Description of the Activity   Chosen predictable and repetitive storybooks with which children have become very familiar. Have children pair up with a buddy to look at the storybook together. Encourage children to pretend to read the book and to retell the story to each other ["Lois, can you read the duckling story to Ashanti?"]. Children who are less capable should be paired with more capable peers, whereas more capable children may also be paired with other children of equal skills.

This activity develops the following behaviors and concepts that are related to early literacy:

Print Awareness   Print—book conventions, awareness of graphic symbols

Phonological Awareness   Perception and memory—words, phrases

Oral Language   Vocabulary—words and sentences; narrative skills—books, narrations of fictional story; literate discourse—conversations, decontextualization

ADULT–CHILD INTERACTIVE BEHAVIORS

High Demand/Low Support

Children read and tell the story to their peers. They will:
> form a written story based on pictures using reading intonation and wording

Support Strategies

Open-ended questioning   Make children aware of their listener's perspective.
> Do you think David understood that?

Providing feedback   Request children to clarify information, if necessary.
> Tell Tamiko who went up the mountain with him.

| | Cognitive structuring | Tell children to use pictures as a reference for them to organize and sequence their stories. |

| | Task regulation | Have children look at books of familiar stories. |

| | Instructing | Directly elicit peer interactions. |

> Ask Jessica whether she knows what a ladder is.

Help children focus on individual pictures.

> Read something about this picture to Annie.

Medium Demand/Medium Support

Children will:

> tell the story to a peer using pictures and literate discourse

Support Strategies

| **?** | Open-ended questioning | Encourage use of metalinguistic words. |

> What did the bear say?
> What does this word mean?

| | Cognitive structuring | Encourage children to make connections among the pictures to form a story. |

> Why is the lion roaring? The picture we saw before shows us why.

Help children sequence events.

> What happens next?

| | Task regulation | Give children familiar books. Encourage children to refer to the pictures. |

> What happens in this picture?
> Let's see what's on the next page.

| | Instructing | Directly elicit peer interactions. |

> Tell Louis what the bear did.
> Tell me what Mary just said to you.
> Show Cora this picture.

Low Demand/High Support

Children will tell very familiar repetitive stories to their peers. They will:

> tell the story to a peer using pictures

The three little pigs
the pigs wit beeffu wufthefud
Brianna

Support Strategies

? Open-ended questioning

Ask children questions about individual pictures.

What do you see?

Task regulation

Have children look at their favorite, often repeated books. Choose familiar books with repetitive rhyming verses.

Brown bear, brown bear, what do you see?

Give children choices.

Is this a big worm or a little worm?

Instructing

Provide models by expanding on children's utterances.

Yes, that's a cow. A brown cow.

Ask direct questions about the pictures.

What's this?

Direct children to initiate or respond to social interaction.

Tell Maya what this is.

Have children practice repeated phrases in the book before they read it to a peer. Model, and have children repeat.

That's a koala bear. What's that?

Comments/Adaptations

Comments   Introduce a daily quiet reading time in the library area where chil-
                  dren choose books to look at and read.

Home Link   Parent Activity: Getting to Know Books; Going Places—The Library;
                  have children take home a favorite story to read to their siblings or
                  parents.

INTERVIEWS

Main Purpose	To use structured conversation as a tool to acquire knowledge
	Children learn that language can be used to obtain, give, and document information.
Materials	Tape recorder; pictures; labels
Description of the Activity	Have children identify topics of interest and related questions that can be answered by peers or other people in the class, school, home, or community. Interview this person, record the interview on a tape recorder, and share it with the class. Encourage children to discuss the information presented. For the presentation of the interview, prepare simple visual materials (e.g., pictures, labels for objects) to accompany the conversation on the audiotape. Identify interesting simple questions that all children can answer ["What's your favorite food?"]. When listening to the tape, write each child's name and response to the question on a list. Have the children ask the same questions of a parent or older sibling at home, then bring these responses back to class. Make a frequency chart to display how many family members answered with similar words.
	This activity develops the following behaviors and concepts that are related to early literacy:
Print Awareness	Print—book conventions, awareness of graphic symbols
Phonological Awareness	Perception and memory—words, phrases
Oral Language	Vocabulary—words and sentences; narrative skills—narrations of real events; literate discourse—conversations, decontextualization, interpretive/analytic discourse

ADULT–CHILD INTERACTIVE BEHAVIORS

High Demand/Low Support

Children participate in the interview and generate appropriate questions. They will:

> make interpretations and use cognitive and decontextualized language

Support Strategies

? **Open-ended questioning**	Encourage children to make interpretations and use cognitive and metalinguistic words.

What do you think of that?
Do you remember what she said about traffic safety?
What did he mean when he said it depends on the weather?

 Providing
feedback

Encourage children to evaluate the accuracy of their comprehension.

Are there things you didn't understand?
Do you know what all of those words mean?

Holding in
memory

Summarize parts of the interview for the children, and have them add comments.

The doctor said that she went to school for 4 years before she started working in the hospital. Why do you think doctors need to study for so long?

Instructing

Model questioning to obtain information.

We want to know whether it is dangerous to be a firefighter. I could ask her, "Is your work dangerous?" What else shall we ask?

Medium Demand/Medium Support

Children will:

participate in an interview by asking simple questions, add comments to the discussion, and generalize experiences to other settings

Support Strategies

 Open-ended
questioning

Encourage children to talk about their own experiences.

Have you ever tried that?
Did anything similar ever happen to you?
Do you know anybody else like that?

 Holding in
memory

Summarize parts of the interview for the children, and have them add comments.

 Task
regulation

Provide visual props and pictures related to the content of the interview as reference for the children. Generate three to five questions that children can rehearse prior to conducting an interview.

 Instructing

Model conducting an interview of another teacher, principal, or classroom volunteer by using the class-generated questions.

Low Demand/High Support

Children will:

ask questions and generate simple sentences to describe people and events

Support Strategies

?	Open-ended questioning	Ask children general questions about the information presented.
		    Where does a nurse work?
		    What does a pilot do?
		Ask children about other information they would like to know.
		    What else would you like to ask Monte?

	Task regulation	Ask children to comment about objects and pictures related to the content of the interview. Who is in this photograph? Limit the list to three questions for interviews that children conduct on their own. Represent each question with a picture cue.

i	Instructing	Provide a model.
		    Ask Roberto, "What do you like to play?"
		Model, and elicit a response.
		    Monica's brother plays basketball. What does Monica's brother do?
		Provide many opportunities to rehearse the three questions.
		    Everybody, what's the first question?
		    Let's practice our questions while we line up.

Comments/Adaptations

Comments	Focus on issues of personal and cultural relevance. Interviewees might include a child's parent, sibling, or babysitter or the school principal or other school staff, such as the nurse, custodian, office manager, bus drivers, librarians, or computer specialists.
Link with Print Awareness	Develop fill-in-the-blank sheets to gather the information from each child; and then discuss responses, write answers on paper, and encourage children to read each others' responses. Gather these responses into a class book that can be checked out and shared with families.
Home Link	Ask parents to help their children interview people in their family or neighborhood (e.g., the store owner in the neighborhood, the crossing guard, a trusted neighbor or relative in a profession; a child's parent who is a dentist or a banker).

MOVIE REVIEWS

Main Purpose

To use narrative skills and literate types of oral discourse

Children learn to retell stories and events and to use forms of oral discourse that reflect opinions, beliefs, and critical judgments.

Materials

VCR/TV; videotape

Description of the Activity

Watch TV shows and short films appropriate for children. During the show or film, occasionally ask children to relate what they just saw, predict what might happen next, and express opinions and feelings about events and topics. Encourage children to ask questions during the viewing. When possible, relate topics to personal experiences. After the entire show or film has been viewed, have children relate the story or event. Discuss the accuracy of their predictions and opinions about characters and events.

This activity develops the following behaviors and concepts that are related to early literacy:

Print Awareness

Print—awareness of graphic symbols, writing

Phonological Awareness

Perception and memory—words, phrases

Oral Language

Vocabulary—words and sentences; narrative skills—narrations of fictional story; literate discourse—conversations, decontextualization

ADULT–CHILD INTERACTIVE BEHAVIORS

High Demand/Low Support

Children will:

> make predictions, interpretations, and judgments and relate elements of the story or event in a coherent sequence

Support Strategies

? **Open-ended questioning**

Encourage children to make predictions.
> What do you think will happen next?

Encourage children to make interpretations and judgments.
> Now, what did she mean by that?
> Do you think that was a good thing to do?
> Do you agree? Why?
> Did you like what she did?

	Providing feedback	Request children to clarify information, if necessary.

> How did she ride home if she lost her horse?

Request children to reinterpret information.

> You thought the fox would eat the eggs. Do you want to change your prediction now?

Cognitive structuring

Review the separate elements of story structure and how they are connected to each other. Point out contradictions in children's narrations.

> You said he didn't have a boat, but he crossed the ocean.

Help sequence events.

> What happened first?
> What did he do after she left?
> First, say what their names are.

Instructing

Ask questions about specific elements of the story.

> Where did it happen?
> Who is the story about?
> How does the story end?

Medium Demand/Medium Support

Children will:

> make predictions, interpretations, and judgments and relate elements of the story or event in a coherent sequence

Support Strategies

Open-ended questioning

Ask children general questions.

> What's the movie about?
> What happened?

Encourage children to relate events to their own personal experiences.

> Have you ever seen a manatee?
> Has this ever happened to you?
> What's your house like?

Cognitive structuring

Help children sequence events.

> What happened first?
> How did it end?

Define the notion of pretend, and explain differences between fictional and real events. Use a visual display to sequence the beginning, the middle, and the end of the movie.

| | **Task regulation** | Use parts of the movie with highly salient clues for prediction points. |

> We saw the caterpillar spin the cocoon, and now we see a little tear in the cocoon. What do you think will happen next?

| | **Holding in memory** | Summarize the story up to a point at which children can continue. |

| | **Instructing** | Ask direct questions about whether an event is real or fictional. |

> Could a raven really carry a boy across the ocean?
> Is this for real?

Model providing rationale for a prediction.

> Remember the magic penny in her pocket? I think she's about to make a wish.

Low Demand/High Support

Children will:

> relate events with a beginning, a middle, and an end; generalize experiences to other settings; and distinguish fiction from real events

Support Strategies

| **?** | **Open-ended questioning** | Encourage children to express their opinions and feelings. |

> What did you like about the story?
> What made you scared?
> What made the girl happy?
> Why was she sad?

| | **Providing feedback** | Encourage children to elaborate and relate story events. |

> Yes, I think he is scared. What is he afraid of?

| | **Task regulation** | Freeze a scene, and ask children to comment. |

> What do you see here?
> Could this really happen?

| | **Instructing** | Model. |

> I liked it when they all danced together.

Ask direct questions to elicit opinions and feelings.

> Did you like this?
> Was it scary?
> Was he sad?

Use a simple story frame (see the Book Review/Story Grammar activity) to help children organize events. Use the same frame (e.g., characters, beginning, middle, end) for many different movies.

Comments/Adaptations

Comments

Select videotapes that are culturally sensitive (e.g., documentaries about other countries, stories with characters who are from diverse cultures or who have disabilities). Show videotapes of class activities or field trips. Use videotapes that address interpersonal themes, if appropriate.

Link with Print Awareness

Write a few of the children's predictions on a large piece of paper. When the movie or story is over, review the predictions and ask children whether any of these events occurred.

Adaptations

Make sure the soundtrack enables children with visual impairments to follow the storyline.

Home Link

Parent Activity: Movie Reviews

FOREIGN LANGUAGES: LET'S SAY IT ANOTHER WAY!

Main Purpose

To develop vocabulary, narrative skills, and literate discourse

Children learn about the symbolic and arbitrary nature of language and print. They learn that objects, people, and events can be represented through the use of different symbolic systems. They learn about the conventions of language and print and their role in the communications of a specific group or culture.

Materials

Paper; crayons; objects presenting information about different cultures

Description of the Activity

During circle time, tell children different ways of saying and writing common words (e.g., hello, good-bye, thank you, yes, no) in foreign languages. If children in the class speak languages other than English, then choose their language and have them translate the words. Make labels in different languages for objects in the classroom, and draw children's attention to them during daily activities. Display boxes of products containing print in more than one language, such as Canadian products with English and French words. The purpose of this activity is not for children to learn specific words in foreign languages but for them to become aware that oral and written languages are specific to social groups and cultures. Encourage discussion about other countries, cultures, and traditions. Use storybooks from other countries or cultures that use words or phrases from other languages.

This activity develops the following behaviors and concepts that are related to early literacy:

Print Awareness

Print—book conventions; awareness of graphic symbols

Phonological Awareness

Perception and memory—words, phrases, phonemes

Oral Language

Vocabulary—words and sentences; literate discourse—decontextualization, interpretive/analytic discourse

ADULT–CHILD INTERACTIVE BEHAVIORS

High Demand/Low Support

Children participate actively in discussions about other countries, cultures, and traditions and say words they know in foreign languages. They will:

seek definitions of words, use cognitive and metalinguistic words, and make interpretations

Support Strategies

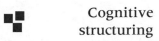

Open-ended questioning

Ask general questions.

What's it like in Mexico?
What do people eat?
What's the weather like?
Which kinds of plants grow there?

Encourage children to make interpretations and use decontextualized language.

What do you think neko means?
What did you notice about the signs in the International District?

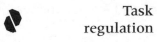

Cognitive structuring

Explain that different words and signs are used in different languages to represent the same object.

Task regulation

Provide visual and other contextual cues (e.g., pictures, objects, maps) to help children identify the meaning of foreign words.

Instructing

Ask direct questions.

How do you say hello in Korean?
How do we say gato in English?

Use peers as models. Provide models, and repeat request.

The Koreans say agno. How do you say hello in Korean?

Medium Demand/Medium Support

Children participate actively in discussions about other countries, cultures, and traditions and say words they know in foreign languages. They will:

seek definitions of words, use cognitive and metalinguistic words, and make interpretations

Support Strategies

Open-ended questioning

Encourage children to talk about their personal experiences with other countries and cultures.

What did you see when you visited your grandma in Puerto Rico?
How does your mother make tamales?
How do you say goodnight in Mandarin?

| | Cognitive structuring | Help children sequence events. |

Help children sequence events.

> First, you light the candles. Then what?

Task regulation

Have children talk about a relevant book read in class or at home. Have children talk about objects they have brought to school from home.

Instructing

Model by talking about your own culture and personal experiences.

> Here's a story my grandfather told me about when he lived in China.

Ask children direct questions.

> How do you say hello in Hawaiian?
> What is Ramadan?

Low Demand/High Support

Children will:

> label and comment on objects, pictures, and events and learn common foreign salutations

Support Strategies

Open-ended questioning

Ask general questions.

> What's happening in this picture?
> What do you use this for?

Task regulation

Have children talk about objects that are familiar and present in the immediate environment. Elicit peer support to extend practice.

> Everybody, let's say agno. Now say agno to your partner. What does agno mean in English?

Instructing

Ask direct questions.

> What's this?

Ask children to label or describe an object or picture following a peer model. Model, and elicit a response.

> This is a dog. Ma is the Thai word for dog. What's this?

Provide frequent practice opportunities for using foreign words and phrases.

Comments/Adaptations

Comments

This activity can be integrated within a reading of folktales or a flannel board story. Children can create books themselves. Teach children songs in different languages. Make audiotapes of people speaking in different languages and accents. Visit ethnic stores that sell foods, literature, and other objects from diverse cultures.

Home Link   Encourage children to bring books and songs in foreign languages from home and articles or souvenirs from other countries or cultures.

SPECIAL WORDS

Main Purpose	To expand vocabulary and literate discourse

Children learn to categorize words and to develop richer definitions for them. They learn about the attributes of objects and meanings and the use of language to organize and obtain knowledge.

Materials	Butcher paper; flipchart; chalkboard; color felt pens or chalk; pictures; photographs; books; objects
Description of the Activity	Begin with several pictures that belong in one category (e.g., animals, things/people in a circus, occupations) or category of words (e.g., describing words, action words). Show the children one picture (e.g., a circus clown), and ask them to describe it. Record on butcher paper the words that they use, and add appropriate words you think of to stimulate their thinking (e.g., a flowerpot hat, floppy shoes, polka-dot shirt, white make-up, painted teardrop). When one category is exhausted, move to action words ["What can this clown do?"] or adverbs ["How does he move?"]. Words can be organized in different formats (e.g., a word wheel). Encourage children to use their new words in describing sentences ["Who can use polka dots and drives a jeep in a sentence?"]. Add other same-category pictures (e.g., a trapeze artist) to keep the discussion going.

This activity develops the following behaviors and concepts that are related to early literacy:

Print Awareness	Print—book conventions, awareness of graphic symbols
Phonological Awareness	Perception and memory—words, phrases
Oral Language	Vocabulary—words and sentences; narrative skills—narrations of real events; literate discourse—conversations, categorical organization, decontextualization, interpretive/analytic discourse

ADULT–CHILD INTERACTIVE BEHAVIORS

High Demand/Low Support

Children will:

    produce appropriate words, use them to describe pictures and relate events, and seek definitions of words

Support Strategies

? Open-ended questioning	Encourage use of cognitive and metalinguistic words.

How do geese know when it's time to fly south?
What does gallop mean?
What does the word beach make you think of?

Have children plan and choose categories.

Here's a clown. Which kinds of things do we want to know about him?

Ask children to summarize.

What did we find out about what police officers do?

| Cognitive structuring | Explain definitions of categories and relationships among objects and events. |

Here we write all of the things we do with a computer and here all of the things we do with paper and pencil.
I know lizards go with snakes because they both are reptiles.
Pants and trousers are two words that mean the same thing.

| Task regulation | Use novel words to encourage children to ask about their meanings. Ask children to define or ask meanings of words suggested by peers. |

Medium Demand/Medium Support

Children will:

relate events, use superordinate labels to indicate categories, and generalize experiences to other settings

Support Strategies

| Open-ended questioning | Ask general questions. |

Who else works in a circus?
Which animals can swim?

Encourage children to relate objects and events to their personal experiences.

We saw a toad yesterday in the park. What did he look like? What did he do?

| Holding in memory | Remind children of categories and words. |

Remember, here are the things we do in a park, and here are the things we do at the library.

| Task regulation | Ask children to choose among categories for a given object. |

A pumpkin. Is it a fruit or a vegetable?

Make discussions more concrete by providing objects or pictures of categories.

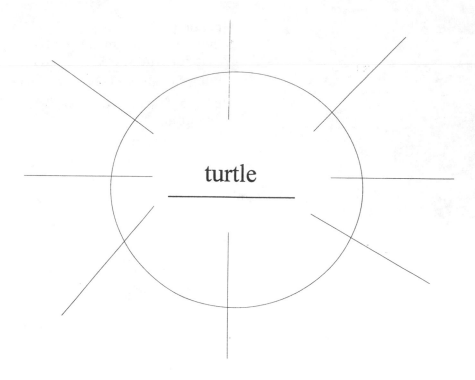

 Instructing

Model, and elicit a response.

> A bicycle is a vehicle. What's a bicycle? Do you know other vehicles?

Low Demand/High Support

Children will:

> use descriptive words and sentences to describe objects and events

Support Strategies

? Open-ended questioning

Ask general questions.

> What can this clown do?
> What does this clown wear?

Task regulation

Have children choose a topic or special word from a short list that you read to the children. Use pictures and props that serve as visual cues.

 Instructing

Provide practice in special words by reviewing lists or collections of words or objects several times. Model, and elicit a response.

> The clown wears big shoes. What does he wear?

Comments/Adaptations

Adaptations   Translate sign language used by children with hearing impairments. Teach basic signs to all children.

Home Link   Send home an activity sheet such as the Word Wheel (see the figure on p. 210) for children and parents to do together.

MY DREAM

Main Purpose	To develop the use of narrative skills and literate discourse
	Children learn to go beyond the immediate context and to think abstractly. They use language that refers to fictional or past events, objects, and situations that go beyond the here and now.
Materials	Paper; pictures; objects; props
Description of the Activity	Propose activities based on children's suggestions and interests that develop fictional scenarios and hypothetical thinking ["I have a dream . . . ," "What if I were a grown-up?" "My dream school," "I live on the moon"]. Emphasize the distinction between fiction and real events ["Could your dog really fly up to the moon, or are you just pretending?"]. Prepare materials and props related to the topics (e.g., costumes for pretend play, books with fictional stories, paper and crayons for children to draw on, paper to dictate words to the adult).
	This activity develops the following behaviors and concepts that are related to early literacy:
Print Awareness	Print—book conventions, awareness of graphic symbols, writing
Phonological Awareness	Perception and memory—words, phrases
Oral Language	Vocabulary—words and sentences; narrative skills—narrations of real events; literate discourse—conversations, categorical organization, decontextualization, interpretive/analytic discourse

ADULT–CHILD INTERACTIVE BEHAVIORS

High Demand/Low Support

Children tell an oral story. They will:

> organize elements of story structure in a coherent manner, make predictions, and explicitly distinguish fiction from real events

Support Strategies

? **Open-ended questioning**	Ask children general questions.
	What if you were an astronaut?
	What do you do in your dream house?

Encourage children to make inferences and predictions.

> Could dogs fly if they had wings?

Providing feedback

Request children to clarify information, if necessary.

> Why would you want a pet dragon?

Reinterpret information.

> Oh, you mean you like firefighters because your uncle is one.

Cognitive structuring

Help children sequence and connect events in a coherent manner.

> What would you do after that?

Point out contradictions in children's narrations.

> Coconut trees grow where it's warm. Would they grow in Alaska?

Task regulation

Have children begin by describing familiar experiences or immediate settings.

> What's our classroom like? What would you like to have?
> What does your dad do at work? Shall we pretend he does something else?

Instructing

Provide models.

> My dream house would have a big swimming pool.

Ask direct questions about whether an event is real or fictional.

> Could a dog really grow wings?
> Is this for real?
> Do elves really exist?

Medium Demand/Medium Support

Children will:

> propose events related to the imaginary theme, draw on personal experiences, and distinguish fiction from real events

Support Strategies

Open-ended questioning

Ask children general questions.

> What would you do in your dream school?

Ask children to provide explanations.

> Why do you want to go to Mars?

Encourage children to relate objects and events to their own personal experiences.

> Have you ever seen a spaceship?
> Has this ever happened to you?

	Cognitive structuring	Help children sequence events.
		What would you do first?
	Task regulation	Have children describe familiar experiences or immediate settings.
		What's our classroom like?
		What's your house like?
	Instructing	Ask direct questions.
		What would you like to be when you grow up?

Low Demand/High Support

Children will:

propose imaginary events and distinguish fiction from real events

Support Strategies

	Open-ended questioning	Encourage children to express their likes, dislikes, feelings, and emotions.
		What do you like the best in our classroom?
		What's your favorite treat?
		What makes you feel good?
		What makes you angry?
	Task regulation	Begin sentences, and have children fill in the blanks.
		My zoo pet would be . . .
	Instructing	Model, and elicit a response.

I would have a kangaroo and keep my toys in its pouch. What would you have?

Comments/Adaptations

Comments   This activity is especially appropriate as a celebration of Martin Luther King, Jr.'s, birthday.

Home Link   Send home a copy of the child's project.

BRAINSTORMING

Main Purpose	To facilitate the use of literate discourse
	Children learn to use literate forms of language as they formulate explanations and hypotheses about events and objects and propose solutions to specific problems.
Materials	Pictures; books; markers; crayons
Description of the Activity	Present children with specific situations that require them to explain an event or process or to solve a problem. Present the situations in the form of a cartoon with characters and empty dialogue boxes. At the end of the brainstorming, ask children to dictate the content of the dialogue. Problems can range from hypothetical situations with scenarios that address social and emotional issues ["Maya lost her mother at the zoo. What should she do?"], events and objects of personal interest to the children (e.g., thunderstorms, birth of animals), or immediate practical problems (e.g., how to make a sandwich). Provide props and objects, and have children solve a problem in small groups.
	This activity develops the following behaviors and concepts that are related to early literacy:
Print Awareness	Print—book conventions, awareness of graphic symbols, writing
Phonological Awareness	Perception and memory—words, phrases
Oral Language	Vocabulary—words and sentences; narrative skills—narrations of real events; literate discourse—conversations, decontextualization, interpretive/analytic discourse

ADULT–CHILD INTERACTIVE BEHAVIORS

High Demand/Low Support

Children will:

> provide explanations, propose solutions, and make predictions and judgments

Support Strategies

? **Open-ended questioning**	Encourage children to make hypotheses and predictions about events.

What could Rebecca do to help Jennie?
What would happen if we turned off the lights?
What would you do if you got lost?

After children have brainstormed and have exhausted their ideas, encourage children to make judgments about proposed solutions.

Which solution do you think would work best?

Providing feedback

Encourage ideas, and acknowledge children's suggestions in a positive manner, regardless of feasibility. Encourage children to evaluate and compare their predictions and hypotheses with actual events.

Did it happen the way you expected?
Which way did you think it would go? Which way did it really go?

Cognitive structuring

Emphasize relationships and similarities between events.

Did you notice that it went farther when you pushed harder?
Chickens hatch from eggs, and so do snakes.

Holding in memory

Remind children of the problem to be solved.

José's mother only speaks Spanish, and his teacher only speaks English. How can they talk to each other?
Remember, we planted the seeds in two different locations.
We want to find out what to do if we get lost.

Medium Demand/Medium Support

Children will:

describe events in a logical sequence and draw from their own experiences in proposing solutions

Support Strategies

Open-ended questioning

Ask general questions to encourage children to describe events.

What did we see?
What happened?
What did Ruth do to make Donna feel better?

Encourage children to compare the proposed situation to their own experiences.

Has this ever happened to you?
When someone pushes you, how do you feel?

Ask children to give explanations and make causal inferences between events.

Why did it go faster?
Why do you think they're getting along better now?

	Providing feedback	Ask children to provide clarifications.
		    You said, "It blew up." What blew up?
		Provide interpretations.
		    You mean your aunt speaks English and Spanish?

	Cognitive structuring	Help children sequence and organize events.
		    What happened first?
		    What happened after we poured the water?

	Holding in memory	Summarize events. Remember, Dan wanted his mother to see his Lego construction. She couldn't come to school, so Ann suggested we take a photo of it for Dan to take home.
	Task regulation	Provide visual cues such as props, pictures, and drawings of proposed solutions.

	Instructing	Ask specific questions.
		    Who helped José's mother talk with the teacher?
		    Would you be scared if you got lost?

Low Demand/High Support

Children will:

    describe events in a logical sequence and draw from their own experiences in proposing solutions

Support Strategies

	Open-ended questioning	Ask children to describe the problem.
		    What happened?
		    What do you see?
		    Why is Kira angry?

	Task regulation	Provide visual cues that represent objects and events related to the situation. Provide children with choices.
		    Would you grab the toy or ask for a turn?
		    Is he happy or sad?

	Instructing	Model by describing events and relations among events. Enrique couldn't find his mother. He told the clerk, and the clerk used the loudspeaker to tell everyone in the store where to find Enrique. Did his mother hear the loudspeaker message? That's how she found Enrique.

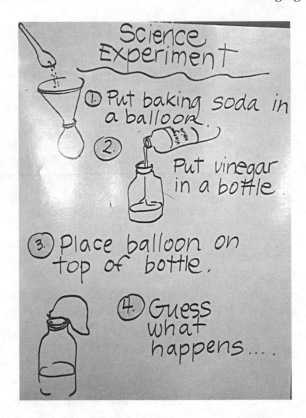

Expand on children's utterances.

> Big. Yes, it grew much bigger when we blew into it.

Ask direct questions.

> How does she look in this picture? And how does she look here? Why is she happy now?

Comments/Adaptations

Comments

This activity presents an excellent opportunity to address important social and emotional events that the children may experience (e.g., neighborhood violence, cultural discrimination).

Home Link

Parent Activity: What Will Happen Next?

LET'S FIND OUT!

Main Purpose

To use language and communication to gain knowledge about the world and to facilitate the use of literate discourse

Children learn to use language to understand and interpret events, to seek explanations and definitions, to categorize objects, to organize and summarize knowledge, to ask questions, to describe events, and to express feelings. Children learn to use different forms of communication and symbolic representation (e.g., oral language, drawings, print signs, photographs) to learn about events and to document new knowledge.

Materials

Project-related materials; paper; markers; pencils; books; notebooks; tape recorder; camera

Description of the Activity

This is a long-term activity that requires significant adult involvement and guidance. The idea is to develop two or three ongoing projects for children to participate in that last the entire school year. It is important that each child get involved in a project in order to learn how to explore and develop a theme in depth. Children will learn about continuity in time and effort. They will learn how events are linked and sequenced. Themes could come from questions or issues the children raise. Adults can observe children over several weeks and decide on two or three topics of interest. For example, children may ask questions about how things are made (e.g., food, paper, buildings, roads), how things work (e.g., cars, trucks, planes, trains), natural events (e.g., rain, snow, tornadoes), or events or people in the community (e.g., a new park, police, doctors, nurses). Pick out the most appropriate topics (for which information is easy to obtain and can be understood by the children) that children suggest. Divide children into two or three groups. Make a plan on how to develop the topic. Define questions and problems. Identify strategies for gathering information (e.g., read books, interview experts, observe). Select a variety of media to represent and document the information (e.g., photographs, drawings, audiotapes). Plan a way to summarize and disseminate the information (e.g., make a book, poster board, or a videotape). Involve children's families and experts from the community. For example, invite a police officer to come and talk about community safety or an architect to talk about how to build a house. Visit a bakery or a paper factory.

This activity develops the following behaviors and concepts that are related to early literacy:

Print Awareness

Print—book conventions, awareness of graphic symbols, letter identification, writing; letter–sound correspondence—single sounds and letters, words

Phonological Awareness	Perception and memory—words
Oral Language	Vocabulary—words and sentences; narrative skills—narrations of real events; literate discourse—decontextualization, interpretive/analytic discourse

ADULT–CHILD INTERACTIVE BEHAVIORS

High Demand/Low Support

Children participate in planning and organizing activities. They will:

> select topics, make predictions and judgments, and organize the narration of information according to temporal and causal sequences

Support Strategies

?	Open-ended questioning	Assist children in planning and organizing events.

> How can we find out where honey comes from?
> Where could we find some books about tornadoes?
> Who could explain to us how the new park was planned?

Providing feedback	Encourage children's ideas, and incorporate them into the project as much as possible. Encourage children to evaluate the feasibility of their suggestions.

> I wonder whether it's possible for us all to go and visit a hospital.
> Do we have enough money to buy a videotape about the National Park?

Ask for clarifications.

> Why do you think we need to take it apart?

Cognitive structuring	Help children find relationships between objects and events.

> The more letters we send, the more responses we might get.

Help children sequence events.

> What should we do first?
> What do we need to do after we write the letter?

Holding in memory	Summarize suggestions, decisions, and plans. Remind children of the purpose of the project. Take notes, and read back plans made by the children.

Task regulation	Assign different tasks to children according to their interest and backgrounds.

| Instructing | Assign specific tasks. |

Sondra, will you draw us a picture of our school?
Ask your parents to help you look in magazines for pictures of bees.

Medium Demand/Medium Support

Children will:

relate events, provide explanations, and organize information

Support Strategies

| | Open-ended questioning | Ask children general questions. |

?

What would you like to know about spiders?

Ask children to provide explanations.

Why do we need to write a letter?

Encourage children to relate objects and events to their own personal experiences.

Is there a bakery near your house?
Did you see any spiderwebs this morning?

| Cognitive structuring | Help children sequence events. |

First, we should take a photograph.

| Holding in memory | Summarize suggestions, decisions, and plans. Remind children of the purpose of the project. |

| Task regulation | Have children describe what they have done in the project so far. Review progress before discussing next steps. |

| Instructing | Assign specific tasks. |

How about if Mercedes puts together all of the signs in this box?

Ask specific questions.

What is bread made of?
What are spiderwebs for?

Low Demand/High Support

Children will:

describe objects and events, follow directions, and participate in displaying information

Support Strategies

?	Open-ended questioning	Ask children to describe an object or an event.
		What are you drawing?
		What do you see?

↻	Providing feedback	Describe what children see or are doing.
		That's a photograph of a queen bee.
		You're painting the box.

	Task regulation	Make the recording of observations or the collecting of information concrete.
		Let's look at our chart and see how many shells we had last week. Count with me. (After counting) How many shells did you bring today? How shall we record that on the chart?

	Instructing	Model by describing objects and events. Expand on children's utterances.
		Honey. Yes, honey tastes sweet.
		Ask direct questions.
		What's this?
		Encourage children to follow peer models.
		Peter is looking for pictures of food. Can you find pictures of food?

Comments/Adaptations

Comments   Involve parents by telling them the topic that their child is researching. Send parents regular updates on the progress of the project. Encourage parent contributions in terms of ideas and direct participation.

Home Link   Parent Activity: Going Places—The Museum

References

Adams, M.J. (1990). *Beginning to read: Thinking and learning about print.* Cambridge, MA: MIT Press.

Ball, E.W. (1993). Assessing phoneme awareness. *Language, Speech, and Hearing Services in Schools, 24,* 130–139.

Ball, E.W., & Blachman, B.A. (1991). Does phoneme awareness training in kindergarten make a difference in early word recognition and developmental spelling? *Reading Research Quarterly, 26,* 49–65.

Beck, I., & Juel, C. (1992). The role of decoding in learning to read. In S.J. Samuels & A.E. Farstrup (Eds.), *What research has to say about reading instruction* (pp. 101–123). Newark, DE: International Reading Association.

Ben-Dror, I., Bentin, S., & Frost, R. (1995). Semantic, phonologic, and morphologic skills in reading disabled and normal children: Evidence from perception and production of spoken Hebrew. *Reading Research Quarterly, 30,* 876–893.

Bentin, S., & Leshem, H. (1993). On the interaction between phonological awareness and reading acquisition: It's a two-way street. *Annals of Dyslexia, 43,* 2–29.

Berk, L.E., & Winsler, A. (1995). *Scaffolding children's learning: Vygotsky and early childhood education.* Washington, DC: National Association for the Education of Young Children.

Blachman, B. (1994). What we have learned from longitudinal studies of phonological processing and reading, and some unanswered questions. *Journal of Learning Disabilities, 27,* 287–291.

Blachman, B., Ball, E., Black, R., & Tangel, D. (1994). Kindergarten teachers develop phoneme awareness in low-income, inner city classrooms. *Reading and Writing: An Interdisciplinary Journal, 6,* 1–18.

Bodrova, E., & Leong, D.J. (1996). *Tools of the mind: The Vygotskian approach to early childhood education.* Englewood Cliffs, NJ: Prentice Hall.

Brady, S., Gipstein, M., & Fowler, A. (1992, October). *The development of phonological awareness and reading acquisition: It's a two-way street.* Paper presented at the annual meeting of the Orton Society, Portland, OR.

Bricker, D., & Cripe, J.J. (1998). *An activity-based approach to early intervention* (2nd ed.). Baltimore: Paul H. Brookes Publishing Co.

Brown, M. (1957). *The three billy goats gruff.* San Diego: Harcourt Brace Jovanovich.

Bruner, J. (1983). *Child's talk: Learning to use languages.* New York: W.W. Norton.

Bus, A.G., van Ijzendoorn, M., & Pellegrini, A.D. (1995). Joint book reading makes for success in learning to read: A meta-analysis on intergenerational transmission of literacy. *Review of Educational Research, 65,* 1–21.

Byrne, B., (1992). Studies in the acquisition procedure for reading: Rationale, hypotheses, and data. In P. Gough, L. Ehri, & R. Treiman (Eds.), *Reading acquisition* (pp. 1–34). Hillsdale, NJ: Lawrence Erlbaum Associates.

Byrne, B., & Fielding-Barnsley, R. (1993). Evaluation of a program to teach phonemic awareness to children: A 1-year follow-up. *Journal of Educational Psychology, 85,* 104–111.

Byrne, B., Freebody, P., & Gates, A. (1992). Longitudinal data on relations between word reading strategy, comprehension, and reading time. *Reading Research Quarterly, 27,* 141–151.

Carle, E. (1969). *The very hungry caterpillar.* New York: Philomel Books.

Chomsky, C. (1972). Stages in language development and reading exposure. *Harvard Educational Review, 42,* 1–33.

Clay, M.M. (1993). *Reading recovery: A guidebook for teachers in training.* Hong Kong: Heinemann.

Cook-Gumperz, J., & Gumperz, J.J. (1981). From oral to written culture: The transition to literacy. In M.F. Whiteman (Ed.), *Writing: The nature, development, and teaching of written communication: Vol 1. Variation in writing: Functional and linguistic cultural differences* (pp. 89–110). Hillsdale, NJ: Lawrence Erlbaum Associates.

Crain-Thoreson, C., & Dale, P.S. (1992). Do early talkers become early readers? Linguistic precocity, preschool language and emergent literacy. *Developmental Psychology, 28,* 421–429.

Cunningham, A.E. (1990). Explicit vs. implicit instruction in phonemic awareness. *Journal of Experimental Child Psychology, 50,* 429–444.

Dale, P., Crain-Thoreson, C., Notari-Syverson, A., & Cole, K. (1996). Parent–child storybook reading as an intervention technique for young children with language delays. *Topics in Early Childhood Special Education, 16,* 213–235.

Diaz, R.M., Neal, C.J., & Vachio, A. (1991). Maternal teaching in the zone of proximal development: A comparison of low- and high-risk dyads. *Merrill-Palmer Quarterly, 37,* 83–108.

Dickinson, D.K., & Smith, M.W. (1996, April). *Grade two reading comprehension: Contributions of preschool, kindergarten, and grade one experiences.* Paper presented at the annual conference of the Society for Scientific Study of Reading, New York.

Dyson, A.H. (1984). Emerging alphabetic literacy in school contexts. *Written Communication, 1,* 5–55.

Edge, N. (1988a). *I can read colors.* Salem, OR: Nellie Edge Resources.

Edge, N. (1988b). *The opposite song.* Salem, OR: Nellie Edge Resources.

Elkonin, D.B. (1973). U.S.S.R. In J. Downing (Ed.), *Comparative reading* (pp. 551–579). New York: Macmillan.

Felton, R.H. (1992). Early identification of children at risk for reading disabilities. *Topics in Early Childhood Special Education, 12,* 212–229.

Forman, G. (1993). Multiple symbolization in the Long Jump Project. In C. Edwards, L. Gandini, & G. Forman (Eds.), *The hundred languages of children* (pp. 171–188). Norwood, NJ: Ablex.

Fox, B., & Routh, D. (1975). Analyzing spoken language into words, syllables and phonemes: A developmental study. *Journal of Psycholinguistic Research, 4,* 331–342.

Fry, P.S. (1992). *Fostering children's cognitive competence through mediated learning experiences: Frontiers and future.* Springfield, IL: Charles C Thomas.

Geisel, T.S., & Geisel, A. (1960). *Green eggs and ham.* New York: Beginner Books.

Goswami, U., & Bryant, P. (1992). Rhyme, analogy, and children's reading. In P. Gough, L. Ehri, & R. Treiman (Eds.), *Reading acquisition* (pp. 49–64). Hillsdale, NJ: Lawrence Erlbaum Associates.

Grammer, R. (1983). Can you sound just like me? Finger Play, and Ready Set. On *Can you sound just like me?* [cassette/album]. Brewerton, NY: Red Note Records.

Gutierrez-Clellen, V., & Quinn, R. (1993). Assessing narratives of children from diverse cultural/linguistic groups. *Language, Speech, and Hearing Services in Schools, 24,* 2–9.

Haddock, M. (1976). Effects of an auditory and an auditory visual method of blending instruction on the ability of prereaders to decode synthetic work. *Journal of Educational Psychology, 68,* 825–831.

Haskell, D.W., Foorman, B.R., & Swank, P.R. (1992). Effects of three orthographic/phonological units on first-grade reading. *Remedial and Special Education, 13,* 40–49.

Hatcher, P., Hulme, C., & Ellis, A. (1994). Ameliorating early reading failure by integrating the teaching of reading and phonological skills: The phonological linkage hypothesis. *Child Development, 65,* 41–57.

Heath, S.B. (1982). What no bedtime story means: Narrative skills at home and at school. *Language in Society, 11,* 49–78.

Heath, S.B., Branscombe, A., & Thomas, C. (1986). The book as narrative prop in language acquisition. In B. Schieffelin & P. Gilmore (Eds.), *The acquisition of literacy: Ethnographic perspectives* (pp. 16–34). Norwood, NJ: Ablex.

Juel, C. (1988). Learning to read and write: A longitudinal study of 54 children from first through fourth grades. *Journal of Educational Psychology, 80,* 437–447.

Juel, C. (1996). What makes literacy tutoring effective? *Reading Research Quarterly, 31,* 268–289.

Katims, D. (1991). Emergent literacy in early childhood special education: Curriculum and instruction. *Topics in Early Childhood Special Education, 11,* 69–84.

Katzen, M., & Henderson, A. (1994). *Pretend soup and other real recipes: A cookbook for preschoolers and up.* Berkeley, CA: Tricycle Press.

Kirchner, D.M. (1991). Reciprocal book reading: A discourse-based intervention strategy for the child with atypical language development. In T.M. Gallagher (Ed.), *Pragmatics of language: Clinical practice issues* (pp. 307–332). San Diego: Singular Publishing.

Leather, C.V., & Henry, L.A. (1994). Working memory span and phonological awareness tasks as predictors of early reading ability. *Journal of Experimental Child Psychology, 58,* 88–111.

Lemish, D., & Rice, M.L. (1986). Television as a talking picture book: A prop for language acquisition. *Journal of Child Language, 13,* 251–274.

LeSieg, T. (1961). *Ten apples up on top!* New York: Beginner Books.

Lewkowicz, N. (1980). Phonemic awareness training: What to teach and how to teach it. *Journal of Educational Psychology, 72,* 686–700.

Lundberg, I., Frost, J., & Petersen, O. (1988). Effects of an extensive program for stimulating phonological awareness in preschool children. *Reading Research Quarterly, 23,* 263–284.

Maclean, M., Bryant, P., & Bradley, L. (1987). Rhymes, nursery rhymes, and reading in early childhood. *Merrill-Palmer Quarterly, 33,* 255–281.

Martin, B. (1970). *Brown bear, brown bear, what do you see?* New York: Holt, Rinehart & Winston.

McCormick, C.E., Kerr, B.M., Mason, J.M., & Gruendel, E. (1992). Early Start: A literacy-rich prekindergarten program for children academically at risk. *Journal of Early Intervention, 16,* 79–86.

McCormick, C.E., & Mason, J.M. (1986). Intervention procedures for increasing preschool children's interest in and knowledge about reading. In W.H. Teale & E. Sulzby (Eds.), *Emergent literacy* (pp. 90–115). Norwood, NJ: Ablex.

McLane, J.B., & McNamee, G.D. (1990). *Early literacy.* Cambridge, MA: Harvard University Press.

Morrow, L.M. (1989). *Literacy development in the early years: Helping children read and write.* Englewood Cliffs, NJ: Prentice Hall.

Ninio, A., & Bruner, J. (1978). The achievement and antecedents of labelling. *Journal of Child Language, 7,* 565–573.

Norris, J.A., & Hoffman, P.R. (1990). Language intervention within naturalistic environments. *Language, Speech and Hearing Services in Schools, 21,* 72–84.

O'Connor, R., Jenkins, J.R., Slocum, T.A., & Leicester, N. (1993). Teaching phonemic awareness to young children with learning disabilities. *Exceptional Children, 59,* 532–546.

O'Connor, R.E., & Jenkins, J.R. (1995). Improving the generalization of sound/symbol knowledge: Teaching spelling to kindergarten children with disabilities. *Journal of Special Education, 29,* 255–275.

O'Connor, R.E., Jenkins, J.R., & Slocum, T.A. (1995). Transfer among phonological tasks in kindergarten: Essential instructional content. *Journal of Educational Psychology, 2,* 202–217.

O'Connor, R.E., Notari-Syverson, A., & Vadasy, P.F. (1996). Ladders to literacy: The effects of teacher-led phonological activities for kindergarten children with and without disabilities. *Exceptional Children, 63,* 117–130.

O'Connor, R.E., Notari-Syverson, A., & Vadasy, P.F. (1998). First grade effects of teacher-led phonological activities in kindergarten for children with mild disabilities: A follow-up study. *Learning Disabilities Research and Practice, 13,* 43–52.

Olswang, L.B., Bain, B.A., & Johnson, G.A. (1992). Using dynamic assessment with children with language disorders. In S.F. Warren & J. Reichle (Eds.), *Communication and language intervention series: Vol. 1. Causes and effects in communication and language intervention* (pp. 187–215). Baltimore: Paul H. Brookes Publishing Co.

Palmer, H. (n.d.). Letter sounds. On *Ideas, thoughts and feelings: Experiences in discovery and independent thinking* [cassette]. Freeport, NY: Educational Activities.

Pellegrini, A.D., Perlmutter, J.C., Galda, L., & Brody, G. (1990). Joint reading between black Head Start children and their mothers. *Child Development, 61,* 443–453.

Peña, E.D. (1996). Dynamic assessment: The model and its language applications. In K.N. Cole, P.S. Dale, & D.J. Thal (Eds.), *Communication and language intervention series: Vol. 6. Assessment of communication and language* (pp. 281–307). Baltimore: Paul H. Brookes Publishing Co.

Pressley, M., Hogan, K., Wharton-McDonald R., & Mistretta, J. (1996). The challenges of instructional scaffolding that supports student thinking. *Learning Disabilities Research and Practice, 11,* 138–146.

Raffi. (1985). Apples and bananas. On *One light, one sun* [cassette]. Cambridge, MA: Rounder Records.

Rogoff, B. (1986). Adult assistance of children's learning. In T.E. Raphael (Ed.), *The contexts of school-based literacy* (pp. 27–40). New York: Random House.

Rubin, H., & Eberhardt, N.C. (1996). Facilitating invented spelling through language analysis instruction: An integrated model. *Reading and Writing: An Interdisciplinary Journal, 8,* 27–43.

Scanlon, D.M., & Vellutino, F.R. (1997). A comparison of the instructional backgrounds and cognitive profiles of poor, average, and good readers who were initially identified as at risk for reading failure. *Scientific Studies of Reading, 1,* 191–215.

Scarborough, H.S., Dobrich, W., & Hager, M. (1991). Preschool literacy experience and later reading achievement. *Journal of Learning Disabilities, 24,* 508–511.

Schade, S., & Buller, J. (1994). *Snug house, bug house.* New York: Random House.

Seeger, P. (1986). *Abiyoyo.* New York: Aladdin Books.

Seuss, Dr. (1974). *Great day for up!* New York: Beginner Books.

Share, D.L., Jorm, A.F., Maclean, R., & Matthews, R. (1984). Sources of individual differences in reading acquisition. *Journal of Educational Psychology, 76,* 1309–1324.

Share, D.L., & Stanovich, K.E. (1995). Cognitive processes in early reading development: Accommodating individual differences into a model of acquisition. *Issues in Education, 1,* 1–57.

Slocum, T.A., O'Connor, R.E., & Jenkins, J.R. (1993). Transfer among phonological manipulation skills. *Journal of Educational Psychology, 85,* 618–630.

Snow, C.E. (1983). Literacy and language: Relationships during the preschool years. *Harvard Educational Review, 53,* 165–189.

Snow, C.E., & Goldfield, B.A. (1983). Turn the page please: Situation-specific language acquisition. *Journal of Child Language, 10,* 551–569.

Snow, C.E., & Ninio, A. (1986). The contracts of literacy: What children learn from learning to read books. In W.H. Teale & E. Sulzby (Eds.), *Emergent literacy: Writing and reading* (pp. 116–138). Norwood, NJ: Ablex.

Snow, C.E., & Weisman, Z. (1996, April). *Grade two reading comprehension: Contributions of home language experiences.* Paper presented at the annual conference of the Society for the Scientific Study of Reading, New York.

Stahl, S.A., & Murray, B.A. (1994). Defining phonological awareness and its relationship to early reading. *Journal of Educational Psychology, 86,* 221–234.

Sulzby, E. (1985). Children's emergent reading of favorite storybooks: A developmental study. *Reading Research Quarterly, 20,* 458–481.

Sulzby, E., & Teale, W. (1991). Emergent literacy. In R. Barr, M. Kamil, P. Mosenthal, & D. Pearson (Eds.), *Handbook of reading research: Volume II* (pp. 727–757). New York: Longman.

Swinson, J., & Ellis, C. (1988). Telling stories to encourage language. *British Journal of Special Education, 15,* 169–171.

Tangel, D., & Blachman, B. (1992). Effect of phoneme awareness instruction on kindergarten children's invented spelling. *Journal of Reading Behavior, 24,* 233–261.

Teale, W.H. (1984). Reading to young children: Its significance for literacy development. In H. Goelman, A.A. Oberg, & F. Smith (Eds.), *Awakening to literacy* (pp. 110–121). London: Heinemann.

Tharp, R.G., & Gallimore, R. (1988). *Rousing minds to life: Teaching, learning, and schooling in social context.* Cambridge, England: Cambridge University Press.

Torgesen, J., Morgan, S., & Davis, C. (1992). Effects of two types of phonological awareness training on word learning in kindergarten children. *Journal of Educational Psychology, 84,* 364–370.

Torgesen, J.K., Wagner, R.K., & Rashotte, C.A. (1994). Longitudinal studies of phonological processing and reading. *Journal of Learning Disabilities, 27,* 276–286.

Treiman, R. (1992). The role of intrasyllabic units in learning to read and spell. In P. Gough, L. Ehri, & R. Treiman (Eds.), *Reading acquisition* (pp. 65–106). Hillsdale, NJ: Lawrence Erlbaum Associates.

Treiman, R., & Zukowski, A. (1996). Children's sensitivity to syllables, onsets, rimes, and phonemes. *Journal of Experimental Child Psychology, 61,* 193–215.

Tunmer, W.E., Herriman, M.L., & Nesdale, A.R. (1988). Metalinguistic abilities and beginning reading. *Reading Research Quarterly, 23,* 134–158.

Vandervelden, M.C., & Siegel, L.S. (1995). Phonological recoding and phoneme awareness in early literacy: A developmental approach. *Reading Research Quarterly, 30,* 854–875.

Vellutino, F., & Scanlon, D. (1987). Phonological coding, phonological awareness, and reading ability: Evidence from a longitudinal and experimental study. *Merrill-Palmer Quarterly, 33,* 321–363.

Vygotsky, L. (1978). *Mind in society: The development of higher psychological processes.* Cambridge, MA: Harvard University Press.

Wagner, R.K., Torgesen, J.K., Laughon, P., Simmons, K., & Rashotte, C.A. (1993). Development of young readers' phonological processing abilities. *Journal of Educational Psychology, 85,* 83–103.

Warrick, N., & Rubin, H. (1992). Phonological awareness: Normally developing and language delayed children. *Journal of Speech-Language Pathology and Audiology, 16,* 11–20.

Wells, G. (1985). Preschool literacy-related activities and success in school. In D.R. Olson, N. Torrance, & A. Hildyard (Eds.), *Literacy, language and learning* (pp. 229–255). Cambridge, England: Cambridge University Press.

Wells, G. (1990). Talk about text: Where literacy is learned and taught. *Curriculum Inquiry, 20,* 369–405.

Wertsch, J.V. (1985). Adult–child interaction as a source of self-regulation in children. In S.R. Yussen (Ed.), *The growth of reflecting in children* (pp. 69–97). New York: Academic Press.

Whitehurst, G.H. (1996, April). *A structural equation model of the home literacy environment on the development of emergent literacy skills in children from low-income backgrounds.* Paper presented at the annual meeting of the American Educational Research Association, New York.

Whitehurst, G.H., Falco, F.L., Lonigan, C.J., Fischel, J.E., Debaryshe, B.D., Valdez-Menchaca, M.C., & Caufield, M. (1988). Accelerating language development through picture book reading. *Developmental Psychology, 24,* 552–559.

Wolf, M. (1991). Naming speed and reading: The contribution of the cognitive neurosciences. *Reading Research Quarterly, 26,* 123–141.

Wood, D., Bruner, J.S., & Ross, G. (1976). The role of tutoring in problem-solving. *Journal of Child Psychology and Psychiatry, 17,* 89–100.

Yopp, H. (1988). The validity and reliability of phonemic awareness tests. *Reading Research Quarterly, 23,* 159–177.

Yopp, H. (1992). Developing phonemic awareness in young children. *Reading Teacher, 45,* 696–703.

Appendix A

Early Literacy Activities for Children and Parents

A Parent's Guide to Easy Times to Do These Activities

Activities that may help your child's early reading skills—what a great idea! And activities that use play as a means of learning about books and print really sound fun. You care and want your child to grow up to be the best reader he or she can be. But when can you find the time to use these activities? You know how little time you have to set aside just for activities like these—even if they are fun and develop early reading skills. Well, if these are your thoughts, then these activities are made for you! They are perfect for you and your child:

- They are written *especially for busy parents* who work, cook, drive to and from errands, and have busy active lives.

- They are designed so that *you can do them while you are doing other things,* such as washing the dishes and driving the car.

- They are *short and easy to do.*

- They are *fun* for both children and parents.

- They *help your child learn skills* that contribute to reading.

To make them easy to use, the activities have been arranged by routines that will be familiar to every parent. So, you can pick the activities that you can do when you are busy with your hands (when you are driving the car or folding laundry) or those that are good at bedtime. Most of the activities take only a few minutes to do—so you can fit one into a trip to the grocery store, when you are waiting in the check-out line, or waiting for the microwave to heat dinner. We know that parents think that reading is very important. These short, easy activities are a parent's dream for how to fit successful learning activities into the family's active daily schedule.

WHEN YOU HAVE NO HANDS FREE

(Driving the car, fixing dinner, doing laundry, bathtime, and so forth) First Sound; Let's Use Words to Describe . . . !; Movie Reviews; Nursery Rhymes; Print in the World; Say it Fast!; Sing a Song; Tell Me a Word that Rhymes with . . . !; That's My Name!; What Did You Hear?; What Will Happen Next?

WHEN YOU'RE SITTING DOWN TOGETHER

(Eating a meal, waiting in the Laundromat, riding the bus, and so forth) Diaries; Let's Use Words to Describe . . . !; Writing Messages

WHEN GRANDPARENTS OR RELATIVES ARE VISITING

Draw a Picture; Getting to Know Books; Let's Dance!; Let's Draw the Building You Made!; Magic Password; Magnetic Letters; Making Signs; Measuring; My Very Own Book; Nursery Rhymes; Recipes; Scribbling; That's My Name!; Writing Messages

WHEN YOUR CHILD AND FRIENDS ARE TOGETHER

Let's Draw the Building You Made!; Magnetic Letters; Making Signs; Measuring; Recipes; Scribbling; Writing Messages

ON A RAINY DAY WHEN YOU HAVE SOME TIME

Art Portfolios; Draw a Picture; Getting to Know Books; Let's Dance!; Let's Draw the Building You Made!; Magic Password; Making Signs; Mapping the Territory; Measuring; My Very Own Book; Print in the Home; Print in the World; Recipes; Scribbling; Storybook Reading Routines; That's My Name!

WHEN YOU HAVE JUST A FEW MINUTES BETWEEN ACTIVITIES

(Waiting in the grocery line, taking a walk, and so forth) First Sound; Let's Use Words to Describe . . . !; Movie Reviews; Nursery Rhymes; Print in the Home; Print in the World; Tell Me a Word that Rhymes with . . . !; That's My Name!; What Did You Hear?; What Will Happen Next?; Writing Messages

AT BEDTIME

Diaries; Getting to Know Books; Nursery Rhymes; Sing a Song; Storybook Reading Routines

ON A WALK OR AT THE PARK

Say it Fast!; Tell Me a Word that Rhymes with . . . !; What Did You Hear?; What Will Happen Next?

SPECIAL TRIPS

Going Places—The Library; Going Places—The Museum; Going Places—The Zoo

ART PORTFOLIOS

Children often put a lot of effort into their drawings. Sometimes they express important things about their feelings and experiences. Why not keep these creative works and collect them in a special art portfolio file? It will be fun to look back at them later with your child and remember special events and experiences together. You can buy a cardboard art portfolio in an art supply store or use a large department store box to store the drawings, collages, and other artworks.

Ladders to Literacy: A Kindergarten Activity Book
by Rollanda E. O'Connor, Angela Notari-Syverson, and Patricia F. Vadasy
©1998 Paul H. Brookes Publishing Co., Baltimore

DIARIES

Give your child a spiral notebook to use as a diary. On a regular basis, encourage your child to draw pictures or dictate some comments about an event that happened during the day. Remember to note the dates. It will be fun to look back at these pages later together.

Ladders to Literacy: A Kindergarten Activity Book
by Rollanda E. O'Connor, Angela Notari-Syverson, and Patricia F. Vadasy
©1998 Paul H. Brookes Publishing Co., Baltimore

DRAW A PICTURE

Children use drawing to stand for writing. When children scribble and draw, they learn that the marks made on paper can mean something. These activities prepare children to understand that writing is a means of communicating a message. Encourage your child to draw or paint a picture and to tell you about the picture. Let your child choose the subject. If your child does not have any ideas that day, then suggest that he or she draw a person, favorite animal, toy or object, or recent event (for example, going to the zoo or the park). Your child may tell you spontaneously things about the picture before, during, or after he or she has drawn or painted the picture. If your child does not say anything, then ask him or her some questions ["What shall we call this?" "What's happening?" "Tell me about your picture"]. Write down exactly what your child says, and read back his or her dictation.

Ladders to Literacy: A Kindergarten Activity Book
by Rollanda E. O'Connor, Angela Notari-Syverson, and Patricia F. Vadasy
©1998 Paul H. Brookes Publishing Co., Baltimore

FIRST SOUND

Have your child choose a word (for example, bear). Ask him or her to identify the first sound of that word (for example, the sound for b is /b/). If your child is unable to find the first sound, then help him or her ["B-b-b-bear"]. Then together try to think of other words that begin with the same sound and that are related to the chosen word (for example, brown, big). Have your child compose sentences with words that begin with the same sound (for example, Big brown bear bought a bagel).

Ladders to Literacy: A Kindergarten Activity Book
by Rollanda E. O'Connor, Angela Notari-Syverson, and Patricia F. Vadasy
©1998 Paul H. Brookes Publishing Co., Baltimore

GETTING TO KNOW BOOKS

In English, we begin to read books at the front, not at the back, and words go from top to bottom and from left to right. Teach your child how to hold a book correctly and to turn pages in the correct direction. When your child begins to show interest in the print and not only the story, run your fingers under the words that you read. Highlight the left-to-right, top-to-bottom orientation of the written text. As your child begins to know some letters, ask him or her to point to a word that starts with the same letter as his or her name.

Ladders to Literacy: A Kindergarten Activity Book
by Rollanda E. O'Connor, Angela Notari-Syverson, and Patricia F. Vadasy
©1998 Paul H. Brookes Publishing Co., Baltimore

GOING PLACES—THE LIBRARY

Your local library is a great place to visit with your child. There you can find books, magazines, videotapes, music, and newspapers for adults and children of all ages. You can check out books for your child and yourself to take home, or you can spend time browsing through materials and searching for information on computers. You can get all kinds of information at the library not only on books but also on events and activities taking place in town, as well as educational programs. Libraries also distribute other useful information such as bus schedules and tax forms. Some libraries even have play areas to keep younger children busy. And, of course, the librarians are always available to assist you. All this and at no charge! Many libraries will issue library cards to children of any age as long as they are accompanied by their parents, and some do not charge overdue fines if children forget to return their books on time.

Ladders to Literacy: A Kindergarten Activity Book
by Rollanda E. O'Connor, Angela Notari-Syverson, and Patricia F. Vadasy
©1998 Paul H. Brookes Publishing Co., Baltimore

GOING PLACES—THE MUSEUM

There are many types of museums that children will enjoy. Science museums have exhibits that help children understand how all sorts of things work. At natural history museums, children can learn all about animals, bugs, oceans, and volcanoes. Art museums introduce children to paintings and sculptures. Find out what is available in your area. Most museums have at least 1 day per month when entry is free of charge. Visit the museum with your child. Talk together about what you see. Read aloud the descriptive labels of the art pieces that your child has picked as his or her favorites. In some exhibitions, you can also watch movies or get information from a computer. Take home the brochures, and use them later to show other people and to tell them what you saw.

Ladders to Literacy: A Kindergarten Activity Book
by Rollanda E. O'Connor, Angela Notari-Syverson, and Patricia F. Vadasy
©1998 Paul H. Brookes Publishing Co., Baltimore

GOING PLACES—THE ZOO

Going to the zoo is always a special treat for both children and adults. Animals are always a great topic for conversations with children. Use this opportunity to encourage language by asking questions and responding to your child's comments. Also point out animal names and other familiar words and letters on the written descriptive labels. Take photographs, and create a scrapbook with pictures of animals that you saw. Have your child dictate labels and descriptions for the photographs. Your child can also draw and write about the zoo trip after you return home.

Ladders to Literacy: A Kindergarten Activity Book
by Rollanda E. O'Connor, Angela Notari-Syverson, and Patricia F. Vadasy
©1998 Paul H. Brookes Publishing Co., Baltimore

LET'S DANCE!

Children learn about rhythm by moving their bodies to music. Exploring rhythm helps children become sensitive to the temporal quality or the duration of sounds. Sing a song or listen to music that has different rhythms. With your child, dance to the different beats, clap hands, or use a drum. Begin with slow, regular, even beats; and later introduce uneven beats with variations in intensity and tempo. Relate movements to personal experiences ["Let's move slowly and pretend we are heavy elephants!" "Let's move fast and pretend we are flying on a plane!"]. Listen to some classical, Latin, or folk music. Talk about how the music makes you feel. What does it make you think of? Ask your child to draw a picture that goes with the music.

Ladders to Literacy: A Kindergarten Activity Book
by Rollanda E. O'Connor, Angela Notari-Syverson, and Patricia F. Vadasy
©1998 Paul H. Brookes Publishing Co., Baltimore

LET'S DRAW THE BUILDING YOU MADE!

Children often build things that need to be torn apart during cleanup time. Encourage your child to make a record of his or her accomplishments before the construction is torn apart. Compliment your child on the construction, then say something to encourage him or her to record it ["I can see you put lots of effort into making your castle so high. Let's draw a picture of it before you put the blocks away. That way we'll always remember what it looks like"]. You might start out by showing your child how to sketch and talk about what you are doing. Encourage your child to join in ["First, I'm drawing the blocks that make up the bottom layer. Now I'm making it higher. See how the color changes to yellow for the top row? Where's a yellow pen?"]. After your child has drawn the picture, ask your child to label the picture ["What shall we call it?"]. Help your child label the picture with meaningful letters or a few words to help him or her remember the construction.

Ladders to Literacy: A Kindergarten Activity Book
by Rollanda E. O'Connor, Angela Notari-Syverson, and Patricia F. Vadasy
©1998 Paul H. Brookes Publishing Co., Baltimore

LET'S USE WORDS TO DESCRIBE . . . !

Although children learn some descriptive words (for example, big) when they are very young, adults need to encourage other kinds of description. Children have strong opinions about food, so a wonderful way to start is to have your child talk about its color, texture, shape, smell, and taste. You can help your child develop a descriptive vocabulary by using these words around mealtime and in everyday conversation. On a walk outdoors, call your child's attention to the rough, spiky leaves of a tree or the striped, velvety petals of a flower. You can encourage your child to describe and classify things in the world around you (for example, help your child find things that are purple, things that taste sweet, or things that are shiny). The possibilities are endless. As you describe and classify with your child, you also develop the essential vocabulary that will help him or her understand the language of books.

Ladders to Literacy: A Kindergarten Activity Book
by Rollanda E. O'Connor, Angela Notari-Syverson, and Patricia F. Vadasy
©1998 Paul H. Brookes Publishing Co., Baltimore

MAGIC PASSWORD

Children learn to rhyme and to understand that words are made up of parts (for example, b-a-t, mom-my, un-der). Have your child enact pretend play activities with toy animals, blocks, and other materials. Tell your child that the animals have to guess a magic password to gain access to or to leave a location (for example, barn, zoo, trap, magic cave). Pretend you are the guardian and the child is the animal. Tell your child that the magic password can be a word that rhymes ["You have to say the magic password. Tell me a word that rhymes with dog"]. Then try asking your child to give you a password that is fragmented into syllables or sounds (for example, Pop-si-cle). When you are reading together or see a sign, point out to your child a written word ["Can you read this word?" (cat) "What word rhymes with cat?" "Can you read this word?" (hamburger) "Can you break it into parts?"].

Ladders to Literacy: A Kindergarten Activity Book
by Rollanda E. O'Connor, Angela Notari-Syverson, and Patricia F. Vadasy
©1998 Paul H. Brookes Publishing Co., Baltimore

MAGNETIC LETTERS

Arrange magnetic letters on the refrigerator, and encourage your child to play with them in a variety of ways when you are in the kitchen together. By taking them off of the refrigerator and putting them back on, your child can learn about colors, shapes, letter names, and sounds. Spell your child's name often, and leave it on the refrigerator so that your child will learn to recognize it. Do the same for other names of people and objects that are important to your child. Older children can read and write simple words with the letters. You can also use the letters to write simple messages. If, for example, you are going to the zoo, then you can write "zoo" and talk about the outing during breakfast. Use the letters to attach pictures or photographs of the words you write (for example, Dad and a photograph of Dad, cat and a picture of a cat). Use a letter to attach a picture of an object with a name that begins with that letter of the alphabet (for example, the letter O and a picture of an orange). You can also play matching games (for example, choosing a letter and having your child find the same letter) and word guessing games (for example, choosing a letter and thinking of words that begin with that letter).

Ladders to Literacy: A Kindergarten Activity Book
by Rollanda E. O'Connor, Angela Notari-Syverson, and Patricia F. Vadasy
©1998 Paul H. Brookes Publishing Co., Baltimore

MAKING SIGNS

Children learn about words and how sounds and symbols go together as they make signs to use in their play. Help your child make signs he or she can use as part of construction activities (for example, Stop, Go around, Open, Closed, Exit). As your child finds a need for new signs, help him or her create meaningful signs.

MAPPING THE TERRITORY

Children can learn that maps represent real places by developing models and drawings of areas familiar to them. For example, landscapes can be created by playing with sand in a sandbox. Help your child to model familiar home or neighborhood features and to talk about how these features are arranged. Encourage your child to enact pretend play scenes using these landscapes as contexts ["How will the bear walk to the store?" "Shall we go down this street?"]. Talk about events that occurred in these contexts ["Remember when we went bike riding? Where did we go?"]. Encourage your child to recall events related to the outing. Use paper and crayons to draw with your child a model of the park or your child's favorite room. Talk about where objects would be located, and add details to the drawing ["Where shall we put the swings? Are they close to the trees or far away?"]. Use print to label objects (for example, stove, table) and activities (for example, cooking, eating).

Ladders to Literacy: A Kindergarten Activity Book
by Rollanda E. O'Connor, Angela Notari-Syverson, and Patricia F. Vadasy
©1998 Paul H. Brookes Publishing Co., Baltimore

MEASURING

Science requires the use of reading and writing skills. For example, writing records of observations and taking measurements are important scientific activities. Practice literacy skills as you and your child do simple science projects. 1) Keep track of your child's height. Make your own growth chart (for example, tape a long strip of paper against a wall), or use an already-made growth chart. Mark your child's height, and then have your child measure with a measuring tape and record the numbers and observation dates. 2) Plant beans or seeds. Help your child measure the growth of the plants and record the heights and dates as well as other observations in a notebook or on a graph. 3) Have a long-jump competition. Mark the starting point of the jump with tape or another object. Use a measuring tape with easy-to-read numbers to measure the jumps. Help your child read the numbers on the tape and record the length of the jumps along with the names of the competitors. 4) Use blocks to measure different objects. Have your child stack blocks next to different objects until the tower reaches the same height as the objects. Help your child count the blocks, record numbers, or draw lines that correspond to the different heights. Compare the differences.

Ladders to Literacy: A Kindergarten Activity Book
by Rollanda E. O'Connor, Angela Notari-Syverson, and Patricia F. Vadasy
©1998 Paul H. Brookes Publishing Co., Baltimore

MOVIE REVIEWS

After watching a television show or a movie with your child, set aside a few minutes to talk about what you watched. Ask your child to tell you about the story or topic and what he or she liked and disliked about the show. This will help your child develop communication and narrative language skills and learn how to express opinions and make judgments. Ask questions that will help your child learn about the sequence and causes of events ["When did that happen?" "What happened next?" "Why did he do that?"].

MY VERY OWN BOOK

With your child, paste photographs or pictures from magazines in a notebook or on sheets of paper that can be stapled together. Write a short sentence to go with the pictures. You can make books about special events (for example, a vacation or a trip) or about topics of interest to your child (for example, dinosaurs, astronauts, fish).

Ladders to Literacy: A Kindergarten Activity Book
by Rollanda E. O'Connor, Angela Notari-Syverson, and Patricia F. Vadasy
©1998 Paul H. Brookes Publishing Co., Baltimore

NURSERY RHYMES

We all know that children take great delight in nursery rhymes. Rhyming during kindergarten helps children to learn to read more easily in first grade. Read traditional Mother Goose nursery rhymes and other rhyming books and songs with your child. Have some pictures of familiar nursery rhymes for your child to color and place in prominent places (for example, the bathroom mirror, the car dashboard, the refrigerator). Encourage your child to say them with you.

Ladders to Literacy: A Kindergarten Activity Book
by Rollanda E. O'Connor, Angela Notari-Syverson, and Patricia F. Vadasy
©1998 Paul H. Brookes Publishing Co., Baltimore

PRINT IN THE HOME

The best way for a child to learn about literacy is to see how reading and writing are integral parts of daily home routines. Have books, newspapers, and magazines in your house; and show your child their value by reading them yourself. Whenever you have a chance, show your child that print is a source of information (for example, cook from a written recipe, use a manual to fix a piece of equipment, look in the telephone book to find a telephone number). Place pictures and bookshelves in your house, especially in your child's room. Use a message board, chalkboard, or the refrigerator to display simple messages, drawings, songs, or nursery rhymes. Create a special place with a small table, chair, and crayons for your child to draw or write. Visit bookstores and libraries so your child has books of his or her own to read and look at.

Ladders to Literacy: A Kindergarten Activity Book
by Rollanda E. O'Connor, Angela Notari-Syverson, and Patricia F. Vadasy
©1998 Paul H. Brookes Publishing Co., Baltimore

PRINT IN THE WORLD

Learning to read and to write is a process that begins at a very early age. Children are continually exposed to many forms of print (for example, signs, labels, logos, symbols). On outings and at home with your younger child(ren), draw their attention to road signs; grocery store, gas station, and restaurant logos; signs in restaurants (for example, men's and women's bathrooms); and letters on cereal boxes. There are so many different kinds of signs in our homes and communities. It will be fun to see which ones your child likes and learns to identify. Suggest that your child might want to make some signs for the house. Give your child some cardboard to draw signs for his or her room, the kitchen, the front door, or your pet's corner.

Ladders to Literacy: A Kindergarten Activity Book
by Rollanda E. O'Connor, Angela Notari-Syverson, and Patricia F. Vadasy
©1998 Paul H. Brookes Publishing Co., Baltimore

RECIPES

Preparing food can help a child understand the relationship between printed directions and the organized actions of one or more people, and the results are delicious. Children learn that print can be used to label and identify ingredients as well as to record and to remember steps in sequence. Let your child help you decide on a favorite recipe to cook together on a rainy day. The recipe could be as simple as a peanut butter and jelly sandwich. Examine labels with your child, and ask sequencing and quantity questions as your recipe progresses ["I have the bread ready. What is our next step?" "How much jelly do you think we should use?" "What happens when there is too much jam?"]. Look for children's recipe books in bookstores or at your local library.

Ladders to Literacy: A Kindergarten Activity Book
by Rollanda E. O'Connor, Angela Notari-Syverson, and Patricia F. Vadasy
©1998 Paul H. Brookes Publishing Co., Baltimore

SAY IT FAST

Breaking down words into syllables and sounds helps the child become aware that words not only have meaning but also are characterized by sounds. It also helps your child understand the sound–letter association involved in reading and writing. During daily activities (for example, driving in your car, walking to the grocery store), play word games with your child. Say a word by breaking it down into syllables ["Look! There's a spi-der!"]. Have your child guess the word ["Can you say that word fast?"].

Ladders to Literacy: A Kindergarten Activity Book
by Rollanda E. O'Connor, Angela Notari-Syverson, and Patricia F. Vadasy
©1998 Paul H. Brookes Publishing Co., Baltimore

SCRIBBLING

Scribbling is the very first step to writing. Even though your child's early attempts to write may not resemble conventional letters and words, do not worry because they will eventually. Encourage your child to write pretend words and messages and to tell you what they may mean. Create a writing scrapbook. Paste photographs or draw pictures, and have your child pretend to write something about the picture. What will your child write? Your child may write a short message consisting of a shape or a straight line or a longer message with full lines of scribbling, perhaps some letter-like forms, and, later, even recognizable words and letters.

Ladders to Literacy: A Kindergarten Activity Book
by Rollanda E. O'Connor, Angela Notari-Syverson, and Patricia F. Vadasy
©1998 Paul H. Brookes Publishing Co., Baltimore

SING A SONG

Singing a song is a fun and natural way to help children become sensitive to the different qualities and sounds of words. During daily activities (for example, driving in your car, bathtime), sing favorite songs with your child, especially songs with words that rhyme. Once your child becomes familiar with the words, you can take turns at singing verses. Eventually, you can invent your own songs together and even play with nonsense words and verses!

Ladders to Literacy: A Kindergarten Activity Book
by Rollanda E. O'Connor, Angela Notari-Syverson, and Patricia F. Vadasy
©1998 Paul H. Brookes Publishing Co., Baltimore

STORYBOOK READING ROUTINES

The first important thing that children need to experience about literacy is the pleasure involved in reading stories together with an adult. You can begin sharing picture storybooks with your child from a very early age. Find a quiet place and time (bedtime is usually a good time) to look at books on a regular basis. You can encourage exploration of the books and print by talking with your child about the pictures, pointing to words as you read, and asking your child to tell or read the story to you (if your child is so inclined). Listen and respond to your child's comments and questions. Associate characters and events in the book with the child's own experience. Story time with your child is a wonderful way to stimulate a love for books and pleasant anticipation for learning to read in school.

Ladders to Literacy: A Kindergarten Activity Book
by Rollanda E. O'Connor, Angela Notari-Syverson, and Patricia F. Vadasy
©1998 Paul H. Brookes Publishing Co., Baltimore

TELL ME A WORD THAT RHYMES WITH . . . !

We use language to communicate ideas and feelings; but we also use language when we tell jokes, invent poems, and use slang. Rhyming is one way of playing with the sounds of words that you can practice with your child. Take turns guessing words that rhyme with each other or that sound the same. Let your child be creative by inventing nonsense words, too, as long as they rhyme. Rhyming helps children learn to read. It helps children understand that not only do words have meaning, but they also are composed of collections of sounds.

Ladders to Literacy: A Kindergarten Activity Book
by Rollanda E. O'Connor, Angela Notari-Syverson, and Patricia F. Vadasy
©1998 Paul H. Brookes Publishing Co., Baltimore

THAT'S MY NAME!

One of the first printed words children learn to recognize is their own name. Find ways for your child to see his or her name in print. Make a name tag for his or her bedroom door and for objects that belong to him or her. Write your child's name on his or her drawings and on letters and cards to family members. Once your child has learned to recognize his or her name, teach your child the letter names, beginning with the first letter. Point out other words in the environment that start with the same first letter.

Ladders to Literacy: A Kindergarten Activity Book
by Rollanda E. O'Connor, Angela Notari-Syverson, and Patricia F. Vadasy
©1998 Paul H. Brookes Publishing Co., Baltimore

WHAT DID YOU HEAR?

At home or on a walk to a park, listen for sounds that may occur and for which the source is not directly in sight (for example, water dripping in another room, a bird or an animal in a tree, a car around the bend). Draw your child's attention to the sound. Ask your child to describe the sound, guess from where it came, and describe what he or she thinks happened. This guessing game can be really fun. It will help your child improve listening skills, problem-solve, and develop the ability to use language to describe objects and events.

Ladders to Literacy: A Kindergarten Activity Book
by Rollanda E. O'Connor, Angela Notari-Syverson, and Patricia F. Vadasy
©1998 Paul H. Brookes Publishing Co., Baltimore

WHAT WILL HAPPEN NEXT?

Reading and writing help us describe and document events in the past and future and in far-away settings. This is an activity to do when reading familiar stories and during familiar routines (for example, mealtime, bedtime, bathtime). Invite your child to tell you what will happen next in the story or what will happen next on your drive to the grocery store. Predicting events helps your child go beyond the immediate here-and-now. It will help your child when he or she begins to read.

Ladders to Literacy: A Kindergarten Activity Book
by Rollanda E. O'Connor, Angela Notari-Syverson, and Patricia F. Vadasy
©1998 Paul H. Brookes Publishing Co., Baltimore

WRITING MESSAGES

In school, your child is learning that print is a tool for communication. Your child is learning how spoken words can be captured on paper and preserved for others to read. Each day, your child's teacher will write a message with the children, telling about important events that take place in the classroom. At the end of the day, the teacher might ask the children to tell about a significant event that happened to them and record it to be reread the following day. You can encourage your child to use written messages at home. Ask your child to dictate a short message to give to an older sibling or other adults in the home, send to friends or teachers at school, or mail to relatives. Encourage your child to write or copy a few words and draw or paste pictures to communicate a message. You can also leave written messages for your child. For example, you can write a short note or draw a picture of an upcoming event or a weekend outing (for example, the zoo, the grocery store, a mountain hike). Writing and reading messages are fun ways to stimulate literacy.

Ladders to Literacy: A Kindergarten Activity Book
by Rollanda E. O'Connor, Angela Notari-Syverson, and Patricia F. Vadasy
©1998 Paul H. Brookes Publishing Co., Baltimore

Appendix B

Glossary

Alliteration Recognition or production of words with common initial sounds.

Blending Combining sounds (e.g., syllables, phonemes) together to form words (d-o-g becomes dog).

Book conventions Book handling behaviors such as turning pages; orienting the book correctly; knowing where the book begins and ends; knowing that print, not the pictures, tells the story; and knowing that text begins at the top left corner of the page and is read from left to right.

Categorical organization The grouping of objects into categories (e.g., animals, food, people).

Compound word Word consisting of two or more elements that have meaning.

Continuous sounds Sounds that can be prolonged without interruption (e.g., vowels, f, l, m, n, r, s, v, z).

Decentration The ability to take into account different points of view or to view an object from a different perspective (e.g., to view a word in terms of its sound as well as its meaning).

Decontextualized language Type of language that refers to objects and events that are detached from the immediate context; deals with the remote and the abstract, such as stories beginning "Once upon a time . . ."

Emergent literacy Perspective that considers literacy a complex sociological, psychological, and linguistic activity that begins in the very early years.

Environmental print Signs, labels, and logos present in the daily environment and community (e.g., road signs, food packages, store fronts).

Interpretive/analytic discourse Type of oral language organized around interpretation and meaning (providing definitions and explanations) rather than experience.

Invented spelling Writing typical of young children, based on an idiosyncratic letter–sound correspondence strategy that differs from the conventional system (e.g., FLR for flower).

Literacy Activities and skills associated directly with the use of print (includes reading, writing, interpreting text, playing alphabet games).

Literate discourse Type of oral language that contains characteristics of written forms of language (detachment from the here-and-now, explicitness of reference and meaning, complex syntactic structures, high degree of cohesion).

Metacognition Ability to reflect on and control one's cognitive processes.

Onset Initial consonant or consonant cluster of a word (e.g., bat: onset is /b/; ship: onset is /sh/).

Phoneme Smallest linguistic unit of sound that can signal a difference in meaning (the sound produced by a letter or letter group).

Phonological awareness The ability to reflect on and manipulate the sounds in spoken words (e.g., to isolate the first sound in spoken words, to produce a rhyming word).

Phonology Aspect of language concerned with the rules governing the structure, distribution, and sequencing of speech sound patterns.

Pragmatic skills Skills that relate to the use of language to communicate in social contexts.

Referent Person, action, or event to which a word refers and for which it serves as a symbol.

Rime Part of a word (vowel and consonants) following the onset (e.g., bat's rime is -at).

Scaffolding Dynamic process during adult–child interactions in which the adult varies levels of task demands and support in response to the child's changing competence.

Segmentation Separation of words into smaller sounds such as syllables or phonemes (e.g., bat can be segmented into b-at or b-a-t).

Semantic intentions Meanings characteristic of children's early two-word utterances. These include agent-action (daddy run) action-object (throw ball), agent-object (mommy book), locative (sit chair), possession (mommy hat), existence (that doggie), negation (no birdie), recurrence (more crackers), and attribution (yellow flower).

Semantics Aspect of language concerned with the rules that govern the meaning or content of words and sentences.

Stop sounds Sound articulated with a complete obstruction of the passage of breath (e.g., b, d, g, h, k, p, t).

Story structure Narrative framework that specifies the underlying relationship of the story components (e.g., setting, episodes, resolution).

Superordinate-level labels Labels that categorize objects and events at an abstract, general level (e.g., animals, people, food) as opposed to basic-level labels that describe particulars (e.g., dog, mama, apple).

Symbol Entity that represents another entity containing similar features.

Symbolic representation Use of a variety of symbolic media (e.g., language, drawing, imaginative actions) to evoke nonpresent realities.

Syntax Organizational rules specifying word order, sentence organization, and word relationships.

Appendix C

Additional Resources

RHYMING

Brown, M.W. (1957). *Goodnight moon*. New York: Harper & Row.

Brown, R. (1994). *What rhymes with snake?* New York: Tambourine Books.

Cauley, L.B. (1992). *Clap your hands*. New York: G.P. Putnam's Sons.

Cole, J., & Calmenson, S. (1991). *The eentsy, weentsy spider: Fingerplays and action rhymes*. New York: Mulberry Books.

Degen, B. (1983). *Jamberry*. New York: HarperCollins.

Edge, N. (1988a). *I can read colors*. Salem, OR: Nellie Edge Resources.

Edge, N. (1988b). *The opposite song*. Salem, OR: Nellie Edge Resources.

Edge, N. (1992). *Make friends with Mother Goose*. Salem, OR: Nellie Edge Resources.

Fleming, D. (1991). *In the tall, tall grass*. New York: Holt, Rinehart & Winston.

Gregorich, B. (1984a). *Beep, beep*. Grand Haven, MI: School Zone Publishing.

Gregorich, B. (1984b). *Gum on the drum*. Grand Haven, MI: School Zone Publishing.

Guarino, D. (1989). *Is your mama a llama?* New York: Scholastic.

Hennessy, B.G. (1989). *The missing tarts*. Middlesex, England: Penguin.

Kalish, M., & Kalish, L. (1993). *Bears on the stairs*. New York: Scholastic.

Langstaff, J. (1991). *Oh, a hunting we will go*. New York: Aladdin Books.

Loomans, D., Kolberg, K., & Loomans, J. (1991). *Positively Mother Goose*. Tiburon, CA: H.J. Kramer.

Martin, B., & Carle, E. (1991). *Polar bear, polar bear, what do you hear?* New York: Holt, Rinehart & Winston.

McMillan, B. (1990). *One sun: A book of terse verse*. New York: Holiday House.

Milios, R. (1988). *Bears, bears, everywhere*. Chicago: Children's Press.

Pelham, D. (1990). *Sam's sandwich*. New York: Dutton Children's Books.

Seuss, Dr. (1957). *The cat in the hat*. New York: Random House.

Shaw, N. (1986). *Sheep on a jeep*. Boston: Houghton Mifflin.

Shaw, N. (1989). *Sheep on a ship*. Boston: Houghton Mifflin.

Silverstein, S. (1964). *A giraffe and a half*. New York: HarperCollins.

Wadsworth, O. (1971). *Over in the meadow*. New York: Scholastic.

Williams, S. (1989). *We went walking*. San Diego: Harcourt Brace Jovano-vich.

Witty, B. (1992). *The racoon on the moon*. Grand Haven, MI: School Zone Publishing.

SYLLABLE SEGMENTATION

Heller, R. (1989). *Many luscious lollipops*. New York: Grosset & Dunlap.

ALPHABET/ALLITERATION

Barrett, J. (1980). *Animals should definitely not act like people*. New York: Aladdin Books.

Dragonwagon, C. (1992). *Alligator arrived with apples: A potluck alphabet feast*. New York: Aladdin Books.

Gregorich, B. (1985). *Elephant and envelope*. Grand Haven, MI: School Zone Publishing.

Grover, M. (1993). *The accidental zucchini: The unexpected alphabet*. San Diego: Harcourt Brace Jovanovich.

Hague, K. (1986a). *Alphabears*. New York: H. Holt.

Hague, K. (1986b). *Numbears*. New York: H. Holt.

Lunn, C. (1989). *Bobby's zoo*. Chicago: Children's Press.

McPhail, D. (1989). *Animals A to Z*. New York: Scholastic.

Merriam, E. (1989). *Where is everybody?* New York: Simon & Schuster.

Nightingale, S. (1992). *Pink pigs a plenty*. San Diego: Harcourt Brace Jo-vanovich.

Shelby, A. (1994). *Potluck*. New York: Orchard Books.

Sloat, T. (1989). *From letter to letter*. New York: Puffin Unicorn.

OTHER FAVORITES

Brett, J. (1990). *Goldilocks and the three little pigs*. New York: G.P. Putnam's Sons.

Brown, M. (1957). *The three billy goats gruff*. San Diego: Harcourt Brace Jovanovich.

Carle, E. (1987). *The very hungry caterpillar* (Rev. ed.). New York: Philomel Books.

Carlstrom, N.W. (1992). *Baby-o*. Boston: Little, Brown.

De Paola, T. (1975). *Strega nona*. Englewoods Cliffs, NJ: Prentice Hall.

Galdone, P. (1970). *The three little pigs*. New York: Houghton Mifflin/Clarion.

Galdone, P. (1975). *The little red hen*. New York: Scholastic.

Kalmain, M. (1988). *Hey Willy, see the pyramids*. New York: Penguin.

Keats, E.J. (1962). *A snowy day*. New York: Viking.

McCloskey, R. (1942). *Make way for ducklings*. New York: Viking.

McDermott, G. (1972). *Anansi the spider*. New York: Puffin Books.

McDermott, G. (1993). *Raven: A trickster tale from the Pacific Northwest*. San Diego: Harcourt Brace Jovanovich.

Perry, S. (1995). *If*. Venice, CA: Children's Library Press.

Piper, W. (1954). *The little engine that could*. New York: Platt & Munk.

Seeger, P. (1986). *Abiyoyo*. New York: Collier-Macmillian.
Sendak, M. (1973). *Where the wild things are*. New York: Harper & Row.
Shaw, C. (1947). *It looked like spilt milk*. New York: Harper & Row.
Slobodkina, E. (1987). *Caps for sale*. New York: Harper Trophy.
Steptoe, J. (1988). *Baby says*. New York: Lothrop.
Testa, F. (1993). *Time to get out*. New York: Tambourine Books.
Tharlet, E. (1993). *I wish I were a bird*. New York: North South Books.

WORDLESS PICTURE BOOKS

Hoban, T. (1983). *I read symbols*. New York: Greenwillow Books.
Mayer, M. (1967). *A boy, a dog and a frog*. New York: Dial.
Mayer, M. (1971). *A boy, a dog, a frog and a friend*. New York: Dial.
Shories, P. (1991). *Mouse around*. New York: Farrar, Strauss & Giroux.
Turkle, B. (1976). *Deep in the forest*. New York: Dutton.

FOREIGN LANGUAGE

Delacre, L. (1989). *Arroz con leche: Popular songs and rhymes from Latin America*. New York: Scholastic.
Dunham, M. (1987). *Colors: How do you say it? English, French, Spanish, Italian*. New York: Lothrop, Lee, & Shepard Books.
McNaught, H. (1973). *500 palabras nuevas para ti* [500 words to grow on]. New York: Random House.
Wyndham, R. (1968). *Chinese Mother Goose rhymes*. New York: Philomel Books.
Yolen, J. (1992). *Street rhymes around the world*. Honesdale, PA: Wordsong.

OTHER MATERIALS

Adams, M.J. (1990). *Beginning to read: Thinking and learning about print*. Cambridge, MA: The MIT Press.
Althouse, R. (1981). *The young child: Learning with understanding*. New York: Teachers College Press.
Borgia, E. (1996). Learning through projects. *Scholastic Early Childhood Today, 10*, 22–29.
Bricker, D., & Cripe, J.J. (1998). *An activity-based approach to early intervention* (2nd Ed.). Baltimore: Paul H. Brookes Publishing Co.
Clark, K. (1994). How do caterpillars make cocoons? *Dimensions of Early Childhood, 22*, 5–9.
Edwards C., Gandini, L., & Forman, G. (1993). *The hundred languages of children: The Reggio Emilia approach to early childhood education*. Norwood, NJ: Ablex.
Geller, L.G. (1985). *Wordplay and language learning for children*. Urbana, IL: National Council of Teachers of English.
Hartman, J., & Eckerty, C. (1995). Projects in the early years. *Childhood Education, 71*, 141–147.
Katzen, M., & Henderson, A. (1994). *Pretend soup and other real recipes: A cookbook for preschoolers and up*. Berkeley, CA: Tricycle Press.

Linder, T.W. (1993). *Transdisciplinary play-based assessment: A functional approach to working with young children* (Rev. ed.). Baltimore: Paul H. Brookes Publishing Co.

Maxim, G. (1997). Developmentally appropriate maps skills instruction. *Childhood Education, 73,* 206–211.

Morrow, L.M. (1989). *Literacy development: Helping children read and write.* Englewood Cliffs, NJ: Prentice Hall.

Neuman, S.G., & Roskos, S. (1993). *Language and literacy learning in the early years: An integrated approach.* San Diego: Harcourt Brace Jovanovich.

Seefeldt, C. (1992). *The early childhood curriculum: A review of current research* (2nd ed.). New York: Teachers College Press.

Strickland, D.S., & Morrow, L.M. (Eds.). (1989). *Emerging literacy: Young children learn to read and write.* Newark, DE: International Reading Association.

Yopp, H. (1992). Developing phonemic awareness in young children. *The Reading Teacher, 45*(9), 696–703.

Index

Page references followed by *t, f,* or *n,* indicate tables, figures, or footnotes, respectively.

PLACE YOUR ORDER NOW!

Please send me

____ **Beginning Literacy with Language** / Stock #479X / Price: $29.95

____ **Ladders to Literacy: A Preschool Activity Book** / Stock #3173 / Price: $49.95

____ **Ladders to Literacy Set** / Stock #3270 / Price: $86.00

____ **Phonemic Awareness: A Classroom Curriculum** / Stock #3211 / Price: $24.95

____ **Read, Play, and Learn! Module Collection 1** / Stock #4013 / Price: $125.00
(includes 8 modules and accompanying box)

____ **Read, Play, and Learn! Module Collection 2** / Stock #4021 / Price: $125.00
(includes 8 modules and accompanying box)

____ **Read, Play, and Learn! Teacher's Guide** / Stock #4005 / Price: $45.00

____ **Read, Play, and Learn! Set** / Stock #4773 / Price: $275.00
(includes Teacher's Guide and both module collections)

____ Check enclosed (payable to Brookes Publishing Co.)   ____ Purchase order attached (bill my institution)

____ Please charge my credit card: ____ Visa   ____ MasterCard   ____ American Express

Credit Card #: _____

Signature (required with credit card use): _____ Exp. Date:_____

Name: _____ Daytime phone: _____

Shipping Address:_____
Orders cannot be shipped to P.O. boxes.

City/State/ZIP: _____ Country: _____

E-mail Address:_____
☐ Please send me special e-mail offers and discounts. (Your e-mail address will not be shared with any other party.)

Photocopy this form and mail it to Brookes Publishing Co., P.O. Box 10624, Baltimore, MD 21285-0624; FAX 410-337-8539;
call toll-free (8 A.M.–5 P.M. ET) 1-800-638-3775 or 1-410-337-9580 (outside the U.S.); or order online at www.brookespublishing.com

FOR ORDERS WITHIN THE CONTINENTAL U.S.

Shipping Rates for UPS Ground Delivery*
If your product total (before tax) is:
$0.00 to $49.99, add $5.00
$50.00 to $399.99, add 10% of product total
$400.00 and over, add 8% of product total
*For rush orders call 1-800-638-3775.
For international orders call 1-410-337-9580.

Prices subject to change without notice and may be higher outside the United States. You may return books and videotapes within 30 days for a full credit of the product price. Refunds will be issued for prepaid orders. Items must be returned in resalable condition.

Product Total $ _____
Shipping Rate (see chart) + $ _____
Maryland orders add 5%
sales tax (to product total only) + $ _____

Grand Total U.S. $ _____

Your source code is **BA 50**

Browse our entire catalog, read excerpts, and find special offers at
www.brookespublishing.com

ANOTHER INNOVATIVE CURRICULUM
THAT MAKES LEARNING FUN

Read, Play, and Learn!

Storybook Activities for Young Children
By Toni W. Linder, Ed.D., with invited contributors

This innovative curriculum provides teachers with a school year's worth of story-related activities centered around themes like enjoying seasonal festivities, sharing emotions, making friends, understanding other cultures, and just having fun! **Read, Play, and Learn!** includes the **Teacher's Guide** and two collections of **modules** linked to popular storybooks. This curriculum makes it easy for teachers to promote general development and boost cognitive, sensorimotor, communication and language, social, and emerging literacy skills.

Module Collections

Based on stories children love, the **Read, Play, and Learn!** modules are a teacher's dream. Boxed 8 booklets to a **Collection**, each fun-filled module offers 2-3 weeks of story-related activities and learning experiences for young children. Included are a brief summary of the storybook, planning sheets, a list of key words and concepts, ideas for modifying the activities for children of varying ability levels, activities for every center in your classroom, sample letters to help keep families informed of classroom activities, and a list of alternative storybooks, songs, fingerplays, and software.

Collection 1

Includes activities thematically linked to the fall semester. One module is linked to each of eight popular storybooks.

Stock Number: 4013 Price: $125.00
1999 • 80 pages each • 8 1/2 x 11 • saddle-stitched
ISBN 1-55766-401-3

The Kissing Hand, by Audrey Penn
Somebody and the Three Blairs, by Marilyn Tolhurst
Picking Apples & Pumpkins,
by Amy and Richard Hutchings
The Little Old Lady Who Was Not Afraid of Anything,
by Linda Williams
The Knight and the Dragon, by Tomie dePaola
Abiyoyo, by Pete Seeger
Night Tree, by Eve Bunting
The Snowy Day, by Ezra Jack Keats

Collection 2

Offers activities appropriate for the spring semester. One module is linked to each of eight popular storybooks.

Stock Number: 4021 Price: $125.00
1999 • 80 pages each • 8 1/2 x 11 • saddle-stitched
ISBN 1-55766-402-1

A Porcupine Named Fluffy, by Helen Lester
First Flight, by David McPhail
Friends, by Helme Heine
The Three Billy Goats Gruff, by Janet Stevens
The Three Little Javelinas, by Susan Lowell
A Rainbow of Friends, by P.K. Hallinan
Franklin Has a Sleepover,
by Paulette Bourgeois and Brenda Clark
The Rainbow Fish, by Marcus Pfister

Teacher's Guide

This manual provides guidance on creating a literacy-rich environment for preschool and kindergarten children of all ability levels. It explains all the basics: how to arrange the classroom, teach children with varying levels of ability, involve families, and encourage learning and development. Best of all the guide includes modifications so teachers can individualize instruction and capitalize on the strengths of every child. It offers background information on the importance of play and literature in early learning, provides an overview of developmental domains, and discusses what to expect at various levels of children's development.

Stock Number: 4005 Price: $45.00   1999 • 256 pages • 8 1/2 x 11 • spiral-bound • ISBN 1-55766-400-5

Order the set and **SAVE!** Teacher's Guide with both collections!
Stock Number: 4773 Price: $275.00

For more on Read, Play, and Learn! visit
www.readplaylearn.com

Ladders to Literacy
A Preschool Activity Book
By Angela Notari-Syverson, Ph.D., Rollanda E. O'Connor, Ph.D., & Patricia F. Vadasy, M.P.H.

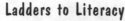

With the preschool activity book, you'll target basic preliteracy skills, orient children toward printed materials, and teach letter sounds. Developmentally appropriate assessment procedures—informal observation guidelines, structured performance samples, and a checklist—will help you measure children's learning.

Stock Number: 3173 Price: $49.95
1998 • 400 pages • 8 1/2 x 11 • spiral-bound • ISBN 1-55766-317-3

Buy the set and **SAVE!**
Ladders to Literacy: A Preschool Activity **and** Ladders to Literacy: A Kindergarten Activity

Stock Number: 3270 Price: $86.00

Phonemic Awareness in Young Children
A Classroom Curriculum
By Marilyn Jager Adams, Ph.D., Barbara R. Foorman, Ph.D., Ingvar Lundberg, Ph.D., & Terri D. Beeler, Ed.D.

Phonemic awareness—distinguishing the individual sounds that make up words and affect their meanings—is an essential preliteracy skill. This supplemental curriculum is brimming with engaging, adaptable language activities proven to increase phonemic awareness in general, bilingual, inclusive, or special education settings. Its developmental sequence builds on simple listening games and gradually moves on to more advanced sound manipulation exercises such as rhyming, alliteration, and segmentation.

Stock Number: 3211 Price: $24.95
1998 • 208 pages • 8 1/2 x 11 • spiral bound • ISBN 1-55766-321-1

Beginning Literacy with Language
Young Children Learning at Home and School
By David K. Dickinson, Ed.D., & Patton O. Tabors, Ed.D.

Drawn from research the authors gathered in the Home-School Study of Language and Literacy Development, this exciting new book demonstrates the impact of early interactions on kindergarten language and literacy skills. Readers will tour the homes and schools of over 70 young children to observe their conversations at ages 3, 4, and 5. Through case studies and transcripts, they'll discover how families talk to children during everyday activities and how teachers support literacy development throughout the school day.

Stock Number: 479X Price: $29.95
2001 • 432 pages • 6 x 9 • paperback • ISBN 1-55766-479-X

Ordering is easy—
just use the order form on the previous page!